# The Golden Years
# of the Hutterites

# STUDIES IN ANABAPTIST AND MENNONITE HISTORY

## № 23

# The Golden Years of the Hutterites

The Witness and Thought of the Communal Moravian

Anabaptists

During the Walpot Era, 1565-1578

Leonard Gross

# STUDIES IN ANABAPTIST AND MENNONITE HISTORY

Edited by Cornelius J. Dyck, Ernst Correll, Leonard Gross, Leland Harder, Guy F. Hershberger, John S. Oyer, Theron Schlabach, J. C. Wenger, and John H. Yoder

*Published by Herald Press, Scottdale, Pennsylvania, and Kitchener, Ontario, in cooperation with Mennonite Historical Society, Goshen, Indiana. The Society is primarily responsible for the content of the studies, and Herald Press for their publication.*

°Out of print, but available in microfilm or Xerox copies.

# The Golden Years of the Hutterites

*The Witness and Thought of the Communal Moravian Anabaptists During the Walpot Era, 1565-1578*

## Leonard Gross

**HERALD PRESS**
Scottdale, Pennsylvania
Kitchener, Ontario
1980

Library of Congress Cataloging in Publication Data

Gross, Leonard, 1931 (Nov. 17)-
    The golden years of the Hutterites.

(Studies in Anabaptist and Mennonite history; no. 23)
    Bibliography: p.
    Includes index.
    1. Hutterite Brethren—Czechoslovakia—History.
    2. Hutterite Brethren—Austria—History.
    3. Czechoslovakia—Church history. 4. Austria—Church history.
        I. Title II. Series.
    BX8129.H8G69 1980        289.7'3        80-10711
    ISBN 0-8361-1227-X

*The photos in this volume are from the Anabaptist Heritage Collection, Scottdale, Pennsylvania. They were taken by Jan Gleysteen, Leonard Gross, and John A. Hostetler.*

*The flower motifs and related designs were copied from original Habaner (Hutterite) ceramics now in the museums of Prague, Olomouc, Budapest, and Rotterdam.*

*The editors of Studies in Anabaptist and Mennonite History herewith acknowledge with gratitude the subsidy from the Hutterian Brethren that has made the publication of this volume possible.*

*289.7
G914
81073115*

# To Irene, Suzanne and Valerie

Who have given themselves
To the idea of community wherein
The spirit of love and peace reigns

Dann so wir von unserm Schöpffer ein pressthaffte natur empfangen haben, die für sich selbs nichts vermag, ist in dem unserm nutz geratten, auf das unsere presten und mangel (sei in geistlichen oder zeitlichen dingen) durch brüederliche und freundtliche beywonung hilff befinde, und darumb was einem mangelt, durch des andern hilf understützt und erstatt werde.

(For since we have received from our Creator a defective nature which is capable of achieving nothing for itself, it turns out to our benefit when our infirmities and shortcomings [both in spiritual and temporal things] find help through warm, brotherly living together, so that what is lacking in one can be supported and complemented through the help of the other.)

Peter Walpot, 1577

# Table of Contents

# Introduction

The Hutterites are a remarkable group because they have maintained continuity both of organization and of idea for four centuries. Socially radical groups tend either to die out by the second or third generation, or else to survive by dropping the radical features. To use Troeltsch's terminology, the sect becomes the church. Among the groups that have died out one thinks in this country of the Oneida Colony, Brook Farm, the Shakers—only three or four old women are left. The Mennonites and Quakers have developed varieties. Some Mennonites, notably those in Holland, have succumbed on the peace issue. So have some of the Quakers. The man chiefly responsible for the bombing of North Vietnam and the invasion of Cambodia was not disowned by the particular branch with which he was associated. The Polish Brethren lasted as a group for a century till their expulsion in 1658, but by that time their radical features had long since been eroded. The question then arises whether a group which has seriously diverged from the original pattern is warranted in keeping the name.

Two factors contribute to continuance of structure, idea, and name. They are persecution from without and isolationism from within. The utopianism of the Polish Brethren was eroded because for a century they were not persecuted and were not isolated. They spoke the language and shared the life of their countrymen, whose manner of life they had at first repudiated. The Hutterites were persecuted and were isolated, being exiles, not speaking the tongue or sharing the life of those who harbored them. The Amish in the United States have persisted by a deliberate self-imposed isolation. That may change. On a recent visit to Goshen, Indiana, I was told that the Amish in that area were too prolific for the resources of the land. No more land was for sale. Hence Amish young men are going into factories. "That," I remarked to myself, "spells the beginning of the end."

This book presents a vast amount of new material on the Hutterites of the second generation by whom the pattern was not eroded. There are so vivid pictures here of stalwart testimonies and martyrdoms. Much of the material reads like the *Täuferakten* of the first period. The arrangement of this work is not geographical but confessional, describing one by one the encounters with three unrelated groups: Catholic, Lutheran, and Calvinist, and two related: the Polish Brethren and the Swiss Brethren. I cannot see much difference between the disputes with the Lutherans and the Calvinists, except that the latter were more theological. In the case of the Polish Brethren the differences lay at the points of Hutterian rigor of discipline and the speculative interest of the Poles. In the case of the Swiss Brethren, not enough is known to provide a complete picture.

In addition to the two factors mentioned above that make for survival, a third should be added, namely the education of the young, to which this work gives considerable attention.

Another significant point is the revival of the pattern without lineal descent in our own day by the Society of Brothers. They have reinstated the original model quite independently of the Hutterian groups of immediate descent. There are such in Canada and the Western half of the United States, who have preserved a number of sixteenth-century documents. So far as I can see, however, the new material in this book is primarily from European archives. Church historians and sociologists will find this an illuminating study.

Roland H. Bainton, Professor Emeritus
Yale University

# Author's Preface

In 1965, when I approached the renowned Basel church historian, Professor Ernst Staehelin, for advice about a dissertation topic, he suggested I develop a historical monograph ("Schreiben Sie eine Monographie, *die* bleibt"). Taking his advice, I settled for a monograph on the Hutterite leader, Peter Walpot. But what at first was to be a biography of a man, gradually developed into a monograph about an era, the Walpot Era. This change in emphasis from the individual to the corporate is in keeping with the brotherhood spirit of the Hutterites. It also seems appropriate to view the movement as a whole during an era when Hutterianism had outgrown its first, youthful decades. This volume therefore attempts to tell the story of the second-generation Hutterites—the fourth and fifth decades of Hutterian history—from their own standpoint, including their vision and their historical development.

Since most of the material included in this volume has been compiled from unpublished sources, many previously unknown historical details had to be pieced together before the process of interpretation could begin. Hence a detailed portrayal of varied incidents seemed the best method of describing second-generation Hutterianism. Chapter Three, for example, details the mission idea as it affected the life and thought of the Brotherhood as a whole as well as of the individual missioners who went out into the world. Chapter Four deals with the Hutterian approach to doctrinal truth. Chapter Five, a major chapter, enters into the realm of social history and offers some insights into the mental and spiritual outlook of one Hutterite, the missioner Paul Glock. Chapters Six and Seven attempt a theological interpretation of one very specific issue: the watershed between the Anabaptists and the Calvinists. Chapter Eight develops new historical material relating to the Swiss Brethren during the 1560s and 70s, which has hitherto been an almost complete void in Swiss Brethren historiography. Finally, Chapter Nine attempts interpretively to set the Walpot Era within the Hutterian history of ideas.

This study is therefore an interpretive attempt to show how the Hutterian movement, beginning in 1528, developed throughout the first century of its continued life, by taking a close look at second-generation Hutterian Anabaptism. It is based chiefly on a particular set of sources, the Hutterites' own—still largely unstudied—codices. In contrast to the scores of interpretive works on the first thirty-five years of Anabaptist history, the period after 1560, with the exception of the Low Countries, has not yet been thoroughly covered. Within Swiss Brethren history such a study is next to impossible because of the dearth of extant in-group documentation;[1] for the Hutterites, however, this is not the case, for among the hundreds of codices they left for posterity, a great many have to do with second-generation Hutterian Anabaptism.[2]

In lifting out the history of the Hutterites, basically from their own standpoint, there is admittedly the inherent danger of being overly sympathetic to the Hutterian cause, and misrepresenting other groups. Nevertheless, this seems to be the natural course to take in describing a movement in a notoriously intolerant century, where black was coal black, and white contained no shades of gray, whether it be the "truth" of the Catholics, or the Protestants, or the Hutterites. With rare exceptions, no denominational group could see, as we do now, that in the sixteenth century there were other sincere, moral, God-fearing people in the differing religious movements.

This volume is therefore not a monograph on Peter Walpot; Robert Friedmann (1931/32) wrote such a work. Nor is it primarily a socioeconomic history; František Hrubý (1933/35), Victor Peters (1965), and John A. Hostetler (1974) have filled this void. Nor is it a general history of Hutterianism; Johann Loserth (1895), Rudolf Wolkan (1918), Lydia Müller (1927), and John Horsch (1931) have written such histories. Nor is it primarily a theological work; Robert Friedmann (1973) covered this aspect. It attempts rather to interpret the nature of second-generation Hutterian Anabaptism from the group's own corpus of writings, set within the history of ideas of Hutterian Anabaptism. Hutterian views of their antagonists are also included, an integral part of the Hutterian idea. Certainly much effort will still be needed to do justice to this era—the details within this volume it is hoped will serve toward that end. The present work is the result of a first modest step toward attempting to note the evolution of the Hutterian idea and its historical reality, and interpreting this development of Hutterian history through its first five decades.

I have deeply appreciated the efforts of the many scholars—at the universities of Basel and Zurich, and in North America, including some dear friends among the Hutterites (all the way from Reardan to Rifton)—who have worked closely with me during the various stages in the development and editing of this thesis. The careful work of Jan Gleysteen, to be seen in his creative pictorial documentation incorporated into this volume, is herewith acknowledged. My gratitude extends as well to the government of the United States for its generous Fulbright scholarship, and to the host of dedicated scholars and archives/library personnel from Austria, Canada, Czechoslovakia, East Germany, West Germany, Hungary, Italy, the Netherlands, Rumania, Switzerland, and the United States, who helped me gather the many codices and documents needed to piece together and develop this thesis.

A final note of deep appreciation is due Professor C. J. Dyck, editor in chief of Studies in Anabaptist and Mennonite History, who entered this study into the SAMH series, and whose critical eye helped transform a manuscript into a book.

Leonard Gross
Goshen, Indiana

# The Historical Emerging of Anabaptism

Throughout the Middle Ages, Roman Catholicism included under its umbrella both church and sect types. Although the church rejected individuals such as Peter Waldo who deviated from basic Catholic dogma, Catholicism did accept into its structure a variety of new Christian types.[1]

The decline in the power and prestige of Roman Catholicism during the fifteenth century, however, produced an almost universal European reaction to, and questioning of, the legitimacy of the mother church whose center lay in Rome. During this same period of decline, Roman Catholicism as an institution no longer seemed able to accept the variety of new Christian types which were surfacing in the late fifteenth and early sixteenth centuries. For this and other (social and political) reasons the Reformation of Martin Luther and others spread throughout many European lands.

Luther began his Reformation with the vision of reestablishing the vigor and intensity of the apostolic brotherhood, a voluntary church of committed believers. But in practice, one all-inclusive, territorial-church type emerged. He ultimately discounted other forms of church renewal and banned various groups which deviated from the magisterial norm. Luther lumped the sectaries all together, disavowed them, and branded them "Schwärmer," a term that he seems to have coined. Zwingli and Calvin also retained a concept of the church which assumed direct responsibility for the welfare of all persons within a given land. They too, with Luther, did not permit the brotherhood-church type of Christian renewal within their structures.[2]

Consequently, it hardly could have been otherwise, in view of the many creative movements that regularly surface throughout church history, that an intense reaction to magisterial Protestantism arose among those who understood Christianity as a brotherhood. But also in Roman lands, individuals and groups continued to react against a church in need of reformation "at its head and among its members." These reactions to both Protestantism and Catholicism resulted, in given instances, in the wide-flung and tenacious Anabaptist movement, one manifestation of which was the birth of the Hutterian Brotherhood.[3]

One distinction between the Protestant and Anabaptist political outlook is basic for the movement depicted in this volume: Luther—and the other Reformers as well—chose to retain the concept of *corpus christianum*, where society was equated with the established church, making society and church in effect coterminous. This neutralized the idea of "world," in the New Testament sense of the term, and made the concept a self-contradiction. On the other hand, the idea of the narrow gate (Matthew 7:13-14), a way of life set apart from society at large, was central to Anabaptist thought. Such a path led to a voluntary community of committed Christians bound together by God's Spirit, who lived in peace and love and shared one another's burdens. The concept of mission was integral to such brotherhood. The Anabaptists believed themselves to be on this narrow path, whereas society was on the broad path leading to destruction. They equated society with the unregenerate world, within which lived seekers after God's truth, souls who desired the strength and peace of brotherhood. Anabaptist mission was established to locate these seekers.[4]

The view of world and life as held by the Anabaptists was a view which they firmly believed to be the New Testament perspective as well, a view which disregarded significant aspects of a 1300-year tradition. Basic to this brotherhood idea was the reality of the kingdom of God on earth, which the Anabaptists believed had withered with the centuries, but which God reestablished in the sixteenth century. For classic Anabaptism, both the temporal as well as the future dimensions of life gave definition to the kingdom of God. Had not Christ established his kingdom of love and peace even now, here on earth? The affirmative, Anabaptist answer to this question also necessitated affirming that the ordering of life had to comply with Christ's Great Commandment (Mark 12:28-34). On the other hand, the full manifestation of the kingdom would come in the future. God's people were consequently to wait for the end time and prepare for its arrival, suffering injustices rather than attempting to right earthly wrongs through coercion.[5]

These were apocalyptic times. Luther counted on the breakthrough of the end time at any moment. Melchior Hofmann staked his life on its coming in 1533. Some Anabaptist sectaries tragically attempted to usher in the kingdom through force. The city of Münster in Westphalia during the 1530s is the classic example of such revolutionary action. A variety of earlier radicals, including Thomas Müntzer, the early Hans Hut, and Karlstadt, each in his own way attempted to usher in the kingdom, advocating the use of coercion to force open the gates for the kingdom. But the great majority of Anabaptists—all those who possessed the inner strength and group discipline to survive the turmoil of the first three years—remained consciously nonviolent. No doubt some of these radicals learned from the tragic experience of the Peasants' War at Frankenhausen, in which Müntzer, and perhaps Hut, were involved. Whatever the reason, one of these radicals, Hans Hut, after his baptism modified his earlier beliefs and became a powerful Anabaptist spokesman throughout the Upper German lands, and his legacy became an essential part of nonviolent Austrian and Moravian Anabaptism. After 1527 the Upper German Anabaptists committed the future to God; for the present, God commanded that Christians live in peace with one another.[6]

However, the firm emphasis upon establishing a kingdom of peace did not deter the Anabaptists from continuing to carry out the Great Commission. The gathered church became the base from which the call to discipleship and community was to go out through mission. After 1527, Anabaptist mission continued to contain a consciously apocalyptic note; but counter to the earlier, revolutionary nature of many other dissidents, the Anabaptists held to the New Testament as programmatic, including a nonviolent approach to effecting Christ's kingdom. They were accused—in a sense, correctly—of wanting to tear down the old church establishment, but the alternative they were suggesting they believed to have been successfully established early within Christian history. It was not a Renaissance utopia, or an illusory dream, or simply a precipitate explosion, the void of which God himself was to fill miraculously. The earliest documents fully substantiate that there was nothing vague in Hutterian doctrine about the kingdom of God. Granted, the Hutterites were dissenters who practiced civil disobedience at times, accepting suffering and persecution as part of the way of Christ. They affirmed only a conditional obedience to the magistracy, but an unconditional obedience to God.[7]

Here may be seen a converging of those ideas which largely determined the nature of Anabaptism. The key idea was Christian obedience: living in accord with the way Jesus lived. This *imitatio* does not imply a sterile imitation, but rather *Nachfolge*, an existential following after the living Christ who himself had exemplified the only way of life. Yet Christian discipleship, the Anabaptists believed, was feasible only within the brotherhood, in the kingdom of God where God's Spirit lodged. Even a disciple filled with the Spirit could not find fulfillment in life except through his brother (Matthew 18:18-20).[8] Only within this spiritual context could peace reign for the Christian brotherhood. A sixteenth-century Hutterite chronicler summarizes this view as follows:

> Swords and spears were forged into pruning knives, saws, and other useful tools and were so used. There was no musket, saber, halberd or any weapon made for defense. Rather each was completely a brother to the other, a thoroughly peaceful people who never helped— much less took part actively—in any war or in bloodshed, or in the payment of war taxes. No revenge was resorted to. Patience was their weapon in all strife (Mt. 23[:29-36]; Mt. 5[:21-26, 43-48]; Rom. 12[:14-19]).[9]

The Protestant churches worked on the basis of an ultimate responsibility for all of society within a given territory; mission was defined in terms of political boundaries. The Anabaptists on the other hand held to an ultimate responsibility for the kingdom of God which they understood to be separate from the world. Although they also felt a responsibility for all people in the world and often gave their own lives to fulfill this responsibility through mission, they considered the pattern and political organization of general society—including its established church—to be one with the kingdoms of this world. In fact the all-pervasive decadence and the constant warfare within the kingdoms of this world, the Anabaptists felt, militated against the fulfillment of the peace which Jesus established upon earth.

But in God's kingdom peace reigned. Hate and war were contradictory to the very concept of the kingdom of God, where Christian love as a way of life was made possible through the reigning of God's Spirit. The church consequently could not fully participate in the life of the kingdom of this world and its ruler (John 16:11).

Such a lofty ideal remained central for the Anabaptists, as God's will for his people. And there is solid evidence from Anabaptist as well as non-Anabaptist sources that a high degree of peace and unity had indeed been established within Anabaptist circles. The Great Chronicle of the sixteenth-century Hutterian Brotherhood contains the following insights:

> Many were convinced and praised them as a devout people that must have been established by God. It would otherwise have been im-

possible for so many to live together in unity, whereas among others, where only two, three, or four live together, they are daily in each other's hair and quarrel until they run from one another.[10]

Such peace and unity characterized the Hutterites in Moravia during much of the sixteenth century.

# Ch. **2**

# The Golden Years of the Hutterites

## Anabaptist Origins in Light of Hutterian Tradition

There is no doubt in the minds of Hutterite chroniclers about the time, place, and circumstances of Anabaptist origins. They report very explicitly their interpretation of events: God intended to reestablish his own people, separate from all other peoples, in the last age of the world. To be sure, Erasmus of Rotterdam, an "educator of the German nation," had nudged the Papacy politely and civilly, thereby anticipating new beginnings. Luther, the Hutterites said, had ripped apart an old house, but built no new house in its place; only an insolent people had arisen as a result of his doctrine, due to his having spurned good as well as bad works—he in fact had been unable to discern the difference between the two. In this regard they considered Zwingli on the same plane as Luther. All in all there had appeared no renewed people as a result of these Reformers' words, and Luther and Zwingli in the end could claim only to have possessed a "blown-up, swollen learning."[1] As a consequence, the Hutterites believed, God needed to reestablish his people upon the earth through other means. The events leading up to the birth of this new reality had occurred in Switzerland; Conrad Grebel, Felix Mantz, and George Blaurock, along with Balthasar Hubmaier, were the leading figures.[2]

The official Brotherhood chronicler of the 1560s, Kaspar Braitmichel, also recounts these earlier events leading up to the birth of Anabaptism in 1525; he then establishes a double linkage between the events of 1525 and Hutterian beginnings. George Blaurock himself had shepherded the very

Tirolean Anabaptist brotherhoods which ultimately became the core of Hutterian Anabaptism in Moravia. Wilhelm Reublin, a Zurich Anabaptist who later surfaced at Auspitz, Moravia, too is mentioned as a person who became part of incipient Hutterianism.[3]

This does not deny the likelihood that pre-Reformation brotherhoods had existed for decades in such areas as Tirol and Salzburg, where oral tradition would have us believe that, already in the fifteenth century, towns such as Zell am Ziller and Zell am See were locations of cell groups led by learned monks and friars, studying newly translated, unpublished fragments of the Bible.[4] Whether adult baptism within any of these cell groups predates 1525 is of course quite another question, still needing a great amount of research. But it is of the highest significance that the Hutterite chronicler, writing at the most some forty years after the Zurich happenings of 1525, interprets the Hutterian heritage as derived from Blaurock and Hubmaier.

The first major link in the story leading to the birth of Hutterianism was Balthasar Hubmaier and the short-lived urban Anabaptism which he developed, first at Waldshut in 1525, and then the next year at Nikolsburg, Moravia. As many as twelve thousand Anabaptists were drawn to South Moravia, with Nikolsburg serving the larger religious community as a sort of "Emmaus."[5]

The events leading to the practice of community of goods are well known: A group of some two hundred, called "Stäbler" (staff-bearers), stood in opposition to the "Schwertler" (sword-bearers). Because of their nonviolent stand, the Stäbler felt compelled to leave Nikolsburg in 1528, at which point they found it necessary to pool all their resources to meet the needs of the entire group.[6] Under the leadership of Jacob Wiedemann, the communal group settled at Austerlitz. The following year another communal group was established at Auspitz, where in 1530 a similar community also was founded by Jörg Zaunring, together with Wilhelm Reublin.

Although there were some tensions, amicable relations prevailed for several years among these and other communal groups in and near Auspitz.[7] The communal idea was taking on form and substance; the Stäbler tradition was setting the doctrinal tone; and Reublin, as seen above, was a link between Zurich and Moravia, providing historical continuity of Zurich Anabaptism.

The other major link between Zurich and Hutterian Anabaptism is in the person of George Blaurock. After his expulsion from Zurich, Blaurock ultimately fled to Tirol. His close friend, Felix Mantz, had already suffered martyrdom. In Tirol he related closely to the Anabaptists already there, who had been won through the efforts of earlier leaders such as Hans Hut, Leonard Schiemer, and Hans Schlaffer. Blaurock most likely served until his death in 1529 with Jacob Hutter as a major Anabaptist leader in Tirol. Soon thereafter Hutter became the acknowledged leader within Tirolean Anabaptism. When persecution grew too intense in the Tirolean mountains, Hutter organized various Anabaptist emigrations to Moravia. Peter Walpot, the Hutterite leader whose name is synonymous with the Golden Years, had been within the crowd that witnessed the martyrdom of Blaurock. Converting to the Anabaptist faith, Walpot too undertook the dangerous journey to Moravia.[8]

By 1531 the Anabaptist brotherhoods in the Auspitz-Rossitz area had formed a loose confederation through the mediating efforts of Hutter. Hutter had undertaken three trips to Moravia and arranged for the coming of the Tirolean immigrants. Unfortunately, disunity gained the upper hand, and by 1533 conditions in Auspitz had deteriorated to such a degree that Hutter, convinced of his apostolic mission and backed by his Tirolean flock, decided to act. Through strict disciplinary measures he "cleaned house" and reorganized so effectively the small brotherhood originally led to Auspitz by Zaunring and Reublin that Hutter became known as the founder of the Anabaptist movement now known as Hutterianism. Two other brotherhoods, the Gabrielites and the Philippites, continued to be plagued by discord and within the next years many of their members joined the Hutterites.[9]

The beginning years were difficult for the Hutterian Brotherhood. The Münster debacle of 1534/35 affected the Moravian Anabaptists as it did all the others, and persecution dislodged the Hutterites. Ferdinand, Archduke of Austria, was able to force the hands of the heretofore tolerant Moravian lords. Month after month, forest and cave provided a primitive habitation for countless loyal brethren. Yet such injustice against the peaceful Brotherhood did not occur without Hutterian protest, for Jacob Hutter sent a letter of protest to the Moravian lord, Johann Kuna von Kunstadt,[10] boldly witnessing to the Hutterian way of life:

> Now we lie on the broad heath, under God's will, injuring nobody. We desire neither to molest nor treat anyone unjustly, not even our greatest enemies—not Ferdinand nor anyone else, great or small. What we do or fail to do—our words and actions, life and walk—is open and clear to all people.... We carry no outward weapons, neither spear nor musket, which everyone can well perceive, for it is evident. All in all our preaching, speaking, and life and walk proclaim that one is to live in peace and unity in God's truth and righteousness as the true disciples of Christ....

Therefore alas and woe and again woe in eternity, you Moravian lords, that you have acquiesced ... to Ferdinand, and agreed to drive the godly and God-fearing people out of your lands, and fear mortal, useless man more that the living, eternal, and omnipotent God and Lord.[11]

Meanwhile Hutter returned to Tirol, but his activities were cut short when he was apprehended and martyred at Innsbruck in 1536.[12] Gradually the friendly barons, in defiance of the royal edicts, began to employ individual brethren and made it possible for the Brotherhood to reestablish itself, until some twenty communities were again functioning.

A short eleven years later, a second wave of persecution began as the result of pressure from Emperor Charles V. But again the Brotherhood withstood the persecution, and during the 1550s was able to consolidate, beginning an era later regarded as the "good years."[13]

The *Vorsteher* or head Brotherhood leader succeeding Hutter in 1536 was Hans Amon, who served until his death in 1542. Leonhard Lanzenstil became the third Vorsteher, and was soon joined by the highly gifted Peter Riedemann. They led the Brotherhood conjointly from 1542 until the latter's death in 1556. Upon Lanzenstil's death in 1565 Peter Walpot was elected to the office. Walpot's years of leadership, extending until his death in 1578, fall within the "Golden Years" of Hutterian history, that variegated, eventful score of years which defines the basic limits of this volume.[14]

## Vorsteher Peter Walpot

Peter Walpot, sometimes called Peter Scherer to denote his vocation as a cloth-shearer, spans the first two generations of Hutterian history. It has already been noted how, as a boy of eight years of age, Walpot witnessed Blaurock's martyrdom at Klausen in the Eisack Valley of Tirol.[15] In 1542 Walpot, twenty-four years of age, was elected to the office of *Diener des Wortes*.[16] This places Walpot's year of birth around 1518.[17] By the 1550s the Hutterites recognized Walpot as a man of great stature. He assumed something of Riedemann's role after the latter's death. In 1565, when Leonhard Lanzenstiel died, Walpot was the obvious choice as Vorsteher, a post he held with constant vigilance until his death on January 30, 1578.[18]

Little is known about Walpot before 1565. Textile workers during the sixteenth century demonstrated high interest in the religious disputes of the day, and it may well be that Walpot's unusual leadership skills were developed in dialogue with fellow textile workers during his travels.[19]

However Walpot's learning and experience developed, he was recognized early as a man of keen ability. Wolf Sailer, a Hutterite hymn writer, dedicated a hymn to Walpot before 1550 admonishing him to remain alert to dangerous times and strife, to act gallantly and diligently, yet to proceed in a Christian manner. Sailer then expressed his hope that God's Spirit might guide Walpot in his mission activities.[20]

Walpot's earliest extant letter was written in 1546 to Anthony Schneider and his three companions imprisoned in Vienna. Walpot penned words of admonition, encouraging them to remain true and steadfast in their faith, and to continue to hold to the unconquerable strength of God, even unto death if need be. He included a word of caution, describing how the devil worked within God's children, trying

> to see if he can bring them to fall, not with one blow, but just like a rich merchant who transports all types of wares to market, so that if one item would not sell, he would have another article to show, and still sell something. . . . Therefore beloved brethren, believe or trust their enticements the less when they try to promise you much, for it is vain deceit; their gentle word is spear and arrow and sword drawn to kill the souls of men.[21]

In a vein similar to his later writing to Paul Glock in 1576, Walpot encouraged the prisoners to

> be comforted in the Lord. He will neither forsake nor neglect you, nor allow you to be tempted beyond what you are able to bear. . . . Believe this with your whole heart, for He is the one who can make the sea restless and quiet, and commands all the winds to be still.[22]

Toward the close of his letter, Walpot revealed something of his activities in the mid-1540s. The letter was written in Silesia, and with him were his wife, Gredel, and six other missioners. Probably around this same time Walpot also served as a missioner in the Danzig area. Later Walpot referred to the times of tribulation that he, along with the whole Brotherhood, had endured during the 1530s and 40s.[23]

In 1565 the Brotherhood chose Walpot to assume the highest office of Vorsteher. Possibly it was about this time that a brother dedicated a poem to Walpot with the acrostic reading: "Gottes geist sei mit dir, herz lieber bruder Petrus Wald bot" ("May God's Spirit be with you, dearly beloved brother Peter Walpot"). The poem includes the wish that God might use the devout Walpot according to divine purpose, so that his work might be fulfilled. The author bears witness to Walpot's vigilance and constant concern for the Brotherhood and the stability of his character. The poem closes with the ever-present Hutterian concern for mission, that God's way might continue to be conveyed to the world.[24]

## The Walpot Era

The period of peace and prosperity which the Hutterites enjoyed during the latter half of the sixteenth century was later looked upon as the Golden Years.[25] This era covers the span of Walpot's years as Vorsteher, beginning in 1565 and continuing well beyond his death in 1578. Although this volume will deal with the nature of this particular Hutterian era primarily from the standpoint of the missioner, scattered references about the nature of Hutterian communities during these years help to complete the story of life in the *Haushaben* (Hutterian communal societies) themselves.

Peter Walpot lived at Neumühl in Moravia, a village which because of Walpot's presence, slowly but surely became the political and cultural center of Hutterian activity. Here were located the archives, library, and communications center of the whole Brotherhood. Epistles were constantly arriving and being sent out, Hutterite brethren themselves often making the difficult rounds from Neumühl to imprisoned missioners hundreds of miles away in Austria, Germany, and Switzerland.[26] Medical supplies were also produced here, not only for the needs of the Brotherhood, but also for the many non-Hutterites whom the famed Hutterite physicians served. (In the 1970s, two buildings were still standing which date from the Golden Years: a large distillery and a mammoth cellar where the distilled medical supplies had once been stored.) Kilns were located here where Hutterite potters created classic works.[27] The village must have impressed contemporaries with broad-ranging activities such as pharmaceutical production, ironwork, wagon-making, an innovative school system—indeed, the whole spectrum of the handsome crafts produced at that time, goods which were in great demand by Moravian lords and other nobility far and wide. The whole culture of Neumühl was possibly in the back of the chronicler's mind when he spoke about the highly organized and variegated vocational programming of these Golden Years of Hutterianism:

> Just as in the ingenious works of a clock, where one piece helps another to make it go so that it serves its purpose; or as in a colony of bees, those useful little animals who work together in their common hive, some making wax, some the honey, some fetching water, or working in other ways, until their precious work of making sweet honey is done, not only for their own needs but that people may also be supplied—so it was among them. There has to be an ordered life in all

areas of existence, for the matters of life can be properly maintained
and furthered only where orderliness reigns—even more so in the
House of God who is himself the Master Builder and Establisher.
When there is no order, there is disorder and collapse, and there God
does not dwell.[28]

In addition to being farmers, millers, dairymen, and builders, the Hutterites were adept in many other occupations and professions. The colorful
list presented in the Great Chronicle includes thirty-nine varied vocations.
Within every division there was a manager who organized the branch he
was responsible for, seeing to it that enough workers were at hand, and that
they had the necessary raw materials. He also was responsible for selling the
products, turning the proceeds over to the Brotherhood coffers.[29]

Community regulations or codes (*Gemeindeordnungen*) covering the
various facets of community life were well worked out. The Shoemakers'
Code was established in 1561. It lists rules for the shoemakers, the sellers,
and the buyers.[30] In 1571 the Millers' Code was established,[31] and in 1574
the Carpenters' Code.[32] Andreas Ehrenpreis, the Vorsteher of the Hutterian
Brotherhood from 1639 to 1662, compiled these and many other codes,
formulated throughout the sixteenth and early seventeenth centuries, and
added some of his own.[33]

## Peter Walpot and the Hutterian School System

The Hutterites established their own schools soon after the movement
began. Schools obviously made it possible for the mothers to help out
sooner in the work of the Brotherhood; yet this was by no means the
primary reason for the Hutterian school. Its basic function was the special
upbringing of the children which could not be matched anywhere in
Europe at that time, for it taught all children the art of reading, and all boys
how to write. Jeronymus Käls (d. 1536) was an early Hutterite schoolmaster
who composed prayers for the children. An even earlier anonymous writing,
possibly the work of Leonhard Schiemer, found its way into the Hutterian
corpus of writings, and was later used by the writer of the "Handbüchlein"
as one of his sources.[34] In the Brotherhood Rechenschaft of 1542,[35] Peter
Riedemann also described the nature of Hutterian schools, where children
learned the meaning of *Gelassenheit* (the quality of yieldedness), a central
Anabaptist teaching which defined in large part the Hutterian community.

But it was Peter Walpot, who, because of the tremendous success of
the missioners in bringing in new converts, found it necessary to establish a
new code for the schools. Up to a certain point in the 1560s, it had been

taken for granted that the schools were providing the correct type of education for the children. Then, almost overnight, the crowded Haushaben created problems which needed attention. On November 15, 1568, a conference was held at Niemtschitz, Moravia, to discuss the school system. In the talk given by Walpot to the schoolmasters gathered from the various schools and to the elders also in attendance, many problems came to light and were dealt with.

The main point on the agenda concerned the practice, of some schoolmasters, of neglecting the direction of the school, busying themselves instead with other projects and leaving school management to the women. The consequence was poor child discipline and the improper use of corrective measures, especially for the boys. Walpot required the schoolmaster to assume full responsibility for all aspects of the school program.

Positive corrective measures were suggested, adjusted to the various types of individuals, rather than simply using the rod as the definitive answer to all problems. One pupil might respond to praise, Walpot suggested, others would need other measures. Often the mere presence of an observant schoolmaster would be all that was required to keep order.[36] Walpot proposed a solution as follows:

> The schoolmaster is not only to be present in the schoolroom for the children's sake, but also in order to be helpful and kind to the sisters, for they need your oversight just as much as the children, since women are women and the weaker vessel. Take care that they may not be aroused in their anger and in their complaints against the children and go about among them with rods, as one does among cattle, and permit the flesh to get the upper hand, so that they quickly become angry, as we have ourselves already experienced. A diligent schoolmaster can prevent such occurrences if he takes his responsibility toward the children seriously and deals with them as if they were his own.[37]

The schoolmaster, for example, upon checking the temperature of the bath water, was not to listen to certain sisters who were accustomed to saying: "Oh, how can you say it is too hot? Don't concern yourself about such things!" The schoolmaster was simply to go ahead with his duties.[38]

The conference apparently fulfilled its purpose, for the accounts which describe the schools during the 1570s speak about a successful educational program. The basic ideas emerging from the discussion were combined into an official school code, drawn up around the time of this conference, carefully outlining the duties of each worker such as those of the day and night nurses. The older girls were to rise at 5:00 a.m. and proceed to their early morning work of spinning. The boys were to rise at six. While these washed and dressed, the small children were to be washed and dressed and prepared for the morning prayer. They were to arrive at the tables in good time. Then the smallest children were to be cared for. They were to be given time to stretch before they were fed. Such a practice, it was noted in the code, had already been alluded to in the older Brotherhood code. The children were also to exercise after the evening meal before being sent to bed. Bedtime was at 6:00 p.m. in winter, and at sunset during the summer months. Regular recesses were to be given so that the children might take care of their natural needs, although at no time was a child to be refused permission to go to the toilet. Not to grant permission could lead to harmful effects. Children who had contagious diseases were to be kept separate from the healthy ones, and children with the same disease were to be grouped together, and kept separate from those with other diseases. The adults examining children for possible disease were to wash and dry their hands carefully before proceeding from child to child. Never was the whole group of children to be punished when only a few were guilty.

The goal of the school program was to teach children Gelassenheit (the attitude of yieldedness to God) by gradually encouraging them to voluntarily submit to the will of God. The schoolmaster, with the entire Brotherhood, was to raise the children in the honor and fear of God, and to subdue any evil inclinations from the time of their youth.

Ten years later, after Walpot's death in 1578, the school code was amended by the new Vorsteher, Hans Kräl. Again in 1585 under Claus Braidl's leadership minor additions were made, as also in 1588. In 1596 the leaders called another conference attended by all the elders, deacons and schoolmasters, who reviewed Walpot's long-remembered address of 1568 in an attempt to meet the school problems of the 1590s.[39]

By all counts the Hutterites maintained good schools. When problems arose, they were carefully dealt with. One reason for the success of the program undoubtedly lay in the support of the total leadership of the Brotherhood, including the ministers and the Vorsteher, all of whom were responsible for the formulation of the code itself. The sisters could now easily fall in line and accept the direction of the schoolmaster, because his authority was upheld by the higher authority of the total Brotherhood, and the still higher and ultimate authority of the biblical mandate.

## Coping with Economic Hardship

The Golden Years also included a period of widespread famine and inflation, from 1569 to 1572, which seriously affected the many thousands of

Hutterites living in scores of Haushaben. To feed a thousand mouths, or even five hundred, the size several Haushaben apparently reached, called for great care and foresight in stocking and distributing provisions. By 1569 economic conditions were already so severe that the Brotherhood found it necessary to establish a special Gemeindeordnung, lasting for the duration of the three-year famine which haunted all of Moravia. The Great Chronicle notes that the general population suffered severely, "a severe punishment resulting from their ingratitude and sins."[40]

The Hutterian Brotherhood managed fairly well under the circumstances. The leaders worked tirelessly day and night, to see that widows and orphans might be cared for. Indeed, even many poor people not belonging to the Hutterian Haushaben were helped. By 1572 the reserves were exhausted, but, as the chronicler adds at the end of his description of this famine, "The Lord knows the right time, and came with his gracious means—to him be praised, and for all his help, high thanksgiving."[41]

It is noteworthy that the Brotherhood had acted decisively in 1569 to meet the oncoming famine. On September 19, 1569, the elders met at Altenmarkt near Lundenburg to determine what course of action to take. They prepared a code which considered the needs of the various types of individuals within the Brotherhood: the sick, the healthy, those whose vocations demanded more nourishment, and those whose tasks demanded less manual effort. In general everyone was to receive breakfast at seven, bread at noon, and a cooked meal in the evening. On Wednesdays and Sundays there was to be meat if it was available. The *Haushalter* (steward) was to be attentive to the special needs of the sick, so that their individual requirements would be met. The sick were to be given whatever they needed or desired, limited only by the supplies on hand. No diligence was to be spared in caring for them. Those with common short-term ailments were to receive beer.

The code specified similar regulations for the entire body of workers, children, guests, and others. If, during the winter, it seemed evident the program could not be maintained, the whole Ordnung would need reconsideration.

The famine also affected the schedules of mothers with young children. When the children reached the age of one year (instead of the normal two), their mothers were to help with the work, entrusting their children to the care of older sisters. Such mothers were to be permitted to return an hour or two earlier than the rest of the workers. When the children were about a year and a half (instead of the usual policy of two years), they were to be placed in the community school unless there was special reason for the child to remain with its mother longer.

The usual regulations were to be continued for the day-laborers working for the nobility, who were not to keep any money but were to give their wages promptly to the Brotherhood. All purchases were to be made by those entrusted with buying and selling. The code closes with remarks which applied to all Brotherhood *Ordnungen:*

> The Haushalter is to preserve carefully this code so that it does not come into the hands of others, out of which disorder and unnecessary talk might arise, evoking more grief than peace. May God grant out of his abundance that, for the sake of our well-being, we adhere to all his rules and regulations, not minimizing their importance, but keeping them diligently, to the honor of his name. This we desire for all those who love God.[42]

## Resolving Conflict Within the Brotherhood

To keep life in the communities smoothly flowing, the Hutterian organization needed constant maintenance. A key to the strength of Hutterianism lay in the Brotherhood's way of handling the problems arising from human relationships. Most personal problems were taken care of immediately. During the Walpot Era, however, three men caused enough of a stir to be mentioned in the Great Chronicle, where personal problems are seen to intertwine with non-Anabaptist theological speculation.

A brother, Ruep Bidmer, held that anyone who said "von Herzen" ("from the heart") was a sinner and a fool and did not possess the Spirit. He left the Brotherhood in 1571, joined the Gabrielites, and thereafter "became a perverted and worthless man."[43]

Five years later, in 1576, Ott Niderlender wrote a letter to Walpot, wherein he asserted that faith in Christ not only took away the burdens of sin, but also the propensity to sin. When some of his own recent signs of weakness were pointed out to him, he said he had only recently entered into the new state of being. He was finally expelled because he was not of one mind with the Brotherhood.[44]

In 1577 still another brother, Herman Schmid, who had been with the Brotherhood for 35 years, wrote a letter to Walpot revealing some of his unusual beliefs about angels, the devil, and sin. The matter was brought to the attention of the Brotherhood, and Schmid was banned. He reconsidered and consented to repent. But after fourteen weeks of repentance he still wanted to retain three points of his doctrine; namely, that angels had never sinned, that they had no freedom of will (and therefore could not sin), and that they were one body with Christ before he came to earth; consequently Christ himself could not have sinned. The Great Chronicle concludes the account stating that Schmid had always been strange in his ways, and warning that the godly should be attentive to all types of temptation which arise in light of the myriad deceits and manifold deceptions of the devil.[45]

Certainly deviation on the articles of faith was not the only cause for excommunication in the cases of these three erring brethren. Yet their positions together with the firm Brotherhood responses suggest that the Hutterites felt strongly about three dangers to the Hutterian way: legalism, perfectionism, and the bondage of the will. The first two options were perennial pitfalls. The third belief would have weakened, if not destroyed, the very foundation of Anabaptism: discipleship and a voluntaristic, gathered brotherhood, both of which presupposed the freedom of the human will. Therefore, on a deeper level, if the rebellion of the erring brethren had not been confronted, it would have sorely threatened the unity of the essential Brotherhood spirit.

## Contemporary Accounts About the Hutterites Written by Outsiders

Hutterite accounts about themselves and their traditions were of course highly sympathetic interpretations. Does another picture emerge from the vantage point of outsiders who had contact with the Hutterites?

The Polish Brethren, with whom the Hutterites had contact during the years 1567-71, are a case in point (see Chapter Seven). Sometime in 1570 a Polish brother wrote a treatise against the Hutterian communal system,[46] describing it as follows: Each Hutterian community was composed of one to three houses, depending on the number of people present as well as the availability of space. All lived communally and all worked. The men lived separately from the women. The beds of the married couples were separated into cubicles with suspended sheets. The Brotherhood owned vineyards, fields, and property, and had great wealth. Each individual had his work assigned, and the people simply obeyed, carrying out the most menial tasks. No idlers were tolerated. The stronger men were sent out to thresh grain and to fell trees. Leaders were granted better meals than the rest of the community, for

while they fill their bellies with fish and meat and wine, they starve the rest on dishes made of water, without butter or any other fat, and a pig's trotter or a hen's leg thrown in for sustenance; and they do not give them beer but only water to drink.[47]

The Hutterites, he said, forbade their members to read the Scriptures, emphasizing their own printed Brotherhood Rechenschaft to a greater degree. The Polish brother who wrote the treatise phrased this polemic with occasional biting hostility. His sole purpose was to convince fellow Polish Brethren that the Hutterites, with their communal living, did not hold the key to an orderly society, which many Polish Brethren had believed to be true. In any case the author of the treatise admitted that he had never visited a Hutterian Haushaben although he had spoken with some Hutterites on a visit to the Polish Brethren at Cracow and Raków.[48] These were the famine years in Moravia when food was scarce; but the charge that the leaders were granted better food than others is true, for reasons which the Hutterites considered scriptural (1 Timothy 5:17f.).

A report from the Czech Brethren should also be noted. Its date is uncertain; the extant copy is dated 1589, yet the original report may have been written in the 1570s. The report contrasts the Anabaptist and Czech Brethren views on baptism, then describes the tensions arising between the Hutterite and non-Hutterite craftsmen, the latter charging that the Hutterites were an economic threat to local craftsmen by robbing them of their jobs, and to the populace as a whole by buying up the food supplies. There is also severe criticism of the Hutterian methods of child rearing. Finally they allege that some Hutterites were guilty of stealing several barrels of beer, and some wood from the forest, which the Hutterites had to return in shame when the deed was discovered.[49]

A report of 1567 from another outsider, an Italian, Varotto, is based on a stay of two months in Austerlitz. It is written without any apparent bias and includes a short description of the Hutterites. It notes that the Hutterites are in greater number than all the other sects and they are rich because many rich persons have given them their property to hold in common. It is their custom that in every land in which they find themselves they live together in one house as in a monastery, and they eat and drink and wear shoes all in common, poor and rich alike in those things that they wear. The fact is that the ministers lead

> an abundant life and hold in their hands the management of everything; on travels where others go by foot with walking sticks, they travel by horse and coach. Among them it is customary that if the members of the sect are wronged by being struck or robbed or having their wives carried off or any other, they offer no resistance; should

they put up any resistance, they are driven away or excommunicated by their ministers.[50]

Varotto's report, although not overtly derogatory, still must be seen as a superficial report; his interest in this richly diversified religious community is merely incidental.

A fourth contemporary report was written by a Tübingen professor, Stephen Gerlach, a relative of several Hutterites, who made a visit to a Hutterian community in September 1578. He was well received as a guest, and with his companion was served a meal which included meat, wine, and beer. He then visited his sister, a Hutterite, and incidentally stated that he had been continuously remembering her in prayer before God. He relates the following reaction:

> At this point, Christman [the husband of Gerlach's sister, Margaretha] interjected that I was not to pray to God, as God does not hear the prayer of the ungodly, but considers it sin. I could not wish him any good. When I accused him of being a proud hypocrite because of such a statement, he left us and walked behind us until my sister admonished him to be more friendly. Then he joined us again and asked me where I had been, what my experiences had been, etc.[51]

Gerlach reports further that the Lord of Löben, a former supervisor in Moravia and present owner of Stignitz, had with his wife attended the Hutterian communion service of the last Whitsuntide. The lord was fond of the Hutterites, Gerlach reports. Journeying on to Stignitz, Gerlach met his second sister, Sara, who was a nurse in the Hutterian school. She told him that children remained with their mothers until they were two, at which age they were placed in the school. The girls learned to pray and to read; the boys learned to read and write, and when they grew older they would learn a trade. Each day the children received fresh air in a nearby field or woods. They prayed each day that "they may be brought up in the fear of God, that they may be kept in the knowledge of God, that their brothers and sisters be kept from all harm." Then, kneeling, they prayed together the Lord's Prayer.[52]

Gerlach's sister, who reportedly had not especially wanted to marry her husband, related to Gerlach how marriages took place:

> On a certain Sunday the elders call all marriageable young men and women together, place them opposite each other and give each girl the choice of two or three fellows. She has to take one of them. She is not compelled, but she is not to do anything against the elders.[53]

Before Gerlach left, he was approached about the "Christian" way of
life. He mentioned how an elder, waiting for him at the gate, began talking
about trees needing to bear good fruit, and that in contrast to the many ungodly in the world, the Hutterites had left everything to follow Christ.
Community of goods was an issue, and the elders attempted to prove the
doctrine from 1 Corinthians 10:24.[54]

Gerlach's report, coming from the pen of an unbiased friend and relative, gives a welcome insight into Hutterianism during the late 1570s.

The Hutterites, to be sure, were fully aware of the precariousness of
their situation, for they well understood the reasons for Moravian toleration.
Perhaps the reason is best expressed by the Hutterite chronicler:

> Some would have liked nothing better than to employ them for
> their services and work. Here they were appreciated more than other
> people; so there were too few of them in the land, since—because of
> their faithfulness—everyone wanted them for his own benefit. But be-
> cause of their religion there were always too many of them in the land.
>
> It was a remarkable set of circumstances: some lords were angry
> and ill-disposed to them because of their faith and did not want them
> to be tolerated in the land; others were angry when they were not
> given more people to work for them, although for many years they kept
> asking. In short, some wanted to have them accepted, others wanted to
> have them expelled; some said the best about them, others the worst.
>
> The whole world was unwilling to tolerate them, yet it had to.
> God divided the sea—the raging nations of this world—so that people
> could be gathered from all lands and dwell together in great numbers,
> acting without fear. This was the work of the Lord, opposed to the
> devil and the world. Indeed, it was an amazing work of God, whoever
> thought about it: some people thought it was good and right for those
> who could do it, others wished they too could live like that; still others,
> the great majority, in their blindness saw it as error and seduction, or as
> a human undertaking (Isa. 11[:10-16]; 49[:8-13]).[55]

As the Hutterites knew, economic reasons helped determine their ongoing presence in Moravia; they were also convinced that it was an "amazing work of God." Tolerant lords of Moravia, such as Johann von Liechten-
stein, Lord of Nikolsburg, helped "God's work" along in their own way by
providing the haven where Hutterite converts from a variety of European
lands could converge. The whole process was an astonishing work, and the
fascinating intricacies of mission activity, effecting surges of families and
groups flowing into a sixteenth-century promised land have been preserved
in documents which graphically relate the drama of the Hutterites in dialogue with the world. Here is the story of Hutterian mission, a story long
unknown in its breadth and depth, yet a story worthy of detailed coverage.

Jörg Rader to Tirol, Hans Langenbach to the Rhine, Claus Braidl to Württemberg, and Peter Hörich to Silesia. Hutterite missioners not only trekked through all parts of the German lands, but also to Switzerland, the Low Countries, Italy, Poland, Bohemia, Slovakia, and even as far as Denmark. Although the Hutterites tried to keep careful record of their mission program, government sources yield evidence of a far greater outreach than the voluminous Hutterian codices would indicate.[2]

These missioners, if apprehended, received a variety of punishments. Some were simply threatened and admonished. One missioner heard that he might be sent to the galleys. A short entry for the year 1567 in the Great Chronicle is by no means atypical: When Burckhart Bämerle, an aged minister, was imprisoned along with his companion, Bärthl Ringel, no ordinary hundred-weights were hung on him, but rather the whole earth; for a ring was fastened to the earth, Bämerle's feet were tied to the ring, and the unfortunate prisoner was pulled up "so that the sun could have shone through him." The prisoner remained steadfast, was later released, but died the same year at Tracht, Moravia.[3]

The Hutterites' great antagonist, the Catholic missioner Christian Erhard, describes the "damage" brought about by the Hutterites and their missioners, who, he reported,

> sneak about in the country and secretly commit serious crimes. Just look at the huge heap of wasps in Moravia; that is where they annually seduce the people.... And these Hutterites are the very same Anabaptists who are hanged and drowned in Tirol, the region of Salzburg, Bavaria, Switzerland, etc., and are scorched and burned according to their deserved reward. Other Anabaptists are not able to seduce the people so secretly, quietly, and treacherously.[4]

Erhard's vituperaton not only shows his disapproval of the toleration accorded the Hutterites in Moravia, which is what he intended, but also demonstrates the effectiveness of the Hutterian mission.

## The Method of Hutterian Mission

Hutterian mission strategy took many forms. Personal encounter was the usual method used, but group-evangelism also occurred, usually secretly held in the open, in barns, and in homes.[5] Missioners were sent out into the world around Easter, and again in the autumn. They met with seekers wherever and whenever possible, sometimes in cellar recesses, sometimes in forests, and at times, at night.[6] The experience of Valentin

Hörl provides an insight into a missioner's arduous travels. With several other brethren he was sent out in 1571 to determine how many souls were left in Tirol who were seeking God's righteousness, and who were desirous of reforming their way of living. Hörl's three comrades had already toured the upper Inn and the Eisack valleys, and Hörl had made inquiries at various localities, including the Adige. The group was planning to meet at a certain place, but something went amiss. Hörl then searched for his comrades in the Puster Valley, and found them on the road just above Schöneck. Because they were finding no one who desired to give himself over to divine obedience they went to Stertzing, and from there directly to Moravia, so as not to misappropriate their funds.[7]

Mission was also carried on through written communication. The mission activity of Hans Schlegel and Simon Kress in the early summer of 1574 in the area of Maulbronn, Württemberg, is an example of both personal and epistolary mission. Kress told Schlegel of his visit to a man whom we know only as Caspar, who had shown genuine interest in Hutterian Christianity. Instead of visiting Caspar, Schlegel merely wrote a letter to him. The probable reason was that circumstances necessitated Schlegel's "hurrying to another place," in all likelihood because the authorities had caught wind of his work. At least Schlegel was able to lend Caspar a printed copy of the Brotherhood Rechenschaft, which he was to return in two or three weeks. The letter expressed Schlegel's hope that the work would bring Caspar blessing and eternal peace. Schlegel apologized for not coming in person, testifying that he was indeed responsible to contact any person showing interest in true righteousness and that he wanted to witness to the truth to the degree that God's grace resided within him. Realizing Caspar might find the Rechenschaft difficult at places, he asked Caspar not

> to desire to understand it with flesh and blood, for flesh and blood cannot reveal [truth] since flesh and blood must lose its own will at this point and die to itself if man is to obey and be made a living person in Christ.[8]

Schlegel further suggested that this is why Christ had commended the narrow way where few were able to enter: "Christ himself is this path and entrance, a way full of derision, pain, and suffering."[9]

It was behind this gate that Christ stood "with his poverty, with his bloody garment and crown of thorns, and with the cup of the bitter cross and suffering." It was this way of life which Christ presented to those who desired divine inheritance. Yet many attempted some sort of compromise to this narrow way, "bending Scripture back and forth so that one might find a wide road that is not so hard, and desiring to break open another gate into heaven." Such persons however were only thieves and robbers. Schlegel suggested therefore that if Caspar desired to seek the kingdom of heaven, he should seek it correctly.[10]

The Hutterites carried this same missionary message to their relatives living in the "world." In April 1574 Margarete Endris, a Hutterite at Wastitz, sent such a letter to her non-Hutterite son Elias, in Horren, Württemberg. Two other children of Margarete, Gretl and Jörgle, had already joined the Hutterites in Moravia. Elias had just written that his two sisters were planning to make the journey. Margarete responded that this would bring her real joy if they came with good intentions and desired to live according to God's will.[11]

But Elias also had wondered on what grounds his Hutterite mother opposed his Protestant faith. Margarete replied that he was deviating from God's truth and the teachings of Christ by turning baptism into child's play, and by transforming the Lord's Supper into idolatry and financial gain, communing and sharing with participants who might still be living in sin, contrary to biblical teachings. Furthermore, she continued, a Christian was a godly person, and this was not the case with Elias, who was instead traveling down the broad way of the devil, thereby demonstrating the works of the flesh. God did not want such "Christians," who only confessed a "holy Christian church" with words but in reality were part of an unholy congregation which disgraced his name. Indeed, her son's congregation did not even demonstrate mutual aid![12]

Margarete expressed the hope that her son would leave the world and change his manner of life, accept the new birth, and separate himself from the world. She pleaded with him not to hesitate:

> Become converted to God and come to his people. For we have no doubt that this is the people of God, the correct way, the narrow gate, the true faith through which one becomes godly and is redeemed in Christ Jesus our Lord and Savior. May you desire to submit to this, you and your wife, and my two daughters if they are still out there. This is our heart-felt request.... From me, Margarete, your loyal mother.[13]

## The Content of the Mission Message

Hutterite missioners proclaimed a uniform doctrine wherever they were active, based on the Brotherhood Rechenschaft, printed in the 1540s and again in 1565. However, a growing tradition built upon the written reports of cross-examinations also contributed to the growing refinement of the mission message. As will be seen below, the writings of such Hutterite missioners as Claus Felbinger and Hans Mändl, for example, were well known to Veit Uhrmacher as well as to the authorities at Innsbruck, for these very writings were carried by missioners in codex form during their travels.[14] Other writings which attempted to present the Hutterian argument more cogently were gradually added to the Brotherhoods' programmatic volumes, such as Leonhard Dax's Refutation, a moving and incisive Concordance and its accompanying apologia and polemic, the ironic and biting "Charges and Allegations of the Blind, Perverse World," and the Great Article Book.[15]

Another solid tract entitled "Valuable Directions and Instructions on How to Turn Unbelievers from Their Error" was composed specifically for missioners, probably by Leonhard Dax during the 1560s.[16] The document begins with an analysis of man's lost state and God's proffered redemption. Adam is to blame for the lost state of mankind, but through Christ salvation has again been realized for the true disciples who remain in his teachings. The redeemed Christian community, composed of these very disciples, remains in conflict with the world, occasioned in part by mission, for the world does not desire to acknowledge God or his messengers, but rather persecutes them. Although the world claims to be Christian, it demonstrates by its actions, such as persecuting innocent missioners, that it is not Christian; and God, at the appropriate moment, will cast down his vengeance upon such ungodly people.

The document continues with a discussion about the world and its magistracy, which exists without God. Since there is a close relationship between it and the established church, the true nature of Christianity and its way of peace lies hidden not only from the world, but also from the established church. Furthermore, the false prophets of these established churches, with their claim of Christian truth, cause the magistrates to believe their words, and lead them to transcend their rightful bounds.

A general appeal is then made for people to turn away from the ways of the world and enter the Christian way of life. For, as the argument continues, the world has created havoc out of biblical precepts, such as the Lord's Supper. Indeed, anyone who eats with an unrepentant sinner shows himself not to be of God's holy community, the church. Partaking in the Lord's Supper, correctly understood, means acknowledging complete agreement and fellowship with one another. Baptism too is of the greatest import to the devil, for if infant baptism were rescinded, then much of his power would be broken, since he "knows that when a person allows himself to be baptized in the Christian manner, he then completely renounces

service to the devil."[17] As for marriage, the priests, who do not even enter
into it, lead wanton lives, which to them is better than to break the man-
made rules of celibacy.

In short, the Hutterites believed that the world simply did not allow
Scripture to bring men to repentance and the forgiveness of sins. The result
was evident: God's punishment continued to prevail in the world. But at
the opposite pole of this retribution lay God's redemption. The Christian
was to live in such a manner that the world and its evil—namely, the false
prophets, persecution, and martyrdom—did not overcome him. For God
granted salvation to his true children, who remained steadfast until the end.

The tract closes with a final appeal to those living in the world. The nature of Christian mission is defined by contrasting the nature of the Christian way of life to that of the world. The following paraphrase captures the
mood of the appeal: The world wants to claim for itself what the Lord has
promised only for the godly, to whom he has shown his grace. The world
wants to cover everything over with the mercy of God without perceiving to
whom he wants to be merciful—namely, not to the ungodly. But sin earns
only death, not the grace of God. One is to follow Christ, who said: "Where
I am, there shall my servants be." He who lives the life of Christ's goodness
will receive eternal life; he who lives a life of evil will receive damnation.
But this does not imply salvation through good works, for salvation rests
only within the atoning power of Jesus Christ. Yet good works are surely to
be there, for Christ is the example. Christians are to do as Christ did and
keep his word by loving one another, the sign of discipleship. For the Christian has died, and his life is hidden with Christ in God, with victory at the
end; although for the ungodly, raging hell will be the reward.[18]

In this tract one may note the Hutterian view of salvation, where a distinction is made between the discipleship-mandate of Christ that entails
bearing fruit, and a works-religion which the author believes he
experienced as a former Catholic priest. The Hutterian call to mission was
an appeal to divine mercy, founded solely upon Christ's redeeming act. Yet
by accepting this mercy, the Christian could not but demonstrate the Christian experience of a transformed life.

## The Results of Hutterian Mission

The majority of those thousands of recruits finding their way to Hutterian communities adopted the new way of life. The Hutterian way was a
way to eternal salvation, but also a way out of material poverty for many.[19]
Many types of immigrants converted to Hutterianism. During the late
sixteenth century, some complaints surfaced about the lack of drive among

some converts; they were nevertheless accepted in the expectation that both spiritual growth and physical dexterity would gradually become manifest. The continuing strength of the Brotherhood suggests that the Hutterian hopes were realized.[20]

The Brotherhood's capability of receiving total strangers into its close communal system is also substantiated by no less a figure than the bold tholic, Christoph Andreas Fischer. Fischer's compliment, obviously intended as an attack, witnesses to the continuing success of the mission program well beyond the Walpot Era:

> Just as doves fly out and continually bring strange doves back with them, the Anabaptists also send out their false apostles annually to seduce the people, both women and men, and bring them into their dove-cotes—as I have been told that in 1604 they enticed more than two hundred persons out of the Empire, leading them into their dove-cotes. And just as newly-captured doves are pampered with wheat, honey, and other things during the first days, until they become accustomed [to their new environment], the Anabaptists also give their new accomplices rich foods and roasts, and very sweet hypocritical words. But afterwards comes the time to "go and work, and be satisfied with cabbage and beets."[21]

It was incomprehensible to populace and magistrate alike that well-to-do farmers would voluntarily forsake productive farms by night for no apparent reason but to join with the distant Hutterites. A passion for private riches and prestige was transformed into a desire for total surrender to God, and a life of complete sharing within a brotherhood. On the other hand, economic reasons led some poverty-stricken families also to make their way to Moravia, the "promised land" of the Hutterites.[22]

Although most of the converts became a part of the expanding Hutterian movement, adapting themselves willingly, a few disenchanted souls returned to the land of their birth. In the winter of 1577, for instance, a handful of young men went to Moravia to look around, returned to their homeland disillusioned, and told the magistrates that they had no desire to return to Moravia. Others, however, returned to the Hutterian fold, sometimes bringing with them their families or other acquaintances.[23]

## The Missioners' Farewell Service

At the time of departure of one or more missioners, the community held a special farewell service. A poem, still extant, was sung for the occasion, entitled "A New Song, Written in 1568, on the Theme of 'When the Brethren Depart for Other Lands.'" The impressive ceremony developed as a prayerful litany in which the missioners, in dialogue with the gathered community, solemnized under God the commission placed upon them.[24] The following résumé offers an insight into what must have been a most meaningful experience to both church and missioners, the latter perhaps never to return.

First of all, attention was called to the original mandate for mission: God has granted his salvation through the coming of Christ to all who accept his counsel and follow his teachings. Hence, as the Father sent Christ, so Christ also sent his disciples to proclaim the gospel. God continues to send his disciples so that people may turn from their evil ways. The message these disciples are to proclaim is that everyone without exception must someday appear before God and account for his deeds and for every idle word.

Then followed a petition to God for perseverance in proclamation, and for divine guidance in scriptural interpretation, that God's covenant be preserved, that the missioners refrain from idle talk in their striving to seek God's honor and glory, and that people far and wide might hear the message of the need to repent by separating themselves from the sins of the world in order to enter into salvation.

Next a reminder was given about the stark reality of divine punishment: Whenever God had desired to punish people, he first warned and taught them. If they did not repent, he brought on punishment. But God is still sending out his Word, proclaiming to the people how they should change in their ways, separate from the worldly Babel and all its impurity, submit to God, and become part of his community. Since the last hour is near, the godly are to be prepared. They are to gather Christ's chosen ones according to his command.

Attention then turned to the missioners themselves: They, God's chosen emissaries, will have to bear the pangs of misery within the world, confident of gathering the fruit resulting from the proclaimed seed.

At that point the missioners responded to the gathered community, acknowledging their call and requesting the continuing prayers of the church, so that God would comfort the missioners with the presence of his Spirit and protect them from suffering. The spirit of the service is well expressed in one of their hymns, a prose résumé of which follows:

> As we depart, our dear brethren, we embrace you with the arms of our hearts, in the pure love of Christ.... May God bless you, the whole Brotherhood, with the pure peace of Christ. May God keep you faith-

ful, that you honor his name.

God alone knows, O dear brethren, whether we shall see you again on this earth. Keep us faithful and devout, O God, on Your heavenly throne. If it be our lot nevermore to be in your presence, God continues to comfort us evermore, in that after this suffering, we shall look upon one another for ever and ever. For in the kingdom of eternal peace which we await, no one can separate us from, or rob us of, the eternal crown if we remain upright and steadfast in this present life, until the end.

O God, help us to attain this goal, through Jesus Christ Your dear Son. Amen.

In response to this confession of faith, the community then affirmed:

> May events unfold as pleases God, that you may be an honor and glory to him, and a comfort to all the children of the entire holy Brotherhood. Commend yourselves to God from the depths of your hearts, that he may constantly accompany you. May God lead you, dear worthy brethren. May he grant you increase, to be fruitful on this earth. May God, who said that "Your increase will be great," bless you as manna, and may you give him the praise with joy and victory for eternity.

A final prayer, spoken by the missioners, brought the ceremony to a close:

> We commend our task to You, O God, You, who have prepared everything. If You desire to call us home from these dangers soon, come to the aid of Your tender children, that we may cross the Jordan properly. Remain with us on the journey.
>
> Your Word has spoken to us. We have perceived that You will be with us always, until the end. You have prepared joy for the godly. Praise be to You at all times, glory be to Your Holy Name, through Christ in eternity. Amen.[25]

Another Hutterian document found in a seventeenth-century codex sheds light upon the farewell services of missioners and the nature of the later Hutterian mission.[26] A missioner goes to the front of the assembled congregation and announces that he and others have been chosen through the counsel of the Lord to go out into foreign lands to gather a church. He acknowledges the immensity of the task and the limitations of man's resources; yet God has demanded obedience in service to the church. Indeed, since God has previously been able to use simple folk for his work, the missioners hope that God may grant them renewed opportunities.

Within the farewell service, various points were brought to the attention of the community. If mission was to be successful and bring people to Moravia, the Hutterites would constantly have to keep in mind that they were to be living examples of a unity wherein life and doctrine merged. The newcomers were to be accepted with joy. Patience was to be the rule in case the incoming people did not immediately comprehend their new vocations. There were not to be hard words such as "Oh, you coarse Swiss; you cavilling Rhinelander; you bad Hessian!"[27] Rather, humility was called for toward everyone. For each person should consider how he had been accepted into the community with love and friendliness, and that the stranger was unaccustomed to everything: the language, the work, even the food and drink.

The missioner then admonished the youth to follow the instruction of the adults and to learn from them, and even accept punishment and counsel with gratitude. They were to commend themselves to the elders as they would to parents, not begrudging them their food and drink, but trusting them, and accepting their advice. He admonished the adults to care for the sick, the elderly, and the widows and orphans.

At this point the missioner asked for the prayers for the church, and for pardon if he had caused any hurt. He thanked the community for the love shown him from the time of his youth. Then in closing he announced that the missioners would soon depart.

After this a member from the congregation arose and praised the missioners, referring to them as sheep among raving wolves, as people facing possible death, as mirrors to the world. The possible harsh treatment of prison towers and chains was acknowledged. Then there was prayer for successful mission.

Finally, following apostolic custom, the congregation accompanied the missioners to the town gates. There, after the missioners were blessed, the parting became a stark reality, leading to certain hardship, probable persecution, possible death.

If the missioner returned, he was received "as if he were the Lord himself." The successes of the mission were lauded, and the reports of imprisoned missioners eagerly awaited. Prison epistles were handed to the addressees, greetings delivered, and reports made, some of which found their way into the Great Chronicle.[28]

## Confessional Encounters During the Walpot Era

The reports of returning missioners are our main source for understanding the nature of the encounters between the Hutterites and the of-

ficials of the various established churches regarding questions of faith. Some
of the cross-examinations of imprisoned Hutterites were cruel grillings, carried out under torture. Others were genuine discussion, with give-and-take
on both sides. Most of the sessions, however, lay between these two poles.

Virtually the whole problem of conflict during the Walpot Era revolved around the fact that the Hutterites held to an entirely different approach to mission from that of the established churches. Protestant mission
was generally limited to the confines of established magisterial boundaries.
The Anabaptists, on the other hand, believed firmly with the psalmist that
all the earth is the Lord's and the fullness thereof, and all that dwell therein
(Psalm 24:1). This idea demanded an obedience to Christ's mission
mandate, despite tribulation through the devil's workmen or the depths of a
watery grave. Consequently Hutterian mission led devout messengers
throughout Europe, searching out individuals and groups who were open to
the Hutterian message, whether their background was Catholic, Lutheran,
Zwinglian, and Calvinist, or Swiss Brethren, Italian Anabaptist, and Polish
Brethren.

Within the following account of Hutterian mission, a way of life and
its rationale slowly unfolds which differs radically from that of any other
sixteenth-century religious group. The unique Hutterian position found
expression, as has already been noted, in the testimonies of Hutterite witnesses under torture, but also in exhaustive deliberation and lengthy
epistles, as well as in open exchanges on the nature of faith. Where genuine
discussion occurred, such as that between Leonhard Dax and the
superintendent at Alzey, a growing awareness of an outside, in this case
Calvinistic, doctrinal stance can be noted in the Hutterian answers (see
Chapter Six). Very likely a similar growing awareness of the nature of the
Anabaptist faith also resulted for the interrogator. Paul Glock paused to
reflect upon both his Swiss Brethren and Catholic opponents' positions, giving them just consideration and finding some grounds of mutual agreement
as a result of the personal encounter; there is also evidence that Glock influenced the Catholic and Swiss Brethren prisoners as well. These, however,
were the exception. For throughout the sixteenth century the overt winner
in disputations was of course invariably the establishment. In this sense,
Luther himself "lost" in 1521 during his Worms encounter with the Roman
Church. Anabaptist-Reformed colloquies of the earlier decades yielded
similar results for the religious establishment, since the Zwinglian-Calvinist
church also considered itself the sole repository of truth for all inhabitants.

When the Hutterites in Moravia served as their own "protocol
secretaries," it was also a foregone conclusion that in the written accounts

they would emerge the victors. Death at the hands of the world did not deter them from proclaiming victory, for they measured victory not in terms of worldly values of profit and gain, but from the perspective of God who is both reconciler and judge, and that of Scripture which is the rulebook revealing his justice. And the same Scripture that revealed God's mercy was also clear about God's judgment upon a disobedient world. This position is suggested by the motto: "Die Wahrheit ist untödlich ewiglich" ("Truth can never be killed"), found embossed on leather covers of numerous Hutterian codices.[29] This motto, probably taken from Balthasar Hubmaier, hints at the "rules of the game" upon which the Hutterites could proclaim victory; namely, that victory, lying outside human hands, judgments, and norms, is based in the ultimate truth of God's Word and of coming judgment.

During the Walpot Era, Hutterite prisoners were granted little chance to speak out and fully express their position, even in their cross-examinations. But when they were permitted to answer they usually demonstrated—granting their own presuppositions—a coherent logic, both in rejecting other positions, and in defending their own. But the possible effect of such witness upon the sometimes numerous listeners was usually reduced by an intentional interruption on the part of the examiner for the purpose of cornering the witness and making him recant, or at least proving him to be enough of a public threat to merit further imprisonment.

At times, however, such unjust grilling backlashed, and the prisoner's witness gave rise to new waves of response among the people in favor of the victim's mission, indeed, a response which at times touched the nobility, and even a few magistrates. At least the system did not always work according to plan, as can be noted specifically in the encounters between the Catholics and Hans Arbeiter, the Lutherans and Paul Glock, and the Calvinists and Leonhard Dax.

That the cross-examiners intentionally thwarted the Anabaptist argument by cutting into discussion before the Anabaptist could clinch his argument is asserted by both Hans Arbeiter and Paul Glock. Yet little of this interruption of argument appears in the "protocols" of the various confrontations, for the simple reason that most of the accounts were undoubtedly written at a later date, sometime after the brisk debate and tense argument itself had taken place. The Hutterian Rechenschaften are in that sense interpretations of the original cross-examinations rather than verbatim accounts. Answers which were cut short during the encounters are presented in the written version as completed replies. The accurate citations of biblical passages, down to such detail as chapter and paragraph footnotings, give the impression that the actual discussions had been just as neat and logical. Yet first-person quotations attributed to the various individuals entering the discussion reveal at least the mood and general content of the original wording.

Obviously it must be assumed that the Hutterite spokesman some-times also misinterpreted his opponent, but we have made no attempt to guess when this occurred. Yet after a man has undergone the long and exhausting process of debate and argument, sometimes under torture, he is usually in a position to interpret reliably on paper those things he himself said, or at least intended to say, to his antagonist. The Hutterian issues and answers emerge clearly.

The importance of the intention of these Rechenschaften dare not be underrated, for they show very clearly one of the areas of strength among the Hutterites: the concern to motivate human beings for the cause of Christ, and the tenacity to pursue such motivation to its logical result, no matter the consequence. Such a creative rendition of experiences as Leonhard Dax and Hans Arbeiter gave, for example, could only have been written by one who knew how to grasp the initiative and make the most of events not only during the questioning but also in reporting happenings at a later date.

It is difficult to fathom a "way of life" only through the process of analyzing a man's confession of faith. A person's inner experience can never be caught fully in such a logical method. Nevertheless, an analytical approach is necessary to complement the narration of the historical aspects of a man's life, especially if he consciously wrote doctrinally, as a handful of missioners indeed did. Dax was the most systematic in his doctrinal formulations during the Walpot Era. Yet even he fits the lengthy description of Anabaptists and their view of life, granted us by a leading Anabaptist scholar:

> The Anabaptist confessions of faith are not creedal statements in a narrow sense, binding for the church, but are rather testimonies or personal statements, making clear how every brother understood personally the Anabaptist outlook, and how he would indicate his own position (far beyond mere literalism). These statements were Christian documents of a genuine character and of great spiritual depth, not something "learned" or repetitions of what others had said. . . . One cannot help being impressed by this matter-of-fact certitude about things spiritual and by the clarity as to why this "way" was chosen and how it must be pursued. There is no fear whatsoever of suffering and death, and with all the respect due to authorities a courageous stand before judges and other officials becomes apparent. There is much nobility of mind, quite in contrast to the uncouthness of most officials and

the times in general, a dignity which proves in itself that these people went through a real conversion. It is a surprising fact, incidentally, that although each brother defends himself independently and out of a personal commitment, Anabaptist documents by and large show an amazing likemindedness, proving again that whosoever was touched by the Spirit from on high experienced and understood more or less the same truth. The "world" had no attraction for them, but also no dread anymore.[30]

It is true that the Rechenschaften and epistles were not directly "something 'learned' or repetitions of what others had said," yet the growing corpus of writings plus the printed Brotherhood Rechenschaft were certainly significant factors in preserving Hutterian unity.

Looking at the accounts of Hutterian confrontation with the world between 1565 and 1578, one is impressed with the frequent conflict which erupted between missioner and establishment, which in some cases led to the ultimate punishment, martyrdom.

The story of these missioners, sometimes glorious, sometimes tragic, but almost always victorious by Hutterian count is a mirror reflecting Hutterian life. For here personalities, their foibles and valor realistically intertwined, emerge as human beings who deserve a listening ear, an ear which has all too long been virtually nonexistent. Most of this history has heretofore not been published, and can only be found in codices under the accumulated archival dust of centuries.[31] This mirror reveals a cross-section of a group of sixteenth-century Christians who saw the world through dark, yet at times well-focused, glasses. Faith and culture intermingle in a way conforming to the Hutterian way of life, where Christian truth reveals itself in deed and word—all of life being an expression of man's faith, where actions, deeds, and thoughts must be brought into one organic unity in order to correspond to man's sincerely held convictions. To what degree the Hutterite missioners accomplished such a unity can be judged by the unfolding story itself.

# Ch.4

# Hutterian Encounter
# with Catholicism

The absolutist position of sixteenth-century Catholicism took its toll not only among the various Anabaptist brotherhoods, but also within the Lutheran and Calvinist churches. All dissenters were condemned as apostates and heretics. But the Anabaptists, out of all proportion to their number, felt the full weight of Catholic law, in consequence of the Anabaptist view that mission and witness were to extend throughout the "earth of the Lord," which took Anabaptist missioners into officially Catholic territory.

The experience of nine representative Hutterite missioners of the Walpot Era who were caught in the severe policy of the Roman Church throws some light on the encounter between the Hutterites and the Catholics. Five were killed: Hans Jorg, Wolf Binder, Hans Missel, and Hans Platner were all martyrs of the Walpot Era, and Hans Mang died in prison as a result of many months of cruel treatment.[1]

Another imprisoned Hutterite missioner, Valentin Hörl, escaped death because his jailers ignored official protocol by not reporting his case to the higher church officials—an example of the occasional magistrate who had the courage to act upon his better impulse. Throughout Anabaptist history there were instances when civil magistrates, whose official duty it was to enforce law and order, treated the missioners more leniently than did the church officials, who represented "truth." For after these magistrates had learned to know the imprisoned missioners personally, they often showed them sympathy.[2]

The five martyrs named above left few records. Fortunately for the historian, three other missioners incarcerated in Catholic lands during the Walpot Era left extensive records of their prison experiences. Their accounts and confessions of faith are the basis of this chapter. The story of Nikolaus Geyersbühler's imprisonment is apparently taken from the official court transcript itself. Hans Arbeiter wrote his own account of his experiences and debate. Veit Uhrmacher, from within the high, impenetrable walls of the mighty Salzburg prison, found the means to smuggle a long letter out to Vorsteher Peter Walpot recounting his three years in prison.

The varied experiences of these three missioners document the evolution of sixteenth-century Catholic thought and practice in its attempt to regain a vast segment of the European populace. The earlier Catholic policy of absolute severity toward heretics moderated into a policy of leniency, with prolonged efforts to convert erring souls. The newly established Jesuit order created new techniques to cope with the realities of a schism that was deeper and wider than any previous division in the universal church. Whereas Geyersbühler, in the mid-1560s, received the traditional treatment accorded heretics, Uhrmacher's fate in the 1570s demonstrated a slight turn toward more humane treatment. On the other hand, Arbeiter's prison term, although occurring in the 1560s, was very different from the other two in style, method, and outcome. Jesuit ideology was clearly visible here, and with it, a brand-new methodology.

## Nikolaus Geyersbühler, Missioner to Tirol

Tirol, the mountainous Oberland of Austria, played a key role in the formation of the Anabaptist movement in Moravia; it was the place of origin of a large percentage of the Hutterites. Some of the great early leaders were Tirolese—the founder of the movement, Jacob Hutter himself, and Peter Walpot, the staunch leader during the Golden Years of the Hutterites. Tirol also continued to be a rich Hutterian mission field well into the Walpot Era, an important exception to the general rule for Catholic-held territory. And this was four decades after George Blaurock's martyrdom in southern Tirol. A perennial yield of converts resulted from the effort of evangelists who courageously exposed themselves to the risk of death at the stake. Many missioners to Tirol, whose activities are chronicled in contemporary documents, were never apprehended. Many others, of course, were executed.

Nikolaus Geyersbühler was caught in 1566. His story unfolds as a revealing portrayal of both Anabaptist mission strategy and the traditional old-guard, unrelenting Catholic methods of handling heretics. It also affords significant insights into Hutterian homeland communities and doctrine.[3]

Most of the known elements of Geyersbühler's life were told by the brother himself in the torture chamber during hours of intense grilling. The record is almost certainly a copy, perhaps somewhat modified, of the official cross-examination transcript. How the Hutterites obtained the document remains a mystery. Johann Loserth says of this confession that it presents conditions among the Anabaptists less favorably than do other sources. It does clearly differ from other Hutterian confessions, and communicates a vastly different mood. Other records of confessions, generally written some time after the event itself, were a Hutterian interpretation of what had taken place, edited by time and memory. Of all the confessions written during the Walpot Era, this is the only one written in the third person. The confession seems to be the careful and generally objective work of a Catholic court recorder.[4]

### Geyersbühler's Conversion to Hutterianism

Nikolaus Geyersbühler was born in Geyersbühel, in the district of Kitzbühel in Tirol. He later lived in the village of St. Johann. Two of his brothers, Wolf and Jeronimus, converted to Hutterianism. Another brother, George, and a sister lived in the Hopfgarten area near Salzburg.

Geyersbühler's decision to join the Hutterites was not easily made. It took many brethren and many years to convince him of the correctness of the Hutterian way. The first brother who approached him was a Kitzbühler, George Vierstadtler. So many others had come to him, explaining the truth "purely and clearly" from Scripture, that he could not recall the number, let alone all their names. He finally submitted his life to God, accepted the truth, and desired the true Christian baptism.

The witness of his own brother, Wolf, who had come from Moravia upon Nikolaus's request, persuaded Geyersbühler to go to Moravia. After discussing at length the life and faith of the Hutterites he accompanied his brother back to the Hutterian Brotherhood.

Geyersbühler, with many others, was baptized about 1555 at Sabatisch by Vorsteher Peter Riedemann in the presence of a group of witnesses. He was appointed head miller and overseer in the mill and the dairy farm of a Bohemian nobleman, the royal notary, Simon Helden, Lord at Gross-Meseritsch and Niemtschitz near Seelowitz. Geyersbühler also was elected to the important Brotherhood office of *Diener der Notdurft*.

## Geyersbühler's Mission

In 1566 the Brotherhood sent Geyersbühler back to his homeland to gather converts and bring them to Moravia. He bade farewell to his wife, Magdalena, and his four-year-old daughter, Maria, at Niemtschitz, and began the long trek with two other brethren, Peter and Veit Berger. During their weeks of scouting throughout Tirol and beyond, Geyersbühler and the Bergers gathered only seven converts: four from the Salzburg district, two from Bavaria, and one from Kitzbühel. Their failure to find more converts indicates that mission prospects among the Tirolese were declining.

Unfortunately, the group, now numbering ten, was apprehended while passing through the district of Klinger. The seven converts were released because they had not been baptized, very probably with a serious warning never again to consider such a move. But the three Hutterites were held. The Bergers recanted at once and were released. Geyersbühler, however, refused to recant, and was confined in the "Kreuterhaus" prison. Jacob Sauerwein, the district judge of Sonnenburg (Vellenberg Castle), supervised the proceedings. Jesuit and other priests made repeated attempts to persuade the prisoner to renounce his "error," but in vain. Finally on April 19, 1566, Sauerwein received orders from the government chancery to proceed with a cross-examination on the rack. Forty-seven questions were drawn up and the grilling took place ten days later. Geyersbühler answered some questions only in part. He refused to give the names of those who had been with him at the time of his arrest, saying he was certain a full report had been sent to the Innsbruck officials. Nor would he reveal the names of the innkeepers or boatmen who had unwittingly treated him well, nor for that matter, those who had not. The only persons he would name even under torture had either died, or would have had no reason to travel to Tirol, such as his own wife and child.

Accused of having been led astray by a heretical sect, Geyersbühler asserted that he belonged to no sect; the Hutterites held to the true way of life leading to life eternal. Furthermore, he said, he had not been led astray; on the contrary, his fellow members in Christ, through the prompting of divine grace, had encouraged and led him onto the true path where the godly walked who lived in true faith, hope, love, and patience.

## Geyersbühler's Faith

In analyzing the nature of "the true path," one discovers in Geyersbühler's thought the same biblical framework as had been developed by Jacob Hutter, and set in writing by Peter Riedemann. The Anabaptists held a high view of tradition. Sola scriptura, to be sure, was basic; but it was modified by their view of history, leading from the Patriarchs and Prophets to the coming of Jesus and the consequent birth of the church, from which event they interpreted all of Scripture as well as later history. This is one reason why the first years of the Christian Era (Acts 2-4), a time when the waters ran pure, were so utterly important to the Hutterites.

### a. The Disciple within Christian Community

Whereas discipleship was the basic principle in the founding of Anabaptism in 1525 which led to the realization of the gathered church, by the time of Hutter in the 1530s the nature of the church had become the central issue. The individual disciple was seen in the light of Christian community and could ultimately be understood only in view of such a close-knit community of peace dominated by God's Spirit. The nature of sin could be identified only from the point of view of this new creation—not by those living in sin, nor even by confessing Christians who were not experiencing the working of the Spirit *among* brethren. Here was a new dimension added to the inner *sola fide* of Lutheranism, which separated the Hutterian Brotherhood from all who chose to root their lives within general society.

### b. Scripture and Tradition

Whereas for the Roman Catholics tradition rested largely upon the wealth of rules, mores, and customs which had developed over the centuries out of the councils and decrees, Geyersbühler looked to the tradition of the early church as established by the apostles upon the command of Christ. What the apostles had written determined the nature of the church, including the congregational pattern itself. Also included was the reality of brotherly love and mutual sharing. Any deviation from this pattern, he adamantly maintained, resulted in something less than the Christian church.

### c. The Lord's Supper

Two radically opposing views of the nature of the Lord's Supper emerged in the discussion: the Catholics held that the essential and the true body of Jesus Christ resides in the sacrament of communion, which, when eaten, brings forgiveness, a means of receiving and enjoying Jesus Christ. For Geyersbühler, the Christ who is seated at the right hand of the Father could not be brought into the hearts of men by material means, but only through the living Word of God, which does not "dwell in temples made with human hands." Consequently for Geyersbühler the Lord's Supper held a very different significance. He believed that its original intent could be respected only when it was observed among repentant brethren who had accepted God's Word, had given themselves over completely to the church, had submitted to baptism, and were living according to God's will as obedient members of the body of Christ.

### d. Sin and Salvation

The radical difference between the Catholic and Hutterian approach to Christian doctrine is also apparent in a comparison of their respective positions on sin and salvation. For the Hutterites, salvation was a way of life, and the way of life in turn defined salvation as well as the nature of sin. Sin could only be understood in the light of the Christian norm for living, but even then, only by those who had come to understand this Christian norm. Salvation was consequently equated with the good and earnest God-given way of life, which refused to compromise with sin. They taught, as did all Anabaptists, that even though the human tendency to sin is ever present within man, God grants the grace and strength by which man can rise to the standard established by Christ and the early apostles; after true repentance, past sins are forgiven through Jesus Christ *and* through the brethren of the Christian community, into which the believer has been baptized.

Affirming one another in prayer was another facet providing strength for such community. Marriage stood with baptism and the Lord's Supper as one of the three main Christian ordinances which also helped to fulfill salvation within the gathered community.

The broader implications of the Hutterian concept of salvation can be seen in the differing views toward holy days. From the Hutterian standpoint, the whole system of holidays, Sundays, and the Lenten season were simply human attempts to balance out the wanton Shrove Tuesday (Mardi Gras or Fastnacht) and other similar occasions. Special holy days consequently were a worldly phenomenon. But God's people had no need for special days of fasting and solemnity, but rather rejoiced in God's atonement, which sanctified the Christian brotherhood 365 days of the year. Since Christ had done away with the old covenant, they believed, each day was the "day of the Lord," established by God that man might praise and honor him, and live without sinning. (In order to avoid unnecessary offense, however, the Hutterites did observe Sunday and the Twelve Apostles' Day.)

From the Catholic viewpoint, the supreme heresy of the Hutterian position was the issue of sin. The church taught that it was not possible to live without transgressing and for this reason the church had established the practice of the confessional. This was also the reason for baptizing infants, for they would otherwise be damned.

Geyersbühler believed that he and his Hutterite brethren no longer needed the Catholic type of confession, for they had found the true faith and the way of salvation through God and their Christian brethren. He intended to remain loyal to that faith. He considered yieldedness to God and acceptance of the Christian way of life as prerequisites to baptism. And since baptism had to be requested, it could not pertain to infants. Furthermore, he said, infants did not need baptism to be saved, for Christ had come to save all of mankind, which meant that until a child reached an understanding of his sinful nature, he participated in eternal life, and if he died while still in innocence he would find eternal peace in spite of his unbaptized state. This was true for all children born throughout the world, for God did not differentiate among the children born to Christians, Turks, or Jews. However, when children raised in Christian homes reached an age of understanding, their parents and the Brotherhood pointed them to the Christian faith and the godly way of life; this of course did not happen in heathen homes, so that the children of the Turks and Jews suffered for their parents' unbelief and false teachings.

### e. The Church and the State

The Christian way of life, according to Geyersbühler, also had implications for the relationship of church and state. He said, for example, that the oath was unnecessary, for godly men spoke the truth anyway. This did not imply, however, that justified commands of the magistracy could be disobeyed, for where law did not conflict with God's will and commandments, the Christian was obliged to obey. Geyersbühler also affirmed that there was nothing in Hutterian doctrine which would do away with the magistracy.

Although Geyersbühler did not enlarge on the theme of the nature of the church, his position was based on a well-defined view of the church as a brotherhood. As an individual under God, he affirmed his ultimate responsiblity to God as a Christian disciple; yet fulfillment of discipleship rested in the brotherhood dimension. Therefore Geyersbühler was willing to sacrifice something of his individuality for the sake of community, in order to enjoy the common life within the community of God, as commanded in the New Testament.

## The Significance of Geyersbühler's Testimony

The testimony of Geyersbühler is all the more meaningful as a Hutterian confession of faith, in view of the fact that he could neither read nor write. His was a composite Hutterian testimonial, the result of group consensus. For this reason his views are of special importance for understanding Hutterian faith and life during the 1560s.

## The Outcome

The prisoner, still painfully stretched out on the rack, answered one by one each of the forty-seven questions raised. One of the last questions put to him was whether he had ever recanted, as had Peter and Veit Berger. He answered that he had never recanted, and with God's strength he would strive to be steadfast for the rest of his life; for he was certain of his faith, the content of which was the desire simply to live in accordance with the commands and teachings of Christ and his apostles. Soon after the interrogation Geyersbühler was beheaded at Innsbruck and his body burned.

The protocol of Geyersbühler's cross-examination represents unpretentiously what the Hutterites thought, and the effect of their teaching program upon the memory and the conscience of one brother. His attitude betrays no sign of trying to outbid other "heroes" in prison, or of having nonplussed the questioners, as was the case with some later missioners such as Leonhard Dax, and to some degree with Hans Arbeiter and Paul Glock. Geyersbühler's confession mirrors authentically what actually took place in the room of questioning. No other document has a more genuine ring than this confession of an illiterate miller. His wish was fulfilled that "with the help and grace of God, he would not recant as long as he lived." In their Great Chronicle the Hutterites listed among the "blood witnesses" the name of Nikolaus Geyersbühler, who "sealed and vouched for his faith in Christ Jesus most valiantly with his blood, thereby entering the great flock of Christian martyrs, A.D. 1567."[5]

# Veit Uhrmacher, Missioner to Austria

A second major encounter between the Hutterites and the Catholics during the Walpot Era took place in the province of Salzburg, where during the 1570s the red-bearded clockmaker, Veit Grünberger, more often called Uhrmacher, suffered a six-year incarceration. Uhrmacher's earlier mission activities in Austria had not gone unnoticed among the civil authorities, whose growing dossier on Uhrmacher, "the Anabaptist bishop seducer," included the following facts: Veit Uhrmacher had originally come from

Pinzgau; this missioner often lodged in the Imst area of Austria, and before converting to Anabaptism he had been a Lutheran minister in Nikolsburg for three years.[6]

In the spring of 1570 Uhrmacher and a fellow missioner, Veit Schelch, after completing their mission, were heading back to Moravia. Their presence in the region was known, and there was a price on their heads. When they stopped at an inn at Wald for breakfast, some local peasant patrons suspected that the two strangers were the wanted Anabaptists, and when the two travelers gave thanks before eating their meal, the peasants had no doubt that here were indeed the two Anabaptists—"just as if praying were wrong, so rudely does the devil make his presence known," the Great Chronicle adds.[7]

### The Imprisonment

The innkeeper stood guard over the two men while the peasants went for the Mittersill sheriff, who came with the castle judge, constables, and provosts. The sheriff shackled the men's hands behind their backs and took them to the castle dungeon of Mittersill, some thirty kilometers away.[8]

The sheriff's sympathetic wife and the cook saw that the prisoners received good food and treatment during their five-week stay at Mittersill. Even the sheriff begged the prisoners' forgiveness for having arrested them in the line of duty. Finally the Salzburg court clerk, accompanied by two constables and two provosts, transferred the imprisoned missioners to Salzburg.[9]

The group passed through Stuhlfelden, where a crowd gathered, as if the prisoners had been "sea monsters." They put up at Zell am See for the night. The next day the group climbed the great Hirschbichel mountain and descended to Berchtesgaden for the second night, a journey of eighty difficult kilometers. The next morning, the first Sunday after Pentecost, the group reached Salzburg just as the people were entering church. Uhrmacher and Schelch were put in separate cells in the mighty fortress and never saw each other again.[10]

Three years later Uhrmacher managed to smuggle a letter to Peter Walpot. It is from this letter that the facts of the arrest and incarceration are known. According to the letter, the two missioners were finally cross-examined on January 19, 1573. Uhrmacher's report offers excellent insights into the Catholic process of dealing with heretics at this time.[11]

### The Cross-Examination

Uhrmacher was first carefully prepared for the cross-examination by three men: the cathedral chaplain, the prison priest, and a third individual, "a man of few words." This third man especially urged Uhrmacher to give "good" answers, for this would certainly make it easier for him to find freedom. But Uhrmacher answered: "My lord, we dare not be hypocritical in matters of faith.... For we must defend it. What would our actions be otherwise?"

Uhrmacher's first moments in the courtroom were indelibly impressed on his memory:

> There sat the fellows in their four-cornered hats, each with paper and ink before him and the sheriff bade me sit down on the chair standing there. Then the cathedral chaplain began, bowing to the sheriff and to the other priests.

The following summary of the cross-examination is taken from Uhrmacher's own reconstruction of events, written four weeks following the encounter. The mood is decidedly different from that of both the Lutheran and Calvinist encounters (see below), partly because Uhrmacher was reluctant to confess his faith in terms of systematic theology, and partly because the Catholics actually could say little against Anabaptist piety. The crux of the matter lay in their widely differing views about the relation of the church to the magistracy.

The court encounter began with the Catholics accusing Uhrmacher of belonging to a diabolical sect that persistently led the subjects of the Catholic prince astray. Uhrmacher, certainly aware of the bite in his reply, countered that he could not accept this charge as being true, unless the Catholics considered the teachings of Jesus to be diabolical, for with Jesus lay the center of Hutterian doctrine and the way of life. If he was not common ground, then there was no use for further dialogue.

One member of the court mentioned that there was common ground, to which Uhrmacher replied that there was really no need to testify, for the books he had had on his person at the time he was apprehended were in the hands of the Salzburg officials, and these books were valid affirmations of the Christian faith; all the Catholics needed to do was to read these testimonials, two of which had been written by Claus Felbinger and Hans Mändel, only recently martyred for their faith. Uhrmacher added that if the court authorities refused to accept the content of these writings, he could not make them believe; and if they wanted to live according to this truth, they did not need his words.

This reluctance to respond irritated the court officials. They reminded Uhrmacher that the court was assembled out of a sincere love; he should therefore respond in full to their questions, and not prolong the session, for they had many other demands to which they might be attending. Uhrmacher responded that he had not requested their time; if they were calling his three-year imprisonment "love," God ought to receive them with the same type of love, for he at least was able to penetrate their hearts and knew why they had not convened earlier. The priest responded that love in this instance was to be interpreted in view of the "false apostles and deceiving workers" who pretended to be apostles of Christ (2 Corinthians 11:13); a three-year imprisonment was simply an extension of this love (1 Corinthians 13). Uhrmacher interpreted this as utter nonsense, in that these passages, from his standpoint, were the antithesis of the practice of the established church.

But the court pressed harder for a confession of faith, chiding Uhrmacher to live up to 1 Peter 3:15, that a follower of Christ should always be prepared to give an account of his faith. Uhrmacher finally agreed to comply on condition that his testimony would be understood as a witness to that Great Day of the Lord, which the court itself would some day have to face. Uhrmacher admonished the members of the Catholic court not to speak against their own highest convictions, for otherwise they would be blaspheming against the Holy Spirit, for which there was no divine forgiveness.

The court accepted these conditions, but once again was annoyed by Uhrmacher's charge that the priests were in reality the plaintiffs and judges, in that whatever they were not able to achieve by verbal pressure, the constables and hangmen would carry out; the ecclesiastics questioning Uhrmacher would simply pass their decision on to the prince, who in turn would pass it on to the judge, the judge to the constable, and finally the constable to the hangman; hence the church was really the hangman. Clinching his point, Uhrmacher noted that the Hutterites, a true people of God, had been persecuted and martyred, including Jacob Hutter himself; if the present court was contemplating the same course of action, it had better understand that it too stood under judgment, not by persons, but by the Lord himself, for God would take revenge upon the examiners.

The sheriff took this reprimand as a personal affront and maintained that he had kept a good prison. Uhrmacher conceded that his years in prison had not been intolerable, but he still felt that injustice had been meted out, for prison—even if food, drink, and room paralleled that of a lord—was still prison, and therefore wrong for two men who had not harmed anybody, having in truth merely prayed to God before beginning a meal.

Toward the end of the hearing the members of the court began to see that it would be difficult to move the prisoner. They affirmed the godly living of the Hutterites and their desire to remain true to scriptural witness, one member of the court even commenting that no people on earth could be found more steadfast than the Hutterites. Yet the Catholic court maintained that the Anabaptists held false doctrines and practices, including their doctrines of baptism and communion; for everything depended on having the true faith. Even the Turks, they said, were devout people, certainly more devout than the Catholics; but devoutness was not enough.

Uhrmacher replied that a genuine faith produced good works. He also concurred with the comment from the Catholic court about the Turks being more devout than the Catholics; for the Catholic way of life was hardly Christian, not to mention their worldly methods of treating true Christians.

The cross-examination lasted three hours. In his letter to Walpot, Uhrmacher affirmed that as a simple member of the body of Christ he desired to continue steadfast with all diligence and God's help, not playing with hypocrisy in faith or in suffering. Divine wisdom, he was sure, was greater than human wisdom, and divine weakness stronger than mankind; divine strength would continue to sustain devout prisoners.

Uhrmacher was quite certain, however, that he was not facing execution; he knew that if the members of the court could have released him without losing face, they would have been glad to do so, for the house sheriff had told him not to fear a death sentence, although he would probably have to endure a long prison term. Uhrmacher was sure that no one desired to wash his hands in the prisoner's blood.[12]


## The Outcome

The above presentation is taken from the only known document from Uhrmacher's pen, written February 16, 1573, in the Salzburg fortress. But the Great Chronicle recounts that Veit Schelch, Uhrmacher's traveling companion, yielded to the Catholics and was released, but then returned to the Brotherhood. After a lengthy time of repentance, with great remorse and weeping, he was again accepted into the Brotherhood.[13]

Early in 1576 the Brotherhood was worried about their brother, supposedly still in prison at Salzburg, for there had been no news for months. Walpot wrote to Paul Glock, imprisoned in Württemberg, asking whether he had any information about Uhrmacher. Walpot said he had sent two brethren to investigate the situation.

On August 28, 1576, Glock replied that he had heard that the Brotherhood had lost contact with Uhrmacher; but he hoped and prayed that God might comfort him, for even if one were walled into solid rock, God could still provide an exit. But three weeks before Glock replied to Walpot's letter, Uhrmacher had reached the Brotherhood. He had escaped by making a rope of old rags, letting himself down from an extremely high window, and then climbing over the wall. Without divine help, he was convinced, his escape would have been impossible. The fortress staff itself said afterwards that he had escaped through supernatural means. The Great Chronicle simply states that Veit Uhrmacher escaped through the power and help of God, "for whom nothing is impossible."[14]

Veit Uhrmacher's steadfastness and courage during more than six years of imprisonment earned a place for him in Hutterian verse; two stanzas of a song compare Uhrmacher's escape with the Apostle Paul's at Damascus (Acts 9:23-25; 2 Corinthians 11:32-33):

> Just as it had happened in an earlier time / In the city of Damascus, / Where the governor / Intended to seize the godly Paul, / And lay him low in prison;
> But in a basket on a rope, / He was speedily let down / Through a window in a wall: / In escaping from the [Salzburg] fortress.[15]

Eight years later, in 1584, Uhrmacher again journeyed as a missioner to Austria, this time accompanied by a half-dozen Hutterite comrades. The Catholics caught wind of the mission, "extracting from the poor simple subjects their bodies and souls, including their possessions." The magistracy was determined "to counter such evil activities with [punishment]." The officials ordered a diligent search, but very likely failed to find them, for the expedition is not recorded in the Great Chronicle. Shortly before his natural death in 1586 Uhrmacher apparently was again sent to Austria.[16]

## Hans Arbeiter and the Jesuits

In 1545, itinerant Jesuits obtained a special papal writ granting the privilege of traveling and preaching freely throughout the world, and of accepting confessions everywhere, without obtaining permission from local ecclesiastical and civil officials. By the 1560s, the Jesuit invasion was felt throughout Europe. In 1566, as has been noted, they shared in the court process of torturing and executing Nikolaus Geyersbühler.

The Jesuit purpose was to restore the authority of the Roman Church. Its methods of converting heathen and heretic were determined by the local situation, but the Jesuit missioners soon broke convention and attempted new methods within the radically changed social and religious setting of the Reformation. The Jesuits were determined to effect a Catholic Counter-Reformation. It was the Jesuits who were later, during the seventeenth and eighteenth centuries, instrumental in expelling all Hutterites from Moravia who refused to convert to Roman Catholicism. And it was a Jesuit priest that the Hutterite missioner, Hans Arbeiter, encountered during the Golden Years of the Hutterites.

In 1557, Hans Arbeiter, a member of the Swiss Brethren at Aachen, converted to Hutterianism. Before transferring to the Hutterian community, he explained to his former brethren his reasons for the change, which he felt lay basically in the problem of disorganization and disunity within the Swiss Brethren congregation. By 1561 Arbeiter was called to the Hutterian ministry, and shortly thereafter into mission. While on a mission with Heinrich Schuester in July 1568, Arbeiter and his comrade were apprehended at Hainbach in the Roman Catholic bishopric of Speyer.[17] Arbeiter later wrote about his arrest and prison experiences as follows:

The burgomaster immediately took command of the situation and began an interrogation. When the prisoners refused to swear an official oath, they were given the alternative of supplying the guards with a few rounds of drinks, but Arbeiter and Schuester also refused to do this, believing they were innocent and not bound to any penalties whatever. Instead, the prisoners answered the burgomaster's threats by admonishing him to be careful in his words and conduct, for to treat godly people with arbitrary wantonness had never led to a good end.

The constable and guards were impressed with the Hutterites' confession of faith, to the point that after the interrogation they would not lay hands on them. The burgomaster bound the men himself, against the murmurings of his staff, and put them in temporary quarters for the rest of the night. The next day, a Monday, he visited the market at Neustadt; Tuesday he took ill; and Wednesday he was buried. This turn of events impressed the apprehensive constable, who sought the prisoners' counsel. They commended the matter to God, and assured the constable that God would not hold him accountable for what had taken place.

The prisoners were transferred to the Kierweiler Castle, where Schuester was put into the common prison, and Arbeiter into a dark dungeon deprived of all natural light. Once again the prisoners experienced hostilities at the hands of the officials. At a court hearing, charged with seducing the people, Arbeiter requested that truth might not be called a seduction, for the Hutterites desired to seduce no one; it was rather the people themselves who had been tragically led astray and deceived with an empty hope. He said he could not conceive of a more shameful way of life than that which the general populace was leading; their hope of redemption could never be realized since they lived without repentance, without faith, and without good works; for the unrighteous would never inherit the kingdom of God.

After Arbeiter confessed his faith, his relations with the prison officials improved substantially. The sheriff later volunteered, "Hans, your life is good and I like your disciplined living—I cannot punish you for this. But your faith is not good." He contended that the Hutterites must be in error, for even the kings and the emperors, who had many wise and highly educated people counseling them, condemned the Hutterian faith at their imperial diets. If the Hutterites were right, the highly educated and wise people, of whom there were many, would have recognized the Hutterian position as being correct.

This criticism launched Arbeiter into a lengthy analysis of the relationship of knowledge to faith. The sheriff, apparently not knowing quite how to proceed, asked about Arbeiter's knowledge of Latin, to which Arbeiter answered that he was a thresher by vocation. Doubting the biblical competence of a thresher, the sheriff was not sure whether the prisoner's views were from God or from the devil. The sheriff's deputy, more familiar with the Bible than the sheriff, confirmed Arbeiter's argument as biblical, but asserted that it was based upon the Old Testament and therefore not applicable to the present church. Arbeiter then proceeded to exegete New Testament evidence to support his point of view. At the end of the discussion, the sheriff assured Arbeiter of a speedy release, since the bishop did not want to hold such people as the Hutterites in prison.

Eleven days later the sheriff returned, saying: "Hans, my friend, a good man and friend of mine has come here. He would like to talk with you in good faith." On his way to the bishop's quarters Arbeiter met the man who was to question him. Pretending to know nothing about Arbeiter, the questioner elicited information from him, but refused to reveal his own identity.

Arbeiter described the Hutterian mission program, mentioned that his imprisonment was not due to any evil deed, and explained that his lot was within a long tradition of suffering which the godly had always borne. The questioner countered:

> Yes, Hans, what you say is true, that all those who have ever lived godly lives and still live godly lives must be persecuted (2 Timothy 3:12). And as you say, the false people have always fared well. This is true, Hans.

Arbeiter wrote: "He could appear so friendly and hypocritical that I asked myself what type of man that was who gave so much testimony to the truth." Not knowing quite how to proceed, the examiner admitted that he had already been in Moravia to learn about the Hutterian faith. A Hutterite preacher had approached him saying: "Now, my friend, we don't want to keep from you the fact that we do not baptize our infants." Shocked by such an erroneous practice, the questioner said that he immediately fled, but now he wanted Arbeiter as an actual member of the group to tell him the truth about baptism. Toward the end of this discussion the interrogator angrily charged Arbeiter with lacking knowledge and being too obdurate to let himself be influenced; he threatened that the prisoner would have to take the consequences if he did not submit. More gently, he admonished Arbeiter to pray to God for grace to discern the truth. He promised to visit Arbeiter again, at which time he hoped he would find the prisoner more receptive; meanwhile Arbeiter was to reflect diligently upon their discussion. As he was leaving, the unknown interrogator boasted that he had been able to convince two Innsbruck prisoners, Veitel Schmidt and Peter Kutzenmacher, of their error. But Arbeiter only reaffirmed his desire to be faithful unto death to the truth which he had come to know, and his determination to ask God day and night for his keeping power, so that the questioner would not be able to boast of having led yet one more godly prisoner to recant.

Through the walls of his cell Arbeiter was able to communicate with an imprisoned preacher just above him who informed him that the questioner was none other than Dr. Lamprecht, the Jesuit head priest at the Cathedral of Speyer, and that he had boasted to the bishop that he would be able to induce the Hutterites to recant just as he had the two educated men at Innsbruck.

About ten days later the two met again. Arbeiter stated that although he now knew the questioner's identity, he still held nothing against him as a person; on the other hand, Lamprecht's work and doctrine were abominable since he was not only seducing the Protestants, but also attempting to lead him as an Anabaptist away from the truth. Arbeiter went on to speak about his own Christian experience. Lamprecht interrupted him so often that he could not always fully express himself. By the end of this second hearing there was still no sign that the prisoner would yield.

During a third examination three weeks later, the Jesuit interrogator asked many questions taken from a "booklet of fabrications" he had brought along, undoubtedly one of the several Catholic booklets in existence indicating the procedure to be used against the Anabaptists.[18] The main discussion centered around the theme of baptism and the nature of faith. But when Lamprecht saw he was not succeeding in stirring Arbeiter, he began asking such irrelevant questions as how many apostles there were, and whether the Apostle John died; he finally demanded, "If you are an apostle, then be prepared [to answer], since I am calling you to account!" (1 Peter 3:15).

Arbeiter objected to these questions, believing that Christians have a divine command to avoid useless talk. He simply stated that God had promised to send out his Word through hosts of evangelists (Psalm 68:11); and that Lamprecht perhaps did not know what an evangelist was. As to John, Arbeiter was certain that he had died in peace, as his writings testified.

Arbeiter then made a charge that was frequently on Hutterian lips: Lamprecht was not seeking the honor of God nor his own redemption; nor did he desire to learn from Arbeiter, but was only trying to lead him astray and suppress him. Arbeiter called him a quarreling scholastic and considered this as reason enough not to answer such babble.

We note again how the Hutterites believed emphatically that mind, tongue, heart, and hand must be placed under the obedience of Christ and that such a unified approach was the only way to fulfillment of life. This doctrine explains Arbeiter's constant appeal to Lamprecht that he be a genuine seeker, and willing to listen:

> If you were seeking the honor of God and your own salvation I would have the good confidence in God that he would give me the grace to speak, and you, to understand and to receive.

After another dispute over semantics, Lamprecht finally said that since he had now visited the prisoner three times, and he still showed no desire to recant, he deserved to be drowned in the Rhine.

Arbeiter affirmed his willingness to suffer whatever God would permit, adding emphatically, "If it is in the plans of your omnipotent God, then to-day rather than tomorrow!" He hoped that even if hangman, bishop, and the very devil were to be present, with the help of God he would not be led away from the truth through terror.

This time, upon being returned to prison, Arbeiter found his menu radically altered. Having earlier received four measures of wine daily, he suddenly was given none at all for sixteen days, and his portion of bread was reduced. Arbeiter knew well the significance of the change: since he had refused to recant he was to be starved to death. Although the starvation diet sickened him, inwardly the Lord continued to comfort and sustain him.

On Lamprecht's fourth and last visit to Arbeiter, now emaciated and weak, he expressed great compassion and concern for the prisoner's welfare and still hoped to move him. He asked:

> Dear Hans, how are you doing? Are you ill? Oh my Hans, tell me, what do you need? Are you receiving less to eat or drink? Tell me, I'll do all I can to supply it—although you are taking this cross upon yourself! But now trust me, and follow my advice. I want to help you gain release from prison.

He told Arbeiter not to worry about having given all his possessions over to the Hutterites; he had helped others, and now also wanted to lift Arbeiter out of these miserable conditions. But Arbeiter likened Lamprecht's efforts to convert him to Satan's offer to Christ of the riches of this world. But, Arbeiter persisted, Christ and his servants had taught nothing but the cross, suffering, and martyrdom, precipitated by an imperfect world, whereas Lamprecht was teaching men to seek only a good life according to the flesh.

Continuing in his friendly argument, Lamprecht pleaded with Arbeiter to change only his faith, not his pattern of life. For his manner of living was good and should be followed by all. But in the matter of faith, the Jesuit once again pleaded with Arbeiter to follow him, offering as security his own soul for Arbeiter's. The latter countered that a man could suffer only for his own thoughts and actions; and anyone who allowed himself to be led astray would have to suffer with the seducer. And so Arbeiter once again affirmed that he was living the correct faith which God from the beginning had planted into the beings of his beloved, faithful people.

Lamprecht finally gave up all attempt to appeal to the authority of Scripture and instead asked Arbeiter forthrightly to give up his faith for the sake of Christ's suffering, for with such a faith he would be damned. Arbeiter rejoined that until he was convinced in his heart that he was wrong, he could not change. Then Lamprecht embraced Arbeiter, and with a kiss insisted that his total concern was only for Arbeiter's salvation; God knew that he loved the prisoner, and he had given him the sign of love according to Paul's command (1 Thessalonians 5:26). Arbeiter compared this kiss to the kiss of Joab, who with the words "May the Lord be with you," killed Amasa and Abner (2 Samuel 20:9-10; 3:27).

At this point the infuriated sheriff called Arbeiter a rogue for rejecting the counsel of such a godly and wise man as Dr. Lamprecht, and he threatened the prisoner with execution. Arbeiter was uncertain whether the threat was genuine or merely another trick, for when Arbeiter had been alone with the sheriff, he had actually been quite friendly. This reversal of attitude was evidence to Arbeiter that his various questioners, in spite of their front, were inwardly convinced of the truth, and yet would have rejoiced if the Jesuit priest had silenced the prisoner so that they could continue to cling to their empty hope.

Ten weeks after his fourth cross-examination with Dr. Lamprecht, the head warden brought Arbeiter a letter which granted his release on the condition that he would promise never to return to the bishopric, and that he would not avenge his stay in prison.

The second condition posed no problem for Arbeiter, but he refused to promise never to return, for this would have opposed God's will. As a missioner, he explained, he was indebted to serve where it pleased God, for the whole earth is the Lord's, and belongs ultimately to no man. Many previous bishops, he continued, had also thought they were the lords of the land (Baruch 3:15-24) but were past and gone; likewise, the present bishop would not remain for all time. And, he concluded, if all rulers denied the Hutterites a place to live, the godly could not exist anywhere in the world; consequently he could not submit to such a clause and felt compelled to obey God more than man (Acts 5:29).

At this juncture the head warden angrily threatened to carry out the prince's written command of execution, because if Arbeiter were given the chance he would continue to lead people astray. Arbeiter, unintimidated, replied that if he could move the whole bishopric with the Word of God and turn the people from their wrong living onto a godly way of life, he would be indebted to God to do it and would gladly do it even if it meant giving his own life.

About a week later the warden returned with the same order. Arbeiter said that a rereading was unnecessary; he had understood it the first time. Rather than reread it, Arbeiter suggested, the warden should now write up whatever report he desired, for Arbeiter could not comply with terms that opposed God. Possibly God would never direct him to return, but if he did, Arbeiter maintained, he could only obediently return; he was now ready to accept whatever God would permit the magistracy to decide in his case.

With surprising frankness Arbeiter then told the head warden that magistrates should confine themselves to their express function, namely, protecting the devout from the violent and wanton. For this reason, he said, the Hutterites upheld the office of the magistracy, granting it the respect commanded by God; but the office was exceeding its function when with shameless violence and wantonness it attempted to pervert Arbeiter and Schuester in body and soul. God would punish such magistrates, Arbeiter continued, quoting from Scripture, that "he who imprisons another will himself be imprisoned" (Revelation 13:10); and that "the measure you use will be used on you" (Matthew 7:2).

Arbeiter's attack angered the warden, who resented Arbeiter's presuming to instruct him and said he had no need of Arbeiter's sermon, having access to more reasonable counsel. Once again he threatened to send Arbeiter to the executioner. As usual, Arbeiter replied that he was willing to bear whatever God willed for him, knowing that God would stand by him with divine aid.

The executioner made his appearance about twelve days later, but fortunately, not to hang Arbeiter and his co-prisoner, but to whip them. However, since no official command had been issued against them, he at first refused to do it but finally agreed to comply for a price of six guilders. But before the act could be carried out some enemy soldiers who had been camping in the bishopric made a surprise attack on the castle, during which the executioner left.

Four weeks later in the dead of night Arbeiter finally was taken out into an open field where his four escorts told him that the prince had been gracious to him, but if he ever returned, his treatment would be quite different. Therewith they released him. Before slipping into the night Arbeiter inquired about Heinrich Schuester. The men replied that he was probably back in Moravia; but Arbeiter afterwards found out that Schuester was not released until two days later.

The half-year of prison behind them, the two brethren returned to the Brotherhood clear of conscience, for they had faithfully held to the truth. A joyful reunion took place. Arbeiter found the community in the same healthy state of peace, love, and unity as when he had left it, and as he had described it to others during his mission and in prison.[19]

### The Essence of Arbeiter's Faith

Hans Arbeiter's encounter with sixteenth-century Roman Catholicism provides solid insight into three broad areas: the Hutterian approach to man's relationship a) to God (discipleship), b) to his brethren (the church), and c) to the world (the two kingdoms). Although a Hutterite cannot exist apart from brotherhood, a distinct consciousness of individuality does surface in the course of Arbeiter's discussions, namely, the consciousness of his being an obedient disciple of Christ.

### a. The True Disciple

Arbeiter believed that one quality of the obedient disciple was remaining true to one's own heart. When Lamprecht had charged him with possessing the wrong faith, Arbeiter answered that until he could be convinced in his heart that his faith was wrong—and the Jesuit priest had not convinced him—he could not change, for his tongue and heart were of one accord. He stated:

> Now if I should allow myself to be moved even when I don't believe your words, I would be of a frivolous heart and would be a fool who believes all such mendacious babble, as Solomon says.[20]

For Arbeiter, the individual was directly and personally responsible to God.[21]

*Faith.* Arbeiter charted his own path to faith, which he believed resulted from the new birth, saying:

> I find a new heart and spirit within myself which has a true horror and revulsion from the secret and public sins and vices of the world. And my heart and soul has pleasure and joy in all that pleases God. Also I find within myself the grace needed to fight sin and roguery, and to do good. This I have not received of myself, but have received it from the Lord.[22]

A godly manner of living was an inseparable part of faith for Arbeiter. When Lamprecht admonished him to return to the old Catholic faith, Arbeiter confessed that before he had accepted his present faith he had been an impure, ungodly person, living as other people generally live, in idolatry and drunkenness; gambling, cursing, and insulting others. He then added:

> If I then had the true faith and if I were then a good "tree" or man while bearing despicable fruit, then Christ's words would not be true when he says, "A good tree or person brings forth good fruit, and an evil tree or person brings forth evil fruit."[23]

Lamprecht charged Arbeiter with being a Pharisee, claiming to keep the commandments of Christ and condemning everyone else. Arbeiter countered, that with such false judgment the Catholics kept the people in unrighteousness, for when a sinful person desired to change his ways, the Catholics only blasphemed and derided him by saying:

> Oh, you also want to be an Anabaptist, a heretic, and Pharisee, and want to be better than all of us, and want to reach for the stars and bribe the Lord with good works.[24]

Developing the point to its logical conclusion, Arbeiter drove home his analysis of the Catholic position. He claimed that according to Catholic reasoning it would be better for a person to be ungodly than godly. For when one rejects all the sins that can enter the heart, and sides with godly living and faithfulness, he is called a Pharisee and Anabaptist; but the person who does not shudder at sin, and lives in abominations, repenting only with his lips, is promised redemption by the Catholics. God, in the Prophets, had already lamented these ways of Catholicism, Arbeiter added, namely, promising life—against God's will—to the ungodly, while at the same time damning the souls of the godly whom God desired to redeem.

Later, when the two were discussing faith in calmer tones, Arbeiter tried to demonstrate to Lamprecht that none of the sinners and the ungodly who opposed the truth could claim to have the true faith which came from God, to whom, therefore, they were not pleasing. Arbeiter noted that through faith God purified the hearts of the Gentiles who accepted the gospel (Acts 15:9), and that Paul had said that if one believed the truth from his heart he would become godly, and if one confessed with his lips he would be saved (Romans 10:10). Yet since no godliness resulted from Catholic faith—indeed the Catholics remained thoroughly immersed in their sins and iniquities; in whore-mongering, drunkenness, greed, lying, cursing, and blaspheming against God—they had never possessed a faith which was pleasing to God. The only other alternative was that the apostles had not spoken the truth.

When Lamprecht suggested that Arbeiter take on the faith he had possessed as an infant, Arbeiter could only express amazement, for in his eyes infants were unable to have faith because they knew neither good nor evil; since they had no knowledge of the good, how could they have faith? He referred to the Apostle Paul's statement that "faith comes from what is heard, and what is heard comes by the preaching of Christ" (Romans 10:17).

The path of faith had taken Arbeiter from his homeland for the sake of that purified and majestic "treasure," the kingdom of God (Matthew 13:44). He admitted that he had not yet fully received this treasure, but he hoped that, with the help of God, no one would prevent his obtaining it (Romans 8:35 ff.). For this faith, Arbeiter was willing to suffer, because God's grace was given not only for man to believe in Christ with words, but also to share in Christ's suffering (2 Corinthians 1).[25]

*Knowledge and Faith.* Another aspect of faith arose when both the sheriff and the Jesuit offered higher education as proof of the correctness of their position. Arbeiter spoke to this by contrasting godly wisdom with worldly knowledge: knowledge resulting from higher education was not in itself pleasing to God; what was pleasing to God, however, was divine wisdom, defined as seeking after God, keeping him in view, and abstaining from evil (Job 28:28). Furthermore, one who had little knowledge, yet feared God, was better than one who had much learning, yet transgressed against God's commandments (Ecclesiasticus 19:24). Arbeiter was certain that the many vile people within the Catholic Church could lay no claim to divine wisdom (Jeremiah 8:8-13), for these very people, in their iniquities— and indeed all hypocrites—invalidated all claim to possessing divine truth (Acts 28:26-27) by judging those who held to the truth and calling them a false sect.

Arbeiter then introduced scriptural examples to substantiate his point. God had always brought about great things through those who were lowly and small, the very ones disregarded by the world (e.g., Ezekiel 21:26). Such had been the case with the people of Israel when confronted by the Pharaoh. Even Gideon, Elijah, Amos, and David had not been held in high esteem by the world, the latter having been disregarded by his own father.

Turning to the New Testament Arbeiter noted that the long-promised salvation through Christ (Psalm 12:6) had been revealed to simple shepherds at Bethlehem. Neither had Christ chosen his servants from the Sanhedrin at Jerusalem, nor from the schools of advanced learning, but rather from simple fishermen (Acts 4:13). Furthermore, Christ had testified that his heavenly Father withheld his divine wisdom from those who were in their own eyes high and wise, revealing it rather to the simple (Matthew 11:25-26). Paul had admonished the believers to consider faithfully their divine calling, for not many wise ones according to the flesh, nor many powerful or noble ones, had been called, but rather the simple (1 Corinthians 1:26 ff.).

Lamprecht also questioned Arbeiter's ability to know the true faith, branding him as an uncultured thresher who could not understand Scripture and who had better believe and follow him, a well-educated man, learned in many languages, and widely traveled. Arbeiter remembered Solomon's advice, to "answer a fool according to his folly, lest he be wise in his own eyes" (Proverbs 26:5), and responded, "Oh dear friend, you don't know how to know; your knowledge only puffs up, and is nothing but pride" (1 Corinthians 8:1). He compared the Catholics to the Pharisees, who had said to the blind man whom God had just healed, "You were born in utter sin, and would you teach us?" (John 9:34). Arbeiter also recalled the words of Jesus: "But because I tell the truth, you do not believe me" (John 8:45).

Arbeiter was convinced that being widely traveled did not necessarily result in wisdom and godliness. Some men traveled widely simply to go to war. As to being widely traveled, Arbeiter believed that he had as much reason to boast as Lamprecht. But his own understanding of divine discipline and wisdom, and his own desired godliness did not result from his extensive travels. Indeed, wherever Arbeiter had traveled, he had seen person after person living disgracefully in ungodly practices.

As to learning, Arbeiter said that divine righteousness was taught neither at Rome nor at Speyer in higher institutions of learning, but rather only in the school of God and David, the location of which was still unknown to the Catholics.

Lamprecht's many languages did not add up to faith in Arbeiter's eyes, for those who had sentenced Christ to the cross also knew Latin, Hebrew, and Greek, as substantiated by the placard placed on the cross (Luke 23:38). Arbeiter recalled the time when not one swineherd in and around Rome did not know Latin; to know such languages in the sixteenth century was a worldly art and not a sign of divine piety or discipline. Lamprecht retorted that Arbeiter was nothing but an uncultured, silly thresher who lacked knowledge, and who was not open to further teaching; if he would not submit, he would experience the drastic consequences meted out by the authorities.

Arbeiter compared his situation to that of Eve. The serpent had suggested to her that she was a simple and foolish woman who in her unknowing state needed additional knowledge, and that she would then become as God. When Eve submitted to the serpent's demands, unrighteousness resulted for her and those of her offspring who followed in unrighteousness. Arbeiter praised God for having given him the strength to perceive the poison of the Catholics, and he trusted that God would continue to keep him from such false advice, doctrine, and living.[26]

### b. The Church: The Godly Person's Relationship to His Brethren

Throughout Arbeiter's dialogue with Lamprecht, three concepts intertwine, which cannot be separated in Anabaptist thought: the nature of baptism, of children, and of the church.

*Baptism and the Nature of Children.* Arbeiter maintained that neither Christ nor his apostles had commanded infant baptism. Hence the Hutterian Brotherhood, basing its community pattern upon apostolic precept, was not so presumptuous as to create a baptism which differed from the baptism of Christ. Lamprecht looked upon this position as being a most dangerous heresy, stating his belief that unbaptized children who died were damned. Arbeiter, in his theological naïveté, replied that in conversation with many preachers—Lutheran, papal, and Zwinglian—he had never met a man so brash as to damn the very innocents that Christ pronounced blessed. Arbeiter charged that under the law of Moses such an arrogant person or prophet would have had to die (Deuteronomy 18:20). Indeed, the children Christ blessed were not baptized, nor did he baptize them. Neither did children, or parents on behalf of their children, desire baptism from Christ or from the disciples. In fact Christ commanded the apostles to baptize only after he had arisen from the dead. Neither did John baptize infants, but only those individuals who repented. Arbeiter asked on what basis the Catholics were so bold as to baptize infants, without their knowledge, will, or desire, and without divine command or scriptural foundation.

Arbeiter added that he could prove that no greater error, abomination, idolatry, or seduction had ever entered the world than infant baptism. For if the ungodly within false Christendom had not been baptized as infants, they could not have taken comfort in the illusion of its false hope. If baptism had remained within the tradition of Christ (Matthew 28:18-20) and true to the custom of the apostles (Acts 2:38), the conventicles of the godly (Luke 12:32-34) would not have been so small and few in number. Then God-fearing parents would have raised their children with all diligence in the fear of God, and would have set them a good example and witness, so that the children also would come to faith and be accepted into the church through baptism, as members of Christ's body. As they grew, the children could have been told "You are not Christian, but heathen," so that children who had reached the point of reason would begin to fear and to be ashamed, and would attend in all seriousness to living blamelessly, so that they could be made a part of the church of Christ (Colossians 2:6-7). Yet since almost all the original Christian traditions, especially baptism and the Lord's Supper, had become perverted, the poor, blinded people thought of themselves as possessing from their youth the correct faith and the Christian way of life; for infants were considered saved as soon as they were "puddled" ("gesudlet").

Here Lamprecht interrupted the discussion, crying: "Hear, hear, this man calls holy Christian baptism a puddle-bath!" But Arbeiter defended his position: Christian baptism was by no means a puddle-bath. Yet what the impure and ungodly had trumped up and established on their own was soiled, impure, filthy, and an abomination before the eyes of God, no matter how highly the world honored it (Luke 16:19-31). For as soon as the children were given their puddle-bath, the parents, in their blindness, would praise the Lord and say: "God be praised that my child has not died in heathendom, but has received holy Christian baptism, and has become a Christian who otherwise would have had to be damned." From this point on neither the parents nor the children paid attention to redemption, but they lived as they desired. Many engaged in the most disgraceful iniquities and still claimed to be good Christians; whereas in reality they were merely living under an illusion of having been redeemed. Such a baptism did not nullify the biblical truth that the unrighteous and impure could not inherit the kingdom of God (1 Corinthians 6:9-10). Arbeiter was even convinced that it would have been much better to allow Christ's mandate of baptism to lapse than to pervert it. For in the state of lapse, individuals would spot the illusion sooner and acknowledge the need to establish and preserve the program and mandate of Christ.

Arbeiter, confident of his own knowledge of Scripture, understood the Jesuit's views to be based upon human wisdom couched in lofty phrases, but lacking in a fuller understanding of biblical truths. Arbeiter had recognized, and knew very well, every single biblical passage to which Lamprecht had alluded, and when Lamprecht ran out of proof texts, his only recourse was to affirm that if infant baptism were not correct, it would not have endured so long. Arbeiter answered logically that a long tradition did not guarantee correctness. Many contemporary idolatries and human foibles, such as permitting priests to have a mistress or two, could also be traced far back in Roman Catholic heritage.

Lamprecht then asked where infant baptism was expressly forbidden in Scripture. If it were written: "Thou shalt not baptize infants," he would surely acquiesce. Arbeiter indignantly called this a "great foolishness." If Christ had sent out such blind persons as Lamprecht and his kind to teach and baptize, he would have to say to them: "Baptize no unbelievers who want to disobey my Word; do not baptize children, bells, or muskets." Arbeiter was certain that the Apostolic Era of history had not been radically different from his own era. For Christ was still sending men whom he had endowed with his Holy Spirit (Luke 24:47), as he had promised (John 14:12-31), who would teach the nations all things. Furthermore, Christ had known that only the spiritually minded would gather with him (Matthew 22:1-14). These godly men understood the authority of this message taught to the nations, that they should add no commandments, prohibitions, or amendments to this message found in Scripture, even on the basis of a long-standing tradition. For Christ had given his "law book," and had held to it, as, for example, when he denounced idolatry and drove this custom of long-standing from the Temple.

In a later encounter with Arbeiter, Lamprecht came equipped with a new strategy. He brought a booklet which Arbeiter derisively called a "booklet of fabrications," from which he asked many questions: Was it possible to do good works which were neither specifically commanded by God nor found in Scriptures? Were such works nonetheless divinely commanded? Arbeiter admitted that such works had been done and were still being done. Mary Magdalene honored the Lord greatly in a manner which had not been commanded, yet Christ considered her act a good work (Luke 7:36-50; John 12:1-8; Matthew 26:6-13).

Lamprecht pursued the argument by citing other good works that pleased God even though he had not commanded them. Thus Noah had built an altar (Genesis 8:20), and the Rechabites drank no wine, built no houses or vineyards, which though not specifically commanded by God, still pleased him (Jeremiah 35:5-10). He listed other examples from the booklet, and finally came to the point that although infant baptism was not commanded by God in Scripture, it was still a good work, and pleasing to God.

Arbeiter replied that Noah had erected the altar through divine inspiration of God's Spirit. For God himself had made known that such worship pleased him (1 Kings 3:4, 15), in that such an altar and form of worship was anticipatory of the true worship, in Christ himself, who brought such outward form to an end. That the Rechabites drank no wine was neither deceit nor error nor idolatry; if the Catholic priests had forbidden wine they would have been much better off.

Infant baptism however, Arbeiter was convinced, was quite another matter, having nothing to do with good works. He repeated his belief that no greater error or abomination had entered the world since the birth of Christ than infant baptism. In fact many godly men who early in Christian history acknowledged infant baptism as diabolical and a human seducement had to suffer martyrdom. Certainly all those who had established it, and those who still desired to retain it by adroit reasoning would experience something far more difficult and terrible than what Saul suffered when God rejected him because of his self-contrived form of worship.

In an earlier discussion with the warden Arbeiter had affirmed that God had granted to his church through his Spirit the right to formulate policy which was not explicitly found in Scripture, for Scripture could not contain everything. But none of these addenda could be in opposition to Scripture, as Arbeiter believed was the case with infant baptism and other idolatries. What God in Jesus had established he also willed to be kept. Arbeiter felt that this included baptism (Matthew 28:18-20; Mark 16:15; Ephesians 4:5); and that surely whoever loved Jesus would keep his commandments (John 14:15).

Earlier the warden had also approached the theme of baptism from the angle of the authority of the church: Was it not possible that God established infant baptism through the Christian church, and that he therefore commanded it in this manner? Christ had had more things to reveal which the apostles were not ready to accept (John 16:12-13). One such new revelation was infant baptism.

Arbeiter countered with the affirmation that revelation was never in conflict with Scripture. He even maintained that the Catholics were not a church at all; they were rather a gathering composed of impure spirits such as whoremongers, drunkards, gluttons, and blasphemers (Revelation 18).

*The Church.* The nature of the church was a major issue in Arbeiter's encounter with Lamprecht. Arbeiter maintained that the Catholics did not perceive the true nature of God's people and church (1 Corinthians 3:11, 16-17; 2 Corinthians 6:16-18). Sinners were to acknowledge their sins, to repent, and to forsake them so that they could be made righteous and receive forgiveness (Matthew 16:18-19; 18:15-20; John 20:21-23) in the true churches of Christ.[27] Yet since the carnally-minded and the pharisaical did not acknowledge or believe such teachings, they were perpetually trying to appease God with prayer, fasting, and almsgiving. Under these circumstances such acts did not please God. For such people—who, in addition, were holding onto their own possessions—were not bearing the cross of Christ.

Arbeiter defined the church as being composed of

> those who are separated through the pure Word of God from the spotted fellowship of the sinful world and all of its disgraceful customs and life, and follow Christ alone, according to the command and order, counsel, and will of God.

Thus, for Arbeiter, the church could not include children. We have already noted his rationale for adult baptism; its effect on the parents was to encourage them to bring up their children in the fear of God. Its influence on children was to point out to them that they needed to submit to the new life in the Spirit in order to be godly. Yet whereas Lamprecht believed that unbaptized children were damned when they died, Arbeiter affirmed that they were innocent, and saved, for Christ himself had promised them blessedness (Mark 10:13-16).

Arbeiter did not directly answer the question arising from the Hutterian position as to the exact age at which children are no longer innocent, for there can be no definite answer. He simply told the warden that the Hutterites had no specific age-requirement for baptism. When children came to understand the Lord's Word, followed the faith in obedience, and demonstrated the manner of living which warranted a word of commendation from the godly; and when they could understand the meaning of Christian baptism, doctrine, and life; and when they knew what they were entering into, upon what they were building, and in what they could take comfort—then they could be baptized. Christ had commanded such baptism and the apostles performed it (Matthew 28:18-20; Mark 16:15; Acts 2:38). As to the proper age, Arbeiter stated that a person might be twenty, thirty, forty, or even a hundred years old, and if he manifested no faith or divine understanding, knowledge, or godly life, he was not baptized.[28]

### c. The Two Kingdoms: The Godly Person's Relationship to the World

The Hutterites believed there were times when God's people must decide against the world in order to decide for God (Acts 5:29). This did not mean, however, that the Brotherhood felt no responsibility toward society at large. Indeed, this responsibility was a fourfold obligation: Two of these obligations were held in common by all Anabaptists, namely, 1) mission to the world, and 2) submission to the magistracy in all areas which did not conflict with Christ's commission. But the Hutterites, because of the high visibility of their close cultural pattern, faced two further obligations to society—3) pointing out the proper use as well as the limitations of the power of the magistrate, and 4) working out a semi-official relationship with an establishment which never quite officially tolerated them. Although other Anabaptists spoke to these latter two at times, these obligations were not, in the same sense, basic to their existence. The Swiss Brethren and the Low Country Mennonites lived in a more hostile milieu that usually necessitated a more covert way of life. The Hutterites on the other hand had learned something about the power of the group as a means to greater justice. All four of these aspects are visible in Hans Arbeiter's Rechenschaft.

*Mission.* Arbeiter was imprisoned while attempting to carry out the godly person's primary responsibility to the world: Christian mission. in fact the main point of contention between Arbeiter and the magistracy centered in Arbeiter's very presence in foreign territory, which in itself challenged the claim of the established church to be the true church of Christ. For here was one who proclaimed implicitly, and at times explicitly, that the established church had no right even to call itself a church. And since there was close interaction between the church and the magistracy, the latter also felt threatened by the potential revolutionary force such dissent might, and in fact at times did, provoke. Yet the Hutterian Anabaptists did not directly initiate this conflict. It was caused primarily by the measures taken by an intolerant, sixteenth-century establishment. At any rate, when Hutterian mission came in contact with a foreign magistracy, it nearly always produced conflict.[29]

Arbeiter admitted from the outset of his imprisonment that he had been called to the office of teacher and apostle by his Brotherhood in Moravia for the purpose of pointing others to the way of redemption.[30] As a missioner his mandate was to confront the people of the world with their sins, their abominations, and their vile living—and this with the Word of God. He proclaimed that the individuals leading such a life could in no way be saved unless they repented and took the cross of Christ upon themselves (Hebrews 13:13). For whoever desired to be glorified with Christ would have to suffer with him here on earth in misery, poverty, and tribulation.

Arbeiter also confessed that he was in prison not for any evil deed, but solely for the sake of the Word of God, as had always been the experience of godly preachers sent out by God and his people. For God had laid his Word in their mouths so that they might point out to the people their vices and disgraceful living (Jeremiah 1:9). This message, Arbeiter maintained, could hardly lead anyone astray, as had been charged, for such a call to devoutness was repulsive to all flesh, that is, to all who desired to wallow in their own sins.

Anticipating the Catholic reaction, Arbeiter stated that most of the people in the world believed the godly were opposing them out of jealousy. But the world had always hated and persecuted the godly preachers and missioners. In the course of history they had at times found it necessary to hide in caves; many were even killed (Hebrews 11:32-38). On the other hand, the seducing prophets and carnal clergy who hypocritically led people into a false hope had always been loved by the world (Luke 6:26), and had always been able to live openly in town and country, going to king and prince, eating and drinking with those who lived in luxury and wore costly fashionable clothing.

Arbeiter also asserted that no earthly magistrates had the right to forbid God's missioners from setting foot on their land, for the earth was the Lord's (Psalm 24:1), and the Lord had called the church to mission.[31] Therefore God was to be obeyed and man disobeyed where such prohibition was demanded by rulers and their mandates.

From the Hutterian viewpoint the territorial church and the civil government were but two sides of the same establishment. However, since Arbeiter's cross-examiners claimed to be Christian, he at one point reprimanded Lamprecht for not living up to his name in threatening Arbeiter with the executioner. Arbeiter considered such a threat brazen and shameless, for if Lamprecht had been a teacher or Christian as he had boasted, and Arbeiter had been a seducer, heretic, and an apostate as Lamprecht considered him to be, then the Jesuit ought to have taken Paul's advice and have avoided him and departed, no longer even considering him (Titus 3:10-11). This, Arbeiter said, was the method of God's church when a person turned apostate; if such a person wanted to defend his ungodliness and contradict the truth, the Hutterian Brotherhood would never have been so bold as to teach him against his will; instead, they would have ignored him. Therefore Lamprecht, who considered Arbeiter as apostate, should have avoided him.

The Jesuit, not open to this suggestion, answered: "Oh no, it is not so, my dear Hans. The Lord says, 'Compel them to come into the kingdom of God' " (Luke 14:23). Arbeiter rejoined that the Lord had never commanded false apostles to lead the godly away from the truth into error, but rather he commanded the godly apostles and all believers to "compel" the people with the pure Word of God away from error into correct godly living.[32] Lot had "compelled" the angels to return to his home (Genesis 19:3). The disciples had constrained Christ to enter with them into the hostel (Luke 24:29-30). In like manner the godly often constrained one in whom they still had hope, often bringing him to godliness. But the Lord never had commanded the godly to take people who had no desire to accept his Word and coerce them through brute force, throwing them into prison and letting the executioner take revenge with torture and death. The false prophets of the established churches were presently urging the magistracy to do this, by imploring the magistrates to impose their arrogance and petulance upon the godly. If Lamprecht wanted to use compulsion, there were enough people in the bishopric who were in need of it, many impure people such as whores, drunkards, scamps, and blasphemers. Why did Lamprecht not trouble himself to have these people change their pattern of living? Arbeiter, with these "ungodly" members of the Catholic church in mind, then compared those who were proclaiming Catholic doctrine and preaching, to threshers constantly threshing empty straw.[33]

*Responsibility to the Magistracy.* From the perspective of the Jesuit interrogator Arbeiter obviously did not make his case theologically as to why Hutterites ought to be permitted to dwell in Catholic territory. There were other grounds, however, that Arbeiter could fall back upon, namely, the sociological. For the Hutterites were indeed accepted by Moravian magistrates, and with good reason. Arbeiter described these church-state relations, intentionally including something of the nature of the Hutterian way of life.

In Moravia, he explained, the Hutterites lived under lords who were well aware of the Hutterian religion and culture. The Brotherhood was even respected by the king, for he, by virtue of his repeated journeys there, knew that the Hutterites were living in his realm. If the rumors about the Hutterites had been at all true, the magistracy could not have tolerated them—even God would not have granted them such protection. In fact they often escorted men and women of the nobility on tours through the Hutterian dwellings and schools. They marveled at the fine upbringing of the children, and were impressed with the other well-ordered activities. Furthermore, wherever a magistrate permitted the Hutterites to dwell within his land, the Hutterites reciprocated by giving the magistrate all that God had commanded them to give and all that God had ordained for the magistrate to require of his constituency, such as taxes, ground rent, and customs duties. The Hutterites also gladly performed services for the magistrate, such as building and improving roads, and performing whatever was not contrary to God or to love for one's neighbor.

*The Magistracy, Its Function and the Limits of Its Power.* For Arbeiter, the proper function of the magistracy lay in protecting the godly from the violent and wanton. God had ordained this level of government; the Hutterites consequently honored the powers and paid tribute (Matthew 22:21; Romans 13:1-7). But there were limits to magisterial power, and Arbeiter charged that the magisterial office was transgressing its God-ordained limits by subjecting two Hutterite brethren to shameless violence and coercion, and attempting to pervert them in body and soul. This illicit establishment action, Arbeiter was certain, could not help but evoke God's wrath (Revelation 13:10; Matthew 7:2).

*The Godly and Revenge.* Arbeiter is typically Anabaptist in his reply to the idea of revenge. When the head warden asked him to promise not to attempt to avenge his prison stay, Arbeiter was amazed that the magistrate could have even conceived of such a sin. Christianity meant suffering and love and the fruits of a life lived in the Spirit. For this reason he answered:

> My dear sir, I have previously confessed to you that I am imprisoned here for the sake of truth, and not for the sake of any evil deeds. But if such a vengeful spirit were in me, that I would desire to avenge my imprisonment in this bishopric, or its staff, or someone else, then I would be no Christian but like all of you, and would be suffering in vain.[34]

The willingness to suffer, the idea of discipleship, and the new life in the Body of Christ combine in Arbeiter's testimony. His Rechenschaft reveals that existential note of a creative discipleship effected through the Spirit at work in the community of God's people.

At the end of Arbeiter's Rechenschaft is the following prayer, which served as a further challenge to his brethren to assure that future generations would be able to say with Arbeiter, "How well we are faring in the Brotherhood":

> O God, grant that we may perceive this correctly and receive Your gifts with worthy and thankful hearts, and use them to the honor of Your holy name and for our physical needs to proclaim Your work and fulfill our service to You and to Your children, resulting in the comfort of our souls. May God fulfill this through Jesus Christ, Amen.[35]

# Ch. 5

# Hutterian Encounter
# with Lutheranism

In 1557, eleven years after the death of Martin Luther, eight churchmen signed a document presumably drawn up by Melanchthon, later published under the title: "Proceedings / on How the Anabaptists are to be Treated / Proposed by a Number of Scholars Meeting at Worms."[1]

The document clearly sets the tone for church and magisterial reactions to Anabaptist activity within Lutheran lands in the second-generation era of the Reformation. All Lutheran territory was to be considered the province of the church, within which there was to be religious unity (1 Corinthians 5:3-8). Consequently all dissenters, including the Anabaptists, were to be condemned as seditious and blasphemous, and were to be killed with the sword.[2]

Seditious acts included (1) refusing to acknowledge magistrates as Christians or considering the magisterial office to be sinful, (2) holding possessions in common, (3) holding that settling suits in court is sinful, (4) refusing to take oaths, and (5) encouraging a convert to leave his or her spouse for the sake of faith.

The document also lists religious beliefs which were not seditious and therefore did not demand legal proceedings: (1) the denial of original sin, (2) that infant baptism was wrong, (3) that God is one person, thereby denying the Christian doctrine of the eternal Son and Holy Spirit, (4) that God reveals himself without consideration of the outer Word, the *ministerium*, and without the sacrament, (5) that the sacrament is only a sign, not an application of grace, (6) that justification is effected by works and suffering and one's own fulfillment of the law, or by special inner revelation, and (7) the doctrine of eternal security (once saved, always saved).[3]

## The Anabaptist Response to the Lutheran
## Proceedings of 1557

Both parts of the list in the Lutheran document were broad enough to cover the several types of Anabaptists, including the prototypes leading to Antitrinitarianism. Yet the group hardest hit was the Hutterites, whose missioners did indeed take converts, sometimes one marriage partner only, into a communal way of life. Once it was proved that a suspect was a Hutterite, legal proceedings could easily be brought to bear upon him. Less obvious were the Swiss Brethren and the Marpeck circle (and in another religious context the Mennonites of the Low Countries), whose family life patterns, at least on the surface, merged more easily with the patterns of the general culture.

The Swiss Brethren were nevertheless concerned about the decree and wrote a letter to the elderly Menno Simons in 1557, telling him that they had discussed the Lutheran broadside and had agreed to refute it in writing. Unfortunately, nothing is known about such a document; if it was written, it has disappeared.[4] But an extended reply by the Hutterites has fortunately been preserved. That they were able to carry out such a project at all was due to their effective organization which the more loosely-knit Swiss Brethren congregations lacked, weakened internally as they were by persistent persecution. Furthermore, with their intense mission program, the Hutterites were more visible in Lutheran lands.

The Hutterites were aware that justice would not win the day unless it was nourished. To compose a reply to the Lutherans, they appointed one of their better educated men, probably Leonhard Dax, who finished his lengthy argument around 1561. Dax had formerly been a Catholic priest. The title of this work is: "Handbook Countering the 'Proceedings,' Issued in 1557 at Worms on the Rhine Against the Brethren who are Called Hutterites, and Signed by Philipp Melanchthon and Johannes Brenz, Among Others from Their Midst."[5]

It can be assumed the document, which was never published, was copied numerous times during the Walpot Era as well as later by Hutterite missioners going to Lutheran lands, but only a few copies remain. Presumably the Brethren found the pamphlet less useful after they were expelled from Moravia in the 1620s. Since the work is in fact one of the major Hutterian works, ranking with the best of their doctrinal writings during the Walpot Era, a résumé of the volume is in order.[6]

A typical Hutterian prologue opens the theme with a biblical pronouncement of woe upon those who call evil good, and good evil, and those who turn darkness into light, and light into darkness (Isaiah 5:20). The volume is addressed to the "elect children of God," urging them to pray constantly and remain alert to Satan's children of evil, who try to make God's truth suspect in the eyes of the common people. It appeals to all devout Christians to remain steadfast in the face of persecution and martyrdom, for surely the writers of the "Proceedings" would reap divine wrath for their work. To show the mood of the Handbook, a lengthy excerpt which paraphrases the Proceedings follows, affording an understanding of the Hutterian interpretation of Lutheran legal pronouncements:

> Your Imperial Majesty ought to exterminate and destroy such sects and heretics as Anabaptists (as they call them) with fire, sword, water, and protracted imprisonment. For they precipitate insurrection among the people with their teachings, roam and travel through all the lands, seduce the people and the common simple man who is not acquainted with the law, and they are therefore cursed. Consequently your imperial laws and proclaimed mandates, which would remove them from the face of the earth are justified. For if they were to continue with their doctrine, the Turks and the Romans would come and take our land and people, and a great insurrection would occur against the power of the magistracy. In addition, a noticeable decline of all of Christendom would have to be feared. Your Imperial Majesty has power to prevent such a noticeable destruction, for a false prophet and heretical person, or a blasphemer, says God, is to be killed.

The Hutterites replied to this condemnation:

> Take note here, you godly Christian hearts, of the great foolishness of the falsely famous Christians and Scribes, with what type of reason and lying words they bring against the devout people of God, and hand them over to the powers that be, so that they become drunk with the blood of the saints, until the measure of their damnation and judgment is fulfilled.

The main text of the volume consists of twelve "books," from two to twelve pages in length. Another extended quotation from Book One indicates the root of the matter:

> If the worldly powers and magistrates want to be Christians, they must actually demonstrate and hold to the way and nature of the life of Christ, and have the same Lord of our life, who is Christ, whose footsteps one is to follow, as Paul testifies, saying, "Each is to have the mind of Christ," and as [Christ] himself says, "I have given you an example, that you may do as I have done," and commanded earnestly that one is to learn solely from him. From these words it is clear and

evident that [the Christian] is to hold to the rules and measure of the heavenly Master. It is surely not unknown that Christ laid aside the power of the magistracy, and refused even to be judge between brother and brother ... also escaped from them when they wanted to make him king.

At stake here is the issue of the nature of discipleship and—implicitly—of the two kingdoms, ideas which are central in Anabaptist thought.

Book Two, on why the judicial system lies outside the realm of Christianity, is supported with New Testament quotations from Luke 12:14, Matthew 5:40-42, and 1 Corinthians 5:12-13. Book Three, on oaths, is based primarily upon Matthew 5:33-37. Book Four examines the nature of the true church, and explains that the Lutherans cannot claim to be this church, because they are not walking in righteousness in line with Paul's admonition, nor taking seriously the statement of the Apostles' Creed that requires believing in the "community of the saints." Book Five deals with the issue of infant baptism: true baptism is only for repentant believers, as witnessed in the New Testament. Book Six considers the symbolic nature of the Lord's Supper, as a celebration to take place among Christians who dwell together in unity, and rejects the idea that Christ dwells in the bread and wine as the Catholics and Lutherans maintain. Book Seven discusses the nature of original sin, a doctrine which the Lutherans wrongly accused the Anabaptists of not believing. Book Eight emphasizes the importance of the proclaimed Word, again refuting the charges of misinformed Lutherans. Book Nine examines the doctrine of the Trinity, another doctrine which the Anabaptists are accused of rejecting. Book Ten refutes the charge that the Anabaptists believed in eternal security, that is, in the belief that a person who is saved cannot again fall into disbelief and divine condemnation. Book Eleven considers the accusation that Anabaptists taught works-righteousness (salvation by works) and perfectionism. Book Twelve presents a detailed account of the manner in which Hutterites brought up their children.

The Conclusion of the Handbook is a reminder to the Lutherans that Jesus has rendered null and void that very law upon which they base their justification of executing Anabaptists and has transformed the Old Testament law against blasphemers (Leviticus 24:16) into a new precept, namely, that those who do not live in accord with biblical teachings are to be considered as pagans and sinners, and are to be banned rather than executed (Matthew 18:15-20; 1 Timothy 6:5).

The Handbook closes with the argument that God's program of proclamation has not been entrusted to people such as the Lutherans, who practice brutal and heathen methods of violence, for biblical nonresistance is incompatible with Lutheranism, as demonstrated by the Worms statement itself, which advocates capital punishment; God's messengers, on the contrary, use only the sword of the spirit. Still, the booklet continues with characteristic emphasis, stating that true believers must reckon with imprisonment and the rope, in no small measure occasioned by such works as Proceedings; nevertheless, the godly shall continue to cling to their biblical faith, for they are sure to gain the ultimate victory.

Proceedings became the basis for later Lutheran writings against the Anabaptists. Another example of the attention and energy the Lutherans expended in dealing with Anabaptism is the seven-day conference held at Stuttgart, at the turn of the year, 1570/71. A lengthy protocol, which deals with some points taken almost verbatim from Proceedings, presents in minute detail the questions to be asked during the interrogation of suspects and the actions to be taken against Anabaptists. In 1584 a similar document was issued because of renewed Anabaptist mission activity. Recalcitrant Anabaptists were to be punished in line with their station in life: elders were to remain in severe imprisonment until they recanted or died; other Anabaptists were to receive milder treatment and better food, and after a given time were to be released even if they had not recanted.

To be noted is the generally accurate understanding the Lutheran officials had about Anabaptism, and relatively lenient sentences imposed in legal cases. Melanchthon's recommendation of capital punishment in 1557 was simply too harsh, for the general attitude toward the Anabaptists as well as other deviants had softened throughout Europe by the 1560s and '70s.[7]

It is a moot question whether the success of Hutterian missioners in Lutheran areas was due to leniency, or whether the soil out of which the Lutheran Reformation grew also produced many seekers who desired a more genuine Christian way of life, different from what sixteenth-century Lutheranism afforded. At any rate, missioners regularly made their way into Lutheran lands throughout the Walpot Era. Paul Glock with his unusual nineteen-year incarceration is the most famous of these. His story will follow the account of two plumbers who were unexpectedly detained for three months in Vienna.

## Marx and Bernhard Klampferer: A Quarter-Year Delay in Vienna

Late in July 1573, three Hutterites traveled from Moravia to Vienna. Two of them, Marx and Bernhard, called Klampferer after their plumbing trade, planned to purchase some tools. While they were buying their wares the third member, unnamed, planned to visit his sister, in the employ of Marshal Hans Wilhelm, Baron of Roggendorf, an ardent Lutheran.[8]

When Marx and Bernhard had made their purchases and entered the Baron's courtyard to pick up the youth, events took an unexpected turn. Marx's inquiry whether the visitor was ready to leave led to the discovery that Marx and Bernhard were Hutterites. They were ushered into the presence of the marshal, and it soon became clear to them that they would not leave Vienna on schedule.

The marshal accused them of illegally entering his house. Marx replied that they had not entered the house, but had only stepped into the courtyard, and apologizing for the intrusion he expressed the hope that their question to the boy in the yard had not angered the marshal. He explained that they could hardly have left their young companion to return by himself from a strange town, and they believed the marshal could sympathize with their actions. If he had known that the marshal was offended when someone entered his courtyard, Marx continued, they would have stayed outside, for their people were not the kind who desired to offend or make trouble. The marshal asked whether the three were Moravian Hutterites, also known as Stäbler,[9] who were justifiably called Anabaptists, a sect which crept around in darkness. Marx affirmed that they were Hutterites, but in reality quite different from what many people imagined.

The marshal thought it a sin and a shame that the Hutterites had led their fine young companion astray. Marx doubted that the youth thought of his experiences in such terms, and asked permission to talk to him. But the marshal simply said that he himself had questioned the lad, and found that he could not even recite the Catechism, the Lord's Prayer, or the Ten Commandments. Marx mentioned that there were numerous catechisms— Papal, Lutheran, and Zwinglian, including one by Johannes Brenz, and that although the Hutterites did not often use such Latin and Greek terms, he considered himself to be a "catechumen" who needed daily instruction. As to the Ten Commandments, Marx affirmed, the Hutterites could not laud anyone who failed to obey them, no matter how well one could repeat them from memory.

A protracted discussion on baptism focused on the issue of whether infants could have faith. Marx believed that children were saved without faith by Christ's atonement, for faith came only through hearing (Romans 10:17), and infants were not yet able to listen.

The marshal finally threatened Marx with imprisonment, but said he did not want to carry this out. He would speak to the Hutterite youth, hoping that his sister would meanwhile have been able to convert him to the Lutheran faith. If he remained firm in his convictions, he would be permitted to return to Moravia with the two plumbers.

The brothers left and spent long hours that evening probing and praying about the incident, its alternatives, and possible consequences. Both were worried that the marshal might call the magistrates, or even a clergyman. On the other hand, leaving the town without the youth would also be risky, for spies had most certainly been posted to arrest them at customs, and if they were stopped at the ferry, they might lose all their belongings and tools and be imprisoned as well. They decided to return to the marshal's house.

The next day there was indeed a visiting clergyman at the marshal's home. In essence, the performance was a repetition of the previous day. Marx first requested that the marshal not prevent them from attending to their business concerns. Instead, the marshal demanded that Marx again present his confession of faith for the clergyman. Marx asserted that he had done this the day before, and since neither party could convince the other side of the correctness of its faith, he felt that the only alternative was a parting of the ways. Marx added that he himself had walked the broad Lutheran path, understood it well, and had no need for further clarification, whereas the Lutherans, not having experienced the narrow Hutterian path leading to eternal life, were unable to understand the Hutterian way. Marx admitted that the Lutheran idea of faith was correct as far as it went, but that it lacked two important manifestations: the works and fruits of faith (1 Corinthians 13).

Marx also affirmed the Lutheran belief that divine grace was made possible only through Christ's atonement, but interpreted it to include the fulfillment of Christ's command, without which atonement was of no avail. To hear the Word was not enough; one was to "do" Christ's words (Matthew 7:24-27). The Lutherans held that this interpretation meant earning one's salvation, a doctrine also held by the Jesuits.[10] Marx replied that fulfilling all of Christ's commands and letting one's light shine (Matthew 5:16) still left the Christian an unprofitable servant (Luke 17:10).

The Lutherans also objected to the Hutterian method of preaching and witness. They asked why the Brethren preached clandestinely, slinking about in darkness. Marx asserted that although open preaching took place in Moravia, they could not use the same methods where they were forbidden to speak about the crucified Christ; neither did the Lutherans enter papal stalls and preach openly—nor did Jesus himself always preach openly.

After a belabored discussion on baptism, Marx once more requested to be released. He even offered to pay the marshal if this were the problem. The marshal instead sent for the provost, who took them to prison and chained them in leg irons.

Four weeks later Marx was cross-examined by a gray-bearded clergyman from Krems, Magister Gangolf Wanger, a quick thinker. Wanger claimed to have with him a letter from the Hutterite youth which said that he had by now converted to the Lutheran faith. Marx, not satisfied with a document that might have been forged, or written under pressure, said he wanted to hear from the lad himself whether the Hutterites had taught anything which did not conform to the teachings and command of Christ and his apostles. Another sharp discussion on baptism ensued in which the Lutherans accused the Hutterites of denying to infants the promised grace of God. Marx refuted this charge. He believed that infants were redeemed, for of such was the kingdom of heaven. It seemed to him that it was rather the Lutherans who were denying to children such promises, for they granted more power and faith to the water than to the words and atonement of Christ, who through his sacrifice and merit had made void the fall of Adam in the sight of the Father.

When the clergyman was frustrated by Marx's answers, he either carried on a monologue, or raged and swore. Finally he called Marx a dolt, one of those men who seduced the people and led women away from their husbands, giving them over to other men, and when they located a good corpulent widow, they were sure to lure her off.

During the next two months there were other cross-examinations, but finally the two prisoners were released and returned to the Brotherhood "with unblemished consciences." The younger traveling companion had apparently recanted, for nothing more is known about him. The two plumbers also disappear from the annals of history at this point, presumably indicating they led a normal life in the community. To this degree, Marx's testimony could have been approximated by most Hutterites, and grants insight into the mind of the typical Hutterite who was neither missioner nor minister. Appended to the surviving document is a verse from Revelation (2:10) written by another hand, which brings the story to an appropriate close:

Behold the devil will cast some of you into prison, that you will be tempted and will have tribulation for ten days. Be faithful until death, and I will give you the crown of life.[11]

## Paul Glock's Nineteen-Year Imprisonment

In Hutterian tradition the name of Paul Glock is legendary. In far-off Ukraine, two centuries after his death, the Hutterites were still telling grandchildren about "those wondrous events which had come to pass" in the life of Paul Glock.[12]

Glock's incarceration of nineteen years had in fact made a much larger contribution to Hutterian history than his small window in the Hohenwittlingen prison wall would seem to warrant. But the records found in a score of his letters validate his fame and permit a detailed account of Glock's life and thought. Actually, more is known historically about Paul Glock the man, from his own pen, than is known about any other sixteenth-century Anabaptist. Consequently on the level of Anabaptist cultural and social history, every detail in Glock's story is significant.

The Glock episode presented below is developed through a descriptive, chronological portrayal. What is hereby lost in unity is hopefully gained in richness of striking detail. Nothing needs to be added in way of a fictionalized background of characterization to enhance this historical drama. It bears testimony to second-generation Hutterian Anabaptism, and deserves close attention. Except where interpretive comment noticeably breaks into the narrative, it should be taken for granted that the account presents Glock's own views, faith, and critique of society. In effect, the world is seen through Paul Glock's own eyes. His contribution to Anabaptist history does not lie in his development of Anabaptist thought, where he followed the traditional lines of his era; it lies rather in the person of Paul Glock the disciple, in his deep, unconditional commitment to obedience.

### Glock's Earlier Years

Paul Glock was born around 1530/35 at Rommelshausen, near Waiblingen, Württemberg, and was named Jung-Paul, to distinguish him from his father. Later in life Jung-Paul described his hedonistic, youthful years. He was very fond of the music of violin, drum, and flute. Dressing in silks and satins highlighted with gold and silver ornamentation was part of his style of life. To please his comrades, he would dance with girls of questionable repute, and was finally felled by Satan. But God, from whom Glock had fallen away, drew the youth away from a world which lived without God and which had enticingly deceived Glock so long. As Glock says, "If I had not left that world of unchaste, conditioned upbringing, about which Your Word, O God, has instructed me, I would never have received Your grace."[13]

During his mature years Glock experienced that joy of spiritual fulfillment and optimism which characterized many a Hutterite during the Walpot Era. His youthful love for music continued, serving him well during two long decades of prison life, for singing and writing poetry were then among his few permitted pastimes.

By 1550 Jung-Paul Glock lay in prison for his Anabaptist faith, along with his father and mother. Three leading theologians of the region attempted to counsel the prisoners about truth, but the prisoners stated they were already on the correct path. They did suggest, however, that if the Lutherans would repent and live without sinning they would be willing to attend Lutheran church services. Although we do not know all the facts, Jung-Paul must have found his way to freedom, for in June 1558 he was seized again and delivered to the Stuttgart authorities by Sixt Weselin, the assistant warden of Schorndorf.

The civil and ecclesiastical officials unsuccessfully cross-examined Glock under torture, and in the autumn of 1558 transferred him to the prison of Hohenwittlingen Castle as a recalcitrant Anabaptist. Around Easter of the next year Adam Horneck (Hornikel), another Hutterite, joined Glock there. By September, both had taken ill. Duke Christoph, from Grafeneck near Münsingen, heard of their plight, and ordered the warden, Hans von Talheim, to permit them to exercise three or four hours daily in leg irons within the inner court, but not to let them speak to anyone lest they lead them astray with their seductive teachings.[14]

### Contact Established with Moravia

Spring of 1563 marked the beginning of a thirteen-year exchange of epistles between Jung-Paul Glock and the Hutterites in Moravia. He somehow procured paper and ink and in April 1563 wrote a lengthy letter to his wife, Else, a teacher at the Hutterian school in Teikowitz, in the region of Mährisch Kromau. In this letter of concern and exhortation, Glock expressed the hope that God's grace might daily sustain and strengthen her and the whole Brotherhood; he admonished her to be quiet in demeanor as becomes a woman, reminding her that one woman's speech was all that had been needed to precipitate the fall of mankind. Addressing himself then to the whole Hutterian Brotherhood, he exhorted his brethren to open themselves to the mind and spirit of Christ and to exemplify Christ's reputation to both the godly and the ungodly, becoming a sweet fragrance to those who would be redeemed and a witness to those who would be lost, so that the impenitent sinner would have no excuse. He closed his epistle with a plea for a life of Christian discipleship. He hoped that the Lord might align the hearts of all brethren to the image of Christ and that they might draw their strength from him, for God's people were a mirror to the world, reflecting the life of Christ himself.[15]

## The Cross-Examination of 1562:
### Glock's First Confession of Faith

To his letter Glock attached a lengthy summary of his court hearing of the previous September. Present at the early morning cross-examination were some members of the nobility, some citizens, some doctors of theology, three ministers, and the head warden from Urach, Nikolaus (Klaus) von Grafeneck.[16] The prisoners were told they could free themselves by presenting "correct" answers. Glock and Horneck, not accustomed to parroting the desired formulas, replied that they would speak neither more nor less than what the Lord gave them to utter. Although Glock had previously presented his confession of faith, he indicated willingness to discuss those articles of faith which constituted the underlying cause of his imprisonment: baptism, preaching, communion, the church, oaths, warfare, vengeance, and the magistracy.[17]

At one point during the three-hour session Matthias Hebsacker, a Lutheran minister, made a proposition to the two prisoners. Having recently moved to Urach he too was troubled by the less than ideal conditions in the church, but he was trying to establish a real Christian congregation; the prisoners should be patient and work with him in improving conditions. Glock felt that this was impossible by the very nature of the case, for no living faith could spring out of a dead faith.

By this time, Klaus von Grafeneck was getting hungry and good-naturedly suggested breakfast for the whole group. During the meal the warden questioned Glock further about his view of the magistracy, for Glock had insisted that a magistrate was not redeemed. The prisoner compared the two types of servants God placed on earth: the "Pharaohs" and the "Pauls," who were mutually incompatible. He was certain that this duality between world and church was still a reality within history. At the close of the hearing, a Lutheran minister admitted the futility of any further attempt at indoctrinating the prisoners, to which Glock readily agreed, and the prisoners were returned to their cells.

Imprisonment during the next months was quite bearable. Prison food, consisting of bread, water, porridge, and soup, was better than many a free person in the area was enjoying. In addition, Glock had established good connections with outsiders, including a brother in the faith, Melchior

Waal,[18] who supplied the prisoners with incidentals.

Another "connection" was none other than the Urach warden, Klaus von Grafeneck, and his wife, Margarete. Klaus had provided Glock with a supply of paper and ink so that he could write a complete confession of his faith. Klaus von Grafeneck had already appeared as a sympathetic eyewitness to the trial and execution of Michael Sattler (1527). Furthermore, his wife and at least one daughter were members of the Schwenckfeld fellowship.

For another year Glock was permitted to meet regularly with Adam Horneck, until Horneck was finally granted a new trial and then expelled from the land.

Something of Glock's sadness is contained in a poem written in 1564 after Horneck's departure, asking for the Brotherhood prayers on his behalf in his new loneliness. Added to Glock's feeling of desolation was the report that he must have received about the same time, that his wife and child had died in Moravia. A constant flow of Hutterite messengers to Württemberg who found ways of contacting Glock helped him over his periods of solitude. For two years, word-of-mouth messages took the place of letters.[19]

### Six Months of "Freedom"

During the fall and winter of 1565/66 something highly unusual for a prisoner happened to Jung-Paul Glock. For six months he experienced as pure a freedom as any prisoner would dare dream of: freedom to travel and visit acquaintances merely by promising to return in the evening. His doors were unlocked at night. He ran errands for Warden Hans von Talheim, whose confidence he had won. He dined regularly with Klaus and Margarete von Grafeneck, once planting a vine in their garden. He was sent to Blaubeuren, a distance of forty kilometers, to the home of Head Warden Wolf and Susanna (von Grafeneck) von Zülnhart, where he remained overnight, even washing his hands in the cold, deep-blue waters of the Blautopf, the source of the Blau River.

Neither minister nor magistrate nor castle warden tried to stop him, and when someone talked to him about Christianity, Glock responded openly with the truth. Everyone marveled that a prisoner was free to come and go as he wished, bound only to his word of honor. Glock was in fact anticipating a stay in his sentence and a speedy release from prison.[20]

### Freedom's End

By March 1566 Jung-Paul Glock's circumstances changed abruptly. The Lutheran ministers reasoned that Glock, in exchange for his newly granted freedom, should be willing to concede certain doctrines so that they could report to their congregations that he had finally yielded, and that they had in return graciously granted him great freedom.

The doctrine they selected was whether the princes and lords, and the clergy as servants of the magistracy, were good Christians, and whether they would be saved at death. Glock answered with an utterly honest "No," reiterating his views that the Holy Spirit would surely damn Lutheran and Catholic looseness and roguery.

Glock's resolve was the provocation which ended his half-year of freedom. The ministers convinced the magistrates that the risk was too great to allow Glock further freedom, and that he should be held in prison for the rest of his days or until he admitted that Lutherans were good Christians; for if the peasants were told that their lords, magistrates, and ministers were not Christian, revolution would be imminent.

Glock was returned to the prison and placed in solitary confinement. Not even Warden Klaus and Margarete von Grafeneck were allowed to visit him. His writing paper, purchased with money he himself had earned in the harvest, was taken away except just enough paper to write one more letter. But the darkness of his wretched windowless cell made it difficult to fill even the one sheet. Glock, writing to Vorsteher Peter Walpot, requested that his radical change in circumstances be announced within the home congregations; he could no longer write letters to anyone, but letters could continue to be sent to him through the usual contact person, Margarete von Grafeneck. Later, looking back with some bitterness to this phase of his prison life, he wrote in verse form:

> Since I rebuke them / For leading the lives they do; / And will not admit them to be right / In their profligacy; / They in return want me behind bars.[21]

## Nigh unto Death

In June 1567 Jung-Paul Glock wrote what he believed to be his last letter to Walpot; Glock was suffering from an advanced case of scurvy and felt that he would soon die. Five weeks of the disease had caused such severe mouth wounds that he could no longer even chew bread. His thighs and knees were crippled. Emaciated, he was no longer even able to pace the floor for exercise. Though the arrow of Job had pierced him, he was certain that God would never forsake him.

Where lesser men might have given up in despair, Glock did not simply passively wait for God to save him, but he dictated a note to the "deceiving rogues in the chancellery," telling them that his illness was so severe that he was unable to swallow his twice-daily portion of thin watery broth and bread.

The reply was read to Glock: since God had afflicted him with sickness, he should confess his sins and accept their doctrine, and thus open up the way for immediate help, with medical care. To this Glock could only reply that if he had acted in any way displeasing to God, he would repent. But he would not succumb to hypocrisy and play into the hands of the magistrates and Lutheran ministers in matters of conscience.[22]

These rogues of clergymen, Glock said in his letter to Walpot, were like Job's visitors when they talked to him about faith, baptism, the Lord's Supper, and the church. Putting his finger directly on the doctrinal watershed, he challenged them to show him one Christian congregation produced by Lutheran preaching, doctrine, and faith; if they could, he would join it. The ministers retorted that the Christian church could not be pointed out with a finger but simply had to be accepted in faith. Glock replied that Christ had pointed to his church, saying that his brother, sister, and mother were those who did the will of his Father in heaven (Matthew 12:47).

In his letter, Glock further related that the rogues continued to let him lie crumpled in his illness, without good food or the services of a physician. They wanted him murdered, Glock claimed; but he took comfort in the Lord. He accepted medication and used some of his remaining coins to buy drugs that he felt had kept him alive. He requested the prayers of the Brotherhood—in case he was still living when the epistle arrived. After admonishing Walpot and the whole Brotherhood to remain steadfast in prayer, in communal fellowship, in their love toward God, and in that true obedience to which they had been called in Christ, he took his leave from the Brotherhood in the peace of Christ.

In way of interpretation, both Glock's will to live and his willingness to die may be noted. Indeed, the "theology of martyrdom," considered by some to be inherent in Anabaptism,[23] must be broadly interpreted to include the fighting spirit of Jung-Paul Glock. For he radiated the will to live, to witness, and to return to the Brotherhood in Moravia, where he could again experience fellowship among his dear friends. Other Hutterite missioners have been noted above who demonstrated the same tenacious will not only to do battle with the world, but also to survive.

In his "last epistle," Glock could not conceal the despair intermingled with his Christian hope. Nor did his biting contempt for his oppressors' arguments pass unnoticed among his friends. The Hutterites were down-to-earth and practical; they took literally Jesus' command to love God and neighbor as well as enemy, but they also kept a healthy self-respect. Previously, imprisonment of heretics had almost invariably signaled execution; this was perhaps the reason why captured Anabaptists seemed to take on an other-worldly spiritual quality, where martyrdom was understood as a natural part of the true Christian's pilgrimage. But times had changed. Imprisonment in many regions no longer meant death. Imprisonment itself became a channel to witness as a living human being; it was not only the prologue to a martyr's death. Many managed to escape. As for Paul Glock, the Great Chronicle reports: "They attempted to bring him to recant with severe imprisonment and also with light imprisonment."[24] Despite enduring unexpected prison severity and being dismayed by his helplessness, Glock still fought back. He had dictated a letter to the authorities and had let his condition be known. Through the months and years he had built up a circle of friends with whom he shared in Christian fellowship. For a member of the close Hutterian society, this was most unusual, but Glock was open enough in his relationships to gather those strengthening elements—human beings who could and would demand a bit of justice for their friend.

The prisoner did not die. The next note from Glock is dated April 1569, almost two years later. "I was really very sick," Glock wrote. His battle between life and death had lasted twelve days, and his physical trials turned into spiritual temptation, for a simple recanting would have brought immediate relief. But with meat added to his diet, and medicines, some of which arrived from Moravia, Glock pulled through. He thanked Walpot for the daily prayers on his behalf, as well as for the special medicine from the Brotherhood pharmacy, a cooked berry juice concentrate used as a purgative which was especially effective in bringing him through convalescence. Although Hutterite physicians knew nothing about vitamins, they had an effective medicine to cure scurvy and sent it with exact directions for use. God had taken care of him, he wrote, and he recovered in spite of the officials of the established church who had returned him to solitary confinement on a starvation diet.

It seems odd to our generation that at times the church had proved less flexible than the state in its policies toward dissenters. But the magistrates often learned to know the Anabaptists personally, not as religious competitors, but as fellow humans, whereas the clergy had to deal with them as "heretics." The established (state) church saw its very foundation threatened by a sect it could not comprehend. It correctly felt that the movement, built upon the concept of a voluntary membership, was undermining a thousand-year-old ecclesiastical structure which had become the fabric of a total society.

The magistrates on the other hand saw a Paul Glock or a Veit Uhrmacher as a person who could sing, talk about the weather, crops, and politics; who was furthermore utterly honest, trustworthy, and often rather likable in spite of his harsh judgment toward sin and his constant admonishing of sinners. How else could Glock have won the confidence of his jailer, who "threw away the key" for half a year?[25]


### New Life in Prison

In April 1569 prison life took a definite turn for the better for Paul Glock. His earlier dank, cold prison cell was replaced by a pleasant, well-heated room. His bread-and-broth diet was exchanged for a feast of two daily meals including a measure of wine, and either meat or fish, or something baked. His clothing and blankets were in good supply. He felt a new mood of optimism.

Glock was enjoying the peace of the unofficial détente with the ministers, who found a new source of concern, Vinzenz Forer, a Spanish Catholic priest who was imprisoned next to Glock. Glock carried on a number of discussions with him and had him read the printed Brotherhood Rechenschaft, hoping he would soon see the truth. Forer agreed only with parts of the Rechenschaft and attempted to convert Glock to Catholicism. The two prisoners debated such points of doctrine as whether man inherited original sin, whether a magistrate might be a Christian provided he did not violate his own conscience, and whether a Christian might pay war taxes, even if he himself could not fight.

Their discussions set Glock to thinking about the Hutterites' growing problem of war taxes. In a letter he counseled the brethren to bear suffering rather than compromise their position through payment of the requested "blood-money." With typical Hutterian practicality, Glock suggested a possible alternative solution: perhaps the brethren who were hired out to the nobility could request payment for their services in the form of grain instead of money, making it difficult for the government to collect its "Turk-money." He reported that there had been talk of setting the prisoners free, although nothing had come of it.

Glock's routine changed little during the next few years. He continued to be well treated and well fed. By late 1570 the famine which had spread throughout Moravia and had eroded most of the Hutterian food reserves spread to Württemberg, but an increased prison budget permitted Glock to receive his usual good meals. At times he wove cord for various citizens of Urach to earn a bit of pocket money. He continued to enjoy singing, writing, and reading. And although he at times could have used some of the hundred guilders that still belonged to him back at Rommelshausen, prison life was quite bearable. Messengers from Moravia, some of them Hutterite, regularly took care of his special needs. The Grafeneck family continued to provide him pleasant company. In return, Glock regularly asked the Brotherhood for Hutterian-produced products, such as the famous carved antler-handle knives and spoons, for all the good people who were so kind and faithful to him.

The Grafenecks merited a special expression of gratitude for lodging the many Hutterites traveling to and through Urach. Klaus von Grafeneck, for example, reported to Glock about Ludwig Dörker, a fellow Hutterite missioner, who had spent the night at the Grafeneck castle in Urach; Glock asked Walpot to send them two more pairs of knives in appreciation for their graciousness.

Glock continued to be intensely aware of what his brothers and sisters were experiencing and felt himself to be an integral part of the Brotherhood. Rumors of Brotherhood discord led him to send a brotherly admonition to Walpot to stand firm in the practice of congregational discipline and not to tolerate looseness or factionalism, for the unity of faith and love must reign supreme in God's church. Glock noted with pleasure the recent increase in the number of converts and felt that the Lord was still "seeking out His own."

Toward the end of 1569, Glock reported an improvement in his relations with the Lutheran ministers. Glock even ate with them at times, avoiding the touchy subjects of doctrine. One minister did express his conviction that even if the Hutterian position were correct, it could not be tolerated.

Some ministers had even spoken to their congregations about the communal sharing and mutual aid of the Hutterites, Glock noted. But he added that even though they witnessed to the ideal Christian life, they would not align themselves with this norm and live as they knew they should.

On the other hand, there were a few individuals who began to see the point. During these years a friendship had been developing between Glock and the assistant warden, Simplicius Volmar, who was sympathetic to Glock's cause. Glock had transcribed the complete Brotherhood Rechenschaft and now asked Volmar to have it bound in Urach, feeling sure that Volmar would read the copy diligently.[26]

**Paul Glock's Prison Philosophy**

In 1571, Paul Glock wrote to Walpot about the recently regained freedoms he was enjoying. Hans von Talheim had granted Glock freedom within the castle on the basis of his promise not to attempt an escape. He was to stay in his room when strangers approached, so that the Lutheran ministers would not know about his new freedom. Glock was out almost every day fetching wood, repairing shoes, doing odd jobs, and even earning some pocket money.

In late 1571 Glock's place of residence changed to the Urach castle as a guest in the home of Klaus von Grafeneck. He remained there one full year, until autumn 1572, once again bound only by his word that he would not escape.

It was during this period of Glock's nineteen-year incarceration that the Hutterian Brotherhood decided Glock should escape from prison and return to Moravia. In late 1572 Walpot sent him a communication to this effect.

Glock had often been tempted with this idea, but had always seen it as a temptation, in light of his promise. It was hard for him to accept the Brotherhood sentiment, for his brethren did not understand all the implications of such an act. Therefore Glock attempted to explain his predicament:

> Therefore you should know, dear brethren, that I was never so free in my travels at the [Grafeneck] home that I could have considered it better . . . to leave. Consequently I did not do it.

From autumn of 1571 to that of 1572 Klaus von Grafeneck was partially responsible for Glock's welfare in the Grafeneck household. During this same time Klaus had often told Glock that were he in Glock's predicament, he would flee. Yet Klaus refused to give him an official pardon to leave legally. Therefore if Glock had taken Klaus's suggestion, the other lords, who were responsible for Glock's welfare as a prisoner and who had entrusted him with so much freedom, would have been in deep legal trouble. Furthermore, if he were to escape, future Anabaptists imprisoned in that area would at once be considered suspect, and because of Glock's actions would gain no favor but would be categorized as lying rascals. Hence Glock was unable to consider escape.

As if to allay Walpot's possible doubts about his satisfaction in his position as a hero in chains, or perhaps even an unwillingness to return to the Brotherhood, Glock added that he took no pride in remaining in his situation, but sought only God's glory. Indeed, Glock had conscientiously sought a means through which he might gain freedom without bringing dishonor upon himself and the lords, but alas, he had not yet found it. The government had even issued a new command that Klaus von Grafeneck, along with Glock's guardian, Georg Rüelin, were to be sent back to Hohenwittlingen. Rüelin sympathetically suggested that Glock ask Klaus to issue a command for his release, even though it might bring reproach to the three higher officials responsible for the prisoner's welfare. Glock followed Rüelin's suggestion, but Klaus replied that he could not bear the consequences of allowing Glock to leave, for then he himself might be executed. Klaus, only beginning to realize the full implications of a possible escape by Glock, seemed quite uneasy during Glock's last three days at Urach before he was returned to Hohenwittlingen. Glock's reaction was to think of the verse in Ecclesiasticus (12:9), which warned against trusting the ungodly, and he considered Klaus—in spite of all his kindness—as being hardhearted! Glock reported Klaus's stubborn refusal to his guardian; Rüelin comforted him by promising to do all he could for him.

Glock accepted this unexpected change stoically and in his report to Walpot stated that the new circumstances were not too difficult. He took comfort in the fact that many ungodly men had a much harder fate than he, the famine being a sign of God's wrath pouring out upon an ungodly Lutheranism. He wrote that this act of God had unfortunately not produced any repentance and the people continued to live in deceit, lying, shooting, greed, usury, exploitation, gluttony, drunkenness, haughtiness, immeasurable blasphemy, whoremongering, lewdness, and still other ways that were not compatible with the New Testament view of the church. They had even discontinued permitting Anabaptists and other brethren to lodge in Württemberg.

All in all, Glock held to the hope that God would soon deliver him, but until that time trusted the Brotherhood to accept his imprisonment as necessary for the good of all concerned.[27]

### Paul Glock's Second Confession of Faith

Late in 1572 the prince, council, and chancellors moved from Stuttgart to Urach and remained there for the winter because of a severe epidemic. In their leisure, the chancellors on three separate occasions wandered up to Hohenwittlingen and talked with Paul Glock about matters of faith. On January 18, 1573, Glock was called to the chancellery for a hearing. Present were the princes' two chaplains, Lukas Osiander and Johannes Stecker, the town pastor, Matthias Hebsacker, four chancellors, and the prefect, Jakob von Hoheneck zu Vils, who was next to the prince in rank. The topics to be discussed were infant baptism, the Lord's Supper, magistrates, and oaths.

Glock was to prove that the Lutheran understanding of these matters was incorrect.

In opening the discussion Glock charged that the Lutherans were practicing unbiblical coercion in forcing people to accept their theology. He then proceeded with the topics on the agenda.

The chancellors remained silent throughout the discussion but listened diligently and took notes. Finally the prefect, Jakob von Hoheneck zu Vils, spoke in Latin to one of the court chaplains, who then told Glock that if he would promise never to return, he would be set free. Glock replied that he would leave if the magistrates would give him the letter and seal which he would need to enter other lands. But the magistrates refused. Glock also admitted that he could not promise never to return, but if he should ever return and commit such acts as merited the penalty of the sword, they should execute him. The magistrates did not seem pleased with this. However, after more conversing in Latin, the ministers told Glock that if he would keep his religion to himself and lead no others astray, they would free him.

How easy it would have been for Glock to promise this and be freed! Yet it was impossible. Glock simply stood firmly by his statement that if he were wrong and merited the sword, they should use it, for God had ordained them for that purpose. But if he were correct, then it was only just that others hear his message.

Toward the end of the three-hour session, one of the clergymen charged that Glock had led many souls astray, and—perhaps feeling the force of Glock's charge of coercion—maintained that the authorities had not been attempting to coerce Glock into accepting the "correct doctrine," but only wanted to restrain him from misleading others. The session ended on this note, and the council then commanded that Glock be taken back to the castle and kept there.

All Glock could do was wait. His faith in God never wavering, he wrote, "Thus I am lying [in prison] trusting completely in the Lord Christ, to him be the praise, and I now await with his grace what God permits them to do with me."

A month later, February 23, 1573, two clergymen and a chancellor came to the castle to speak with the two new prisoners, the Swiss Brethren, Leonhard Sommer and Jakob Gantz. At the close of the debate the Lutherans talked with Glock and then left. But they left behind a terse command stating the prince's order:

     . . . the warden is to confine the stiff-necked Paul Glock carefully under lock and key. . . . It has become known to us that you have allowed

Glock his freedom within the castle. If this continues, you will be punished by the prince.

But orders were also given that his food and drink should continue as usual.[28]

### Hans von Talheim's Untimely End

By 1574 Paul Glock was experiencing his seventeeth year of incarceration. With the passing of time also came changes which signaled the arrival of a new generation, with new forces and new events. Glock listed some of these changes in letters to Walpot in the spring of 1574.

The old castle warden, Hans von Talheim, had retired, handing his position down to his son Jakob. Hans had not been so cooperative since the reprimand from his superiors the year before, but his son established a good relationship with Glock, who reciprocated by offering a pair of handsome Hutterian knives to the warden's wife. She was highly pleased with the gift. The new warden and his wife continued to treat Glock well over the next months and years.

Later that year Glock recounted the details of the difficulties he had had with the elderly Hans von Talheim. In Glock's opinion, events showed that divine justice sided with the Anabaptists, for earlier in the year the Swiss Brethren in the area had been able to convince a maid working at the castle to join their Brotherhood. When Hans von Talheim heard about this he fumed and raged, threatening to go to Stuttgart and give a report that would cause regret for all concerned—including his own son, the new warden. The young warden himself told Glock of his father's threat and outraged curses. However, on a Sunday, two weeks after these threats took place, old Hans and his wife were sitting in their orchard protecting their fruit trees against Sunday poachers, when two farmers passing by fell into a brawl. Hans started toward the rowdies, but before he could reach them he fell to the ground and gasped his last words, saying, "Alas, alas!" Glock reported that Hans turned black as the devil and was soon pronounced dead. As the retired warden had apparently been in good health, so Glock reported, this proud Haman (Esther 7) was therefore slain upon the gallows with which he had threatened others, with God himself acting as hangman; God did not always grant the enemies of his people free rein, nor did he cede any detail of his plan for his people.[29]

### Matthias Binder's Imprisonment

The next word from Paul Glock is dated a year and a half later. This time there was a surprise in the salutation: "Paul and Matthias, your brethren in the tribulation and kingdom of Christ; to Peter Walpot and the church of God." Two years before, the Brotherhood had lost track of Binder and had asked Glock for information. Although at that time Glock could provide no details, by 1575 he knew all about Binder's encounters with the authorities, for Binder was now with him.

Matthias had been chosen as minister in 1569 and was later sent as a missioner to Württemberg with Paul Prele. Two years later, on April 15, 1573, the two were seized and imprisoned at Neuffen. Since he was not an ordained minister, Prele was soon released, leaving Binder alone in his struggle with the authorities. Binder, who had known about Glock's imprisonment and unwavering witness, had often taken strength from Glock's example during his own interrogations.

After several transfers between the prisons at Neuffen and Maulbronn, Binder was finally moved in 1575 to Hohenwittlingen where he became Glock's co-prisoner. The Brotherhood soon sent the two brethren news of their families and of the larger Brotherhood.[30]

### Prison Life in Early 1576:
### Reflections and Activities

In February 1576, Paul Glock wrote one of his most expressive letters to Vorsteher Walpot and the Brotherhood. The effects of Glock's year-in year-out imprisonment were beginning to take their toll. Although he still had good food and no special needs, he was confined to his room and had resigned himself to spending the rest of his life in a prison cell. Almost nineteen years of prison was no light punishment for a man who believed himself to be innocent, and believed that others knew it. The temptation to escape—an ever-present possibility for Glock—was no longer as great, for such an act would have deceived those to whom he had given his word. For Glock, truthfulness was a requisite for anyone who deemed himself worthy to be called Christian.

After a warm greeting, Glock explained to his brethren and sisters that he felt constrained to write them a few comforting words, with the admonition that they remain loyal workers in the vineyard of Christ, and not fear the storming and raging of an insolent world. Rumors had reached Glock that the Turks were at Moravia's door. But no matter what tribulation befell the Hutterian community, Glock promised that he and Matthias Binder were determined to remain resolute until death, for they were continuing to take comfort in God. Both were advancing in age—Paul Glock no longer referred to himself as Jung-Paul—and the Lord might soon release them from life and take them to himself. Matthias, who had been suffering from rheumatism for some months, was given a warm room, and with four months of medical treatment, his health improved. Contrary to the wishes of the magistrates, church officials now forbade Paul and Matthias to see each other. Nevertheless, Glock had not become morbid or depressed in his long encounter with the world. His sense of Christian mission remained strong and aggressive. This quality, found in many Hutterites, helped Glock build bridges to the Grafenecks, the castle wardens, and anyone else who came his way. Mission for Glock was much more than speaking about salvation; it involved developing friendship. The many material gifts that Glock gave were tokens of gratitude for such friendship. Never do we hear that Glock gave a knife or other present to a Lutheran minister. If he had, the whole course of his life might have been changed!

Glock's continuing determination to witness to the Württemberg society can also be seen in a plan he formulated in the form of three poems. The poem that seemed to Glock to be most important deals with the inequity of imprisoning Hutterian Brethren as a precautionary or preventive measure while allowing bona fide criminals to go scot-free and continue their malicious acts. The poem related three such cases of men in public positions: a waiter, a warden, and a clergyman. Although it was known that the waiter had stolen many thousand guilders, the magistracy did not hang him. His punishment (to modern sensibilities certainly "cruel and unusual") was imprisonment with a gallows sewn onto his garment and a rope around his neck which he had to wear in public every Sunday when going from prison to church. Anyone who merely stole a horse or a cow would be promptly hanged, but not such a great thief! The warden had also stolen, lived licentiously, deceived people, and even shot at people. But after a short confinement he was allowed to return home and resume his office. Only after the common people had clamored loudly about his continuing misdeeds was he finally brought to justice. The clergyman, who had been living in adulterous relations with his maid, was briefly imprisoned in the tower at Urach.

Glock's poem declared that it would be more just to commit such rascals to prison *before* they committed their evil deeds, than to confine innocent Hutterites. But that, he said, was how the world operates; the righteous were often sacrificed for the sake of the unrighteous, until the end of time, when the righteous would be redeemed from their tribulation, but the ungodly would inherit eternal tribulation.

Glock explained the poem's background. In 1575 several lords and a disguised clergyman had visited the two prisoners to criticize their way of life. Glock replied that he had lived among the people at Urach for a whole

year, and his character was an open book. The clergyman retorted that even
if no one had seen Glock commit even one misdeed, he should still be held
imprisoned, for if released he might possibly start an insurrection. It was at
this discouraging time that Glock wrote the poem. He asked Walpot to
sharpen it and send it back, so that at an opportune moment he could show
it to the clergymen and observe their unguarded reaction.

Toward the end of his long letter to the Brotherhood, Glock asked his
brethren not to be offended if the prisoners did not answer all their letters.
Not only did messengers at times fail to deliver their letters, but it would
also have been too great a risk to answer all the letters since the messengers
would not be able to conceal their bundles. Therefore the brethren should
be content with news of their well-being and thank God that their secret
channel of communication had not been completely taken away from them.

Glock also described some of the prison activities. Binder continued to
work at his trade by sewing at times, and Glock continued his weaving.
They both read and sang, passing their time sometimes joyously, sometimes
sadly, not unlike April weather. In conclusion, Glock admonished the
Brotherhood to hold fast in prayer for the prisoners and to commend itself
in faith to God that his honor might be served and Glock and Binder might
be saved. It was Glock's prayer that God might allow the Brotherhood to
grow and with obedient hearts dwell in true love and unity of faith; for the
present age was drawing to its close and life was becoming more dangerous.
As Glock grew older he also believed more firmly that the end of time was
approaching. He saw many signs pointing to judgment as he viewed the sin
and injustice of the world, and trusted God to keep the whole Brotherhood
devout and faithful.

Six days after Glock wrote, Binder also wrote a letter to Walpot and the
Brotherhood, which consisted of extensive biblical quotations and lengthy
religious considerations intended to comfort and strengthen the Hutterian
community. He admitted that it would be good to be with them in person
again, but for the time being he could only take comfort in their letters. He
closed his epistle with greetings to the Brotherhood, to all the imprisoned
saints, and to the scattered missioners.[31]

## The Brotherhood in Moravia

Paul Glock's epistles must have gradually taken on extraordinary dimensions of excitement for the brethren living in Moravia and Slovakia.
The letters that Glock and Binder wrote in February 1576, were received by
the Brotherhood the week before Pentecost. Walpot read them to the

Neumühl community the Monday after Pentecost and ordered that they be read throughout the Brotherhood.

The hymns and verse written by remote prisoners served greatly in strengthening the Brotherhood by reminding them how the spiritual aspects of life were to be applied to daily living. Poems and hymns were generally bound together as a collection, separate from other volumes of epistles and handwritten tracts.

Unfortunately, many of Glock's epistles to individual brethren must have been lost. But thanks to the well-organized Hutterian Brotherhood center set up by Walpot, this did not happen to letters coming to Neumühl, the Hutterian hub of organization during the whole of the Golden Years.

Correspondence sent out from the Brotherhood, on the other hand, generally was not retained. Two rare exceptions to this were the epistles Peter Walpot wrote to the Hohenwittlingen prisoners in 1576, in answer to Glock and Binder's letters of February 1576. The originals somehow found their way back to the Brotherhood archives.

In the letter to Glock which he enclosed with the corrected poems, Walpot expressed the hope that the two prisoners would continue to hold firmly to their faith, like the mighty oak whose roots reach deeply into the earth so that the strongest wind cannot uproot it. He reported that all was well with the Brotherhood. The Lord's Supper had been held throughout the Brotherhood communities on the fourth Sunday after Easter. The Turks had not yet entered Moravia; they had entered Hungary and were attempting to advance. As to Glock's verse, Walpot commented that only a few improvements were needed to fit the poems to tunes.

Admonishing the two prisoners to continued steadfastness, Walpot wove into his letter the analogy of a ship at sea:

> For in the same manner as merchants do not look at the tempests of the sea, but rather at monetary reward and the only too perishable gain in the future, thus much more do we look upon the heavenly, eternally continuing reward; and in these difficult and wearisome matters we do not consider the toil, but the reward. . . .
>
> For when a ship does not reach its destination but sinks in the middle of the sea, its having traveled far does not make it any less of a liability; but it also incurs greater liability, the greater the cargo it had taken into its hold. . . .
>
> Oh, dear brethren, let us strive the more, . . . for it may not be long until the time of the spiritual summer, when those who love God, having ridden out the storms and tempests of life, will reach a quiet and joyful time. The ungodly, however, enjoying their present summerlike ease, will come into the tempest and snow of winter.

Walpot closed his missive with the wish that God might yet lead the prisoners back to the Brotherhood, if he so willed.[32]

### The Final Exchange of Letters

Late in August 1576, the aging Paul Glock received a long message from Walpot written in the Lenten season of 1576, which merits careful analysis for its insights into Anabaptist thought during the Walpot Era.

Walpot assured the two prisoners in Hohenwittlingen that they were a constant concern of the Brotherhood. Although it would have brought real happiness if the prisoners could again have been united in body with their brethren, at least the Brotherhood was glad for the prisoners' faithfulness, for thus they were truly abiding within the long heritage of all saints. Walpot was confident that the Holy Spirit would permit them to continue to abide in faith and truth. He expressed the hope that God might work through Glock and Binder, fulfilling the work of faith, so that the name of God, so grossly dishonored and disdained throughout the world, would be extolled. For God would most certainly perceive and retain his honor in spite of a crazed generation of madmen. When, in centuries past, God allowed destruction to fall upon the people, he had sent warnings through prophets such as Jeremiah, whose efforts resulted in his being beaten and thrown into prison. Walpot was convinced that the same forces were incurring divine wrath during the 1570s within apostate Christendom, and that judgment lay just outside the door. Glock, Binder, and other missioners were God's spokesmen proclaiming the impending judgment, but this same so-called Christendom was reacting to the present witness of God's people just as people had reacted to Jeremiah. Furthermore, the people as a whole who listened to the words of the biblical prophets and apostles proclaimed to them every Sabbath within their own church services did not understand their message and respond to it; such people would suffer the consequences of this rejection, namely death and bondage, even if they denied the manner in which God operates. Walpot admonished the prisoners to remain staunch and active in their heavenly calling and divinely blessed walk, which had taken them into a valley of sorrow, for theirs would be the victory.

It is possible that Walpot was approaching that older age which is inclined to see in its world a new low point in the depravity of human nature. But it is more likely that a real change was taking place, brought on in part by both past and impending wars. The Turks were still a serious threat and many thought they might become God's tool of retribution. Glock and Binder's descriptions of evil times, similar reports from other traveling brethren, and the fact that the response to Hutterian mission was growing dimmer pointed, as Walpot saw it, to a possible approaching doom. The disciplined, obedient world of the Brotherhood was constantly in tension with the broad, loose, outside world. Walpot was certain that as surely as God dwelt with the one world, he would also allow destruction to prevail upon the other. Later on in his letter, Walpot reminded the prisoners once more about their responsibility to witness in raising a prophetic voice against the sins of the present sick generation.[33]

Even in tolerant Moravia, where all seemed to be well with the Brotherhood, Walpot wrote that a devil had been let loose, for several of the nobles who controlled the land were proving rather difficult at times. He warned the Brotherhood of possible tribulation, for even the populace could be heard murmuring against the Brotherhood. Indeed, God would only need to nudge the world a bit and permit it to happen, and nothing would be more certain than open persecution. Hence Walpot urged the Hutterites on all fronts to be vigilant in mutual prayer and admonition, as long as they were still dwelling in their temporal bodies.[34]

On August 28, 1576, in response to Walpot's Lenten letter, Paul Glock dictated his last letter to Walpot. Glock was aware that there were still those in the Brotherhood who believed the two prisoners should break out of jail and return to Moravia. Glock asked Walpot to remind the Brotherhood that they could still not undertake such an act with a good conscience, although such a move seemed more than justifiable. But in light of the great damage it would create, they had abandoned the idea. Their attempting to escape might completely ruin the work of God, who had his own schedule. Their lives rested in the strength of the Lord's hand; they had commended the matter to him and were content.

The widespread ungodliness that Walpot saw throughout Moravia was also evident in the German states. Glock had been noticing ever-deepening division and conflict between the Lutherans and Roman Catholics and thought that their fighting was also bringing with it their due judgment. Glock reflected on the implications of growing ungodliness: the populace was not concerned with the Day of Judgment, but lived as beasts, not desiring to learn about God; there was preaching, but no faith; there was teaching, yet no followers; there were threats and admonitions, but no change in their way of life, and Hutterite missioners were no longer finding a response. Did all this not signal the last age of the earth? Glock believed that it was all the more necessary to resist the evil ways of the Lutherans and Catholics, such as their war and violence, but also their philosophy and learning, in order to remain true to the Word of God. Had God not promised victory to his people if they remained true to his Word? Even if prisoners like Veit Uhrmacher were walled into solid rock, God could still provide an exit.

Near the end of his letter, Glock mentioned that both he and Binder were experiencing physical pain, but accepted it as part of God's discipline. They were grateful for the gifts that had been sent, cloaks, knives, and a spoon for each prisoner. Glock requested that some larger knives be sent for the castle warden's wife, since she cut great amounts of bread for the prisoners, and the loaves were unusually large. Then he closed the letter, sending greetings to various individuals.

Glock then, in Pauline fashion, closed with the following lines:

> I, Alt-Paul, now imprisoned for nineteen years for the sake of the testimony of Jesus. The Lord will certainly someday free me from my bonds—one way or the other. Amen. End. Date: Wittlingen, August 28, 1576.[35]

## The Outcome

The progression from Jung-Paul to Alt-Paul in nineteen years of prison life could well be expected, but what happened next was as completely unexpected as it was welcome. There are no letters to tell of the incident. The account could only have come orally from "Alt-Paul" and Matthias themselves, finally finding its way into the Great Chronicle.

Late in 1576 a fire broke out in the castle through the negligence of the women of the staff in handling some dried hemp. Glock and Binder, fully aware of the danger, helped to put out the fire and, working rapidly, saved more equipment and supplies than anyone else. After the fire was extinguished, Glock and Binder officially requested to be set free since they had never harmed anyone. They promised that they would never attempt to avenge their time in prison. Soon thereafter—before the "jealous Lutheran ministers" could stop the action—a request was sent to the prince to acquit them. He commanded their release and ordered a traveling allowance for them. Consequently with clear conscience and joy, both Matthias Binder and Paul Glock returned to the Brotherhood around New Year's Day, 1577.

Six weeks after his joyous reunion with his kindred, Glock was elected minister in Walpot's home village of Neumühl, and was confirmed in his calling three years later, during the Lenten season of 1580. One final entry about Glock is noted in the Great Chronicle:

In the year 1585 the faithful and dear brother Paul Glock, a servant of the Word (who was imprisoned continuously for almost nineteen years in the land of Württemberg for the sake of the faith, suffering during this time much tribulation, as has been noted above, then, through God's providence was again set free, returning to the Brotherhood), died in the Lord at Schaidowitz on January 30.[36]

### The Faith of Paul Glock

Paul Glock's primary companion to Scripture throughout his nineteen-year imprisonment was the printed Brotherhood Rechenschaft. He did not attempt to create any new perspectives of faith and life, but was simply defending what had been set down and accepted a generation earlier. Furthermore, Glock continually referred touchy issues to Vorsteher Walpot for Brotherhood counsel. Yet such brotherly counsel did not keep Glock from acting at times counter to Brotherhood suggestions when he felt his brethren did not fully comprehend his unusual personal circumstances. Paul Glock the brother was by no means engulfed in the group to an extent that did violence to Paul Glock the person. He exemplified in his own being and experience this unity of discipleship (individuality) and brotherhood (consensus). His beliefs were "orthodox," in the Hutterian sense, and his total thought pattern fitted the traditional Anabaptist idea of God's people within history bearing witness in the face of a broader society that does not recognize the lordship of God.

### a. The Church

Glock's definition of the church is unequivocal: "There have always been two peoples, the godly and the ungodly." Denying the Lutheran idea of the invisible church, Glock believed that the godly formed a visible church, composed of identifiable disciples and founded on Christian love. Since Glock knew of only one such brotherhood, which was in Moravia, it was there that God's people, in disciplined obedience and mutuality, could grow in faith and love by following the example of Christ. The tending of this flock of Christ required constant vigilance to preserve unity in the Spirit.[37]

### b. Baptism and Faith

Entrance into the church was through baptism, and baptism was for believers. Glock believed it quite simple to show this view of baptism as the biblical position: Faith stems only from hearing the Word being taught (Romans 10:10, 17). Salvation is based on a person's confessing that Jesus is Lord (Romans 10:9). Therefore, since baptism (entering into the Body of Christ) is integral to salvation, and since faith follows teaching, an individual's baptism does not precede either his having been taught or the personal confessing of his faith; baptism instead follows from this. Furthermore, baptism, as a covenant of a good conscience with God (1 Peter 3:21), demands that the convert understand what he is entering.

Glock also believed that there is a closer correlation between faith and works than that evidenced by the Lutherans. He thought the Lutherans interpreted Romans 7:19 too literally, in making allowances for small sins—a bit of swearing, drunkenness, fornication, etc. Glock interpreted Romans 7:19 out of what he thought was the larger Pauline context, but also in view of such passages as Matthew 5 and Luke 10:14. Twice Glock said that he would join the Lutherans if they would change their congregational pattern and repent of their sins.[38]

### c. The Lord's Supper

The Lord's Supper took on special meaning within a brotherhood where there was mutual sharing, for the Supper signified the nature of genuine Christian fellowship, where many members were one with Christ, and as such met one another's needs.[39]

### d. The Trinity

The God whom Paul Glock served was not a composite of three persons. Asked by the Lutherans whether he agreed with them that the Father, the Son, and the Holy Spirit in their essence were three persons, Glock answered that he considered the Father's essence to reside in his divinity, but no one knew his person. The Son's essence resided in his humanity and was consequently two in name but only one in divinity. The essence of the Spirit was not to be found in itself, but in the living Word residing in the Father and Son, and emanating from them both. The Spirit filled the hearts of men, making them intelligent and wise, and thus enabling them to fulfill God's will. Whoever did not have the Spirit had none of God; whoever had the Spirit, had all three. The people of God were recipients of this Spirit, which permitted them as a brotherhood to grow and mature. Glock, in retrospect, related to Walpot that the Lutheran clergy remained in their "madness" by continuing to affirm God as three real persons. Because of his beliefs, they had called Glock a Turk and a Jew.[40]

## e. Mission

The obvious reasons for Hutterian mission are clearly presented in most sixteenth-century Hutterian confessions of faith, and are a direct answer to the inevitable question, "What are you doing in our country?" Leonhard Dax[41] developed an extensive strategy and apologia of missions, but Paul Glock also spoke constantly about mission. Mission meant searching out those who desired to live among God's gathered people in his kingdom, bringing them to Moravia, and sharing with them the good news that God's kingdom indeed existed. Thousands of converts accepted the message and joined the Brotherhood.

But Hutterian mission included a more subtle level of operation, which may readily be seen in the person of Paul Glock. Of course God's people, as the Body of Christ, emanated something of Christ's Spirit simply by living in brotherhood. Yet each member also reflected this same Spirit wherever his path took him.

Part of this witness lay in the concept of truthfulness and genuineness, as when Glock refused to break his promise not to escape, even though he was advised to do so by the Hutterite leaders.[42] Even in prison it was natural for Glock to share the good news of the kingdom of God. He never ceded to Lutheran officialdom.

## f. The Magistracy

In Glock's view, quite in agreement with general Anabaptist teaching, the magistracy, although ordained by God to protect and punish the evildoer, lay outside the realm of the church, since its servants were men of vengeance and therefore could not belong to God's people. Since Christ's peaceful kingdom was not of this world, his servants could not make war within the kingdoms of this world. Those who fought and warred gave evidence by their conduct that theirs was not the kingdom of God, but rather of the evil one. Still, the Christian was to obey the powers that be unless such demands conflicted with a higher obedience.[43]

## g. History

The God of history, however, according to Glock, was not only Lord of his people, he was also active within general society. It was he who had permitted the sacrifice of Christ, judged the nations through famine and turbulence, and knew the correct time and manner to bring history to completion. It was God who warned his people to remain alert to the ever greater threats opposing them, and to remain staunch in their obedience to him until the end, which was near.[44]

## h. Toleration

One Lutheran trait which thoroughly disturbed Glock was the use of coercion in matters of faith. In one of his encounters with the clergy, Glock asked them where God had commanded that the Word be communicated to all the world, and whoever would not believe was to be captured, tormented, and slain into "believing" the gospel. Yet, he observed, the Lutherans and Papists were not above using coercion, even murder when it served their purpose; consequently their ministers and priests were Satan's workmen, for the devil had been a murderer from the beginning.

Glock observed that Christ's method of "coercing" (Luke 13:23) had never included forcing any person into his kingdom through the services of constable, prison, and hangman; instead, he left unresponsive unbelievers alone (Matthew 15:14) or commanded his missioners to shake the dust from their feet as a witness against such people (Matthew 10:14). Christ had "compelled" the Samaritan woman by telling her what she had done, at which point she was inwardly compelled to recognize Jesus as the Messiah; she in turn passed the word on to others. This he believed was the manner of mission Christ had commanded, and any person who would not allow himself to be "compelled" in the manner of the Samaritan woman would reap divine judgment.[45]

## i. Judging

Another heated exchange between Glock and the Lutherans centered in the matter of judging. In response to Glock's persistent and harsh criticism of the established church's failure to deal with obvious sins, the officials charged him with an unchristian attitude, for Christ had clearly said: "Judge not that ye be not judged." Glock, working out of an entirely different milieu, admitted that the "beams" should be taken care of, but also the splinters. The Christian dared not judge before the beams were removed from his own eyes; and even then only by remaining holy, pure, and blameless before God and his church was a man worthy of fulfilling God's command to ban and condemn, exclude and include (John 20:19-23; Matthew 18:15-20). How could the Lutherans pardon an evildoer and allow him to share in the Lord's Supper one day, and hang, burn, or behead him the next? Since the body of the Christian was the temple of the Holy Spirit, he argued, the Lutherans were hanging the temple of God on the gallows (Galatians 3:13). As Christ had forgiven the woman caught in adultery, he taught his followers likewise to forgive. Glock also cited Paul's similar dealing with Philemon's thieving slave.[46]

## j. Authority

Glock believed that the true Christian church takes its charter from Christ and the apostles, and that the substitution of other regulations for those which are biblical transforms it into an institution of apostasy. He was convinced that the Lutheran establishment had taken this route, for it had evidently not received the Holy Spirit of Christ, through whom sin is forgiven.[47]

## Paul Glock as Legend

The name of Paul Glock lingered on in Württemberg into the seventeenth century; through oral history, the stories of Paul Glock continued within Hutterian tradition into the nineteenth. The historical account of Glock, as found in the Great Chronicle and other codices, has remained an important chapter in Hutterian tradition to this day.

In Württemberg, Lutheran church officials objected to the lenient treatment of Anabaptists, especially the release of leaders like Paul Glock. In 1584, Lukas Osiander, the Stuttgart court chaplain, wrote a sharp note, contending that

> Paul Glock did not experience a prison at Wittlingen, but lived the life of a lord, enjoying his usual wine, meat, roasts, warm room, bed, and antechamber. When one thought he was sitting in his room, he was out across the fields delivering messages; this softheartedness towards such an evil rascal as he was made him and other Anabaptists stiff-necked, from whom such [a mild policy of confinement] had not been hidden.[48]

As late as 1590, magistrates of the same area were still troubled by Glock's lenient treatment, as is seen in their interrogation of Hans Schmitt, a Hutterite prisoner, when they probed him about Paul Glock.

In 1608 at Urach, Hans Jacob Vischäss, a clockmaker, was cross-examined as an Anabaptist suspect. He stated that more than thirty years earlier he had often been Paul Glock's companion during his journeys in and around Wittlingen. At various times they had discussed whether the true body of Christ was present in the Lord's Supper. Vischäss affirmed that only in the light of Christ's omnipotence could he begin to believe the bodily presence. Furthermore, if the Lutheran doctrine should prove to be false, he would prefer being an Anabaptist, for as an Anabaptist he would not curse or get drunk. He proved that he was no Anabaptist, for he not only attended Lutheran services, but had also taken communion the year before, as was attested in the Communion Book. The Lutheran officials noted that Vischäss should be under constant watch to prevent his falling into doctrinal error.[49]

In a letter of April 2, 1573, Paul Glock had mentioned being with a clockmaker, presumably Vischäss. Glock had noted that contrary to his usual practice, he would send no gift with his letter, for he needed money to present a return gift for a clock promised to him.[50]

As late as 1800, one particular story was still a topic of conversation among the few hundred Hutterites in Russia, survivors of the Brotherhood's manifold persecutions and repeated flights. According to this story, Else, Paul Glock's wife, had been awaiting the birth of a child when in 1558 Jung-Paul was sent out by the Brotherhood as a missioner. When he returned after his nineteen years of imprisonment, the Brotherhood was preparing for a wedding: Glock's own daughter was about to be married. Father Paul Glock thus arrived just in time to attend the wedding of the daughter whom he had never seen.[51]

In the extant letters of Glock there is no reference to such a child. Glock's wife and a child had died in the early 1560s. On the other hand, if Glock's daughter had been living in one of the Haushaben far distant from Neumühl, Glock might well have written a steady stream of letters to her which did not survive.

The legend revolved around a man who attempted to bring all of human existence—word, thought, and action—into line with his understanding of the mind and life of Christ. In the life of this brother, the concept of Christian discipleship reaches one of the high points within the history of Anabaptism. He was one of those "distinguished Christians," and "venerable and steadfast figures" within Anabaptism, who was, in the words of Adolf von Harnack, "more understandable to us than the heroic Luther and the ironlike Calvin."[52]

But Glock himself, as a prisoner, expresses his understanding of Christian faith in verse, a fitting close to the story of Paul Glock:

It is Christ who is my life; / And death, my highest gain. / In striving toward godliness / Lies my hope and vision. / It is better to die honestly, / Than to live dishonorably, / And inherit the devil's kingdom / Which has caused the undoing / Of the Papal and Lutheran churches.[53]

# Ch. 6

# Hutterian Encounter with Calvinism

One of the early confrontations between the Hutterites and a recognizable form of Calvinism came in 1567 at Alzey, in the Palatinate, three years after the death of John Calvin. By that time Calvinism as a religious movement had expanded vigorously, and as a system of thought had developed into a refined, highly systematic theological system. Calvin's own great work of systematic theology, the *Institutes* (1536, 1559, *et al.*), provided the solid foundation for Calvinistic dogmatic theology. Further development of Calvinism as a system came in 1563, when the definitive Calvinistic *Heidelberg Catechism* was composed, and in 1566, when Heinrich Bullinger wrote his popular *Second Helvetic Confession.*[1] All of these works were in print and available to Calvinist leaders such as the superintendent at Alzey, Gerrit Dircks Versteghe, who cross-examined Leonhard Dax in 1567 and 1568.[2]

By the 1560s the Hutterites too had carefully worked through their faith and doctrine. In 1565, Vorsteher Peter Walpot reprinted the official Brotherhood Confession, which had served well since the 1540s. Further defining of the Hutterian faith came in the early 1560s via the scholarly efforts of Dax. In 1561 Dax composed his "Refutation," an apologia in twenty-six articles countering charges made by the Lutherans against the Hutterites.[3] About the same time, the anonymous Hutterian "Handbook" was composed, probably by Dax, as an answer to the Lutheran broadside of 1557 composed by Melanchthon, "Proceedings. . . . "[4] "Valuable Directions and Instructions on How to Turn Unbelievers from Their Error" was also written about this time, and although anonymous, must have come from

Dax as well, judging from specific personal remarks about Catholicism.[5] A
final anonymous Hutterian polemic, "Charges and Allegations," written
about this same time (1570/78) was directed toward the Catholics.[6] The
document reflects the thought of Dax's "Refutation," and at least to this
degree may be considered as part of the Dax legacy.

Leonhard Dax, building upon Riedemann's Brotherhood Rechenschaft, left an impact upon the development of Hutterian thought by defining Hutterian mission and witness in the same definitive way that
Riedemann had, in establishing the foundational Hutterian brotherhood
charter. Dax in fact developed the definitive Hutterian mission strategy on
three fronts, the Roman Catholic, the Lutheran, and, in his Alzey
confession of faith, the Calvinist.[7]

Not much is known about the background of Dax. Born around 1520/
25 in Munich, he became a Catholic priest about 1544, and was active in
this station for thirteen years, first in Munich, then in Tirol, where he came
into contact with the Hutterites. The Great Chronicle notes that in 1555
Dax, as a priest, tried in vain to convert Hans Pürchner to Catholicism.
Around 1557 Dax himself converted to Anabaptism, separating from the
"idolatrous papal church" and joining the Hutterian Brotherhood which for
him embodied the truth.[8]

Dax's gifts were soon put to use on the mission field. In 1560 he was
active in Tirol and was in the crowd that witnessed the martyrdom of the
Hutterite missioners, Hans Mändl, Jörg Rack, and Eustachius Kotter. Dax
was able to slip through to the prisoners and extend to them his hand in a
final farewell. The martyrs' response was one of great joy, for they praised
God that they had been able to meet a godly believer before their execution. In 1564 Dax was chosen as minister and two years later confirmed.[9]

In the early 1560s Dax composed the numerous writings mentioned
above, all of them missionary in nature, in which he both summarized and
interpreted the Hutterian faith in view of Lutheran and Catholic charges.
However, since Hutterian mission was geared to devout seekers who were
looking for a pattern of life different from current Catholic, Lutheran, or
Calvinistic practice, the works took on an apologetic rather than polemic
tone.[10]

Dax's theological training enabled him to summarize objectively the
argument of his Calvinist opponent in the discussions in 1567 and 1568, an
ability which set him apart from most other late sixteenth-century defenders
of Hutterian faith. The encounter began in early November of 1567, when
Dax became the spokesman for a tiny group of Hutterite missioners to the
Palatinate—Leonhard Dax, his wife Anna, and four others—where they

were caught and imprisoned in the castle of Alzey on the Rhine.[11]

News of the imprisonment reached the Brotherhood, and early in January 1568, Walpot wrote an epistle to the prisoners, encouraging and admonishing them to remain true to the example of that "great cloud of witnesses" through the centuries of history (Hebrews 11). Walpot warned them of the tricks often employed by the ungodly:

> They consider how they can confuse the godly about the truth, as is often the case when brethren, separated from one another, are told with lying words, each by himself: "Look, all the others have recanted and have accepted correction. Why do you alone want to be so unbending and stiff-necked? Recant, or we will do thus and so to you!" With such and similar words they attempt to dishearten the devout.... However, we trust in God...that in the very hour when salvation seems close to the point of being lost, God will help and save.[12]

One other extant letter was written by three other ministers, Kaspar Braitmichel, Valentin Hörl, and Jörg Rader, admonishing the prisoners to remain upon the foundation of truth, the immovable rock of Christ.[13]

After two encounters with the Calvinist superintendent of Alzey, the authorities saw that Dax would not be moved. Near the end of this cross-examination they offered Dax a lucrative position within the Calvinist Church, the job description of which was to keep others from falling into the same "error" that he had fallen into. Dax refused. Finally threatened with execution, Dax resolved to hold fast unwaveringly in the Hutterian faith, and answered that he would defend his faith, and his own faithful people of God, in word and—if death were indicated thereby—in deed; for even martyrdom would not stand in the way of his firmly based faith.[14] Ultimately, on February 25, 1568, the Hutterite prisoners were released and returned to Moravia. Dax was assigned as minister to the community at Damborschitz, where he died August 4, 1574.[15]

## Leonhard Dax's Confession of Faith

Leonhard Dax's reconstruction of his cross-examination is the most systematic and unified of all the Rechenschaften composed during the Walpot Era. This is undoubtedly due to Dax's own bent for dogmatics. Almost all reference to congregational life and specific personal mission assignments is missing, with a bare minimum of information included about his background. The theological frame of reference lies much more deeply imbedded in Calvinism than in Catholicism and Lutheranism; consequently the systematic development of ideas which emerges with such clear-cut logic may indeed mirror the original discussion with relative accuracy. Dax's written apologia also emerges as probably the most cogent articulation of the Anabaptist faith to be written after mid-century.

The subjects discussed by Dax and the superintendent covered nine areas: mission, faith, righteousness, nonconformity, community of goods, baptism and the new birth, the church, the magistracy and the sword, and marriage. The various points at times are logically joined to one another, especially in the questions of the church, the magistracy, and the problem of coercion.

The argument of the superintendent, as condensed from Dax's reconstruction of the prison debate, follows this line: Since the church in the Palatinate is correctly established upon Calvinistic dogma and the truth is proclaimed throughout the whole territory, there is no need for Anabaptism (Hutterianism) to make its appearance in the land. The Anabaptist missioners are consequently attempting to lead astray any and all people who open themselves to their witness, people who are already of the right persuasion. And given the peculiar Anabaptist doctrines, such as baptism, (Hutterian) community of goods, and the views on the nature of church and the magistracy, the whole Anabaptist idea of mission is based upon human, not divine, action. Furthermore, since the Hutterites confess, with the Calvinists, the foundation of Jesus Christ and his righteousness, there really is no reason why the Hutterites should form a separate church body. They should actually join the Calvinist church.

Dax's argument, highly condensed, is as follows: Hutterian mission justifiably extends into the Palatinate, because the church there is by no means correctly established, and God's truth must be proclaimed. Even though the Hutterian creed and view of justification by faith seems on the surface to be similar to that of Calvinism, the Hutterites in fact stand a world apart from the Calvinists on many important issues that determine the authenticity of the church. The differences are serious enough to merit a separation of God's people not only from the "world," as the term is usually defined, but also from other so-called churches, which are churches in name only. Such mission results in a gathering together of the faithful into a godly community where a communal sharing takes place on all levels, among believers who have freely committed themselves through baptism to be God's people, the church. But separation from the world also entails political consequences in light of the fact that God's kingdom, not being of the world, is established upon voluntarism and love, not upon the sword. The church consequently relates to the magistracy on a conditional basis only. Furthermore, separation at times may also have a bearing upon unequally yoked marriage partners, for even marriage is conditional to a higher obedience to God, which conceivably could (although in general practice does not) lead to separation of man and wife.[16]

## a. The Issue of Biblical Interpretation

The encounter between the Hutterites and the Calvinists was unique not only because of the rarity of Hutterian-Calvinist confrontations, but also in view of the Calvinistic approach to faith. In Dax's *Rechenschaft* the cultural and social areas of Hutterian life are conspicuously absent. The Calvinist penchant for a highly systematized dogmatics far surpasses that of either the Catholics or the Lutherans. For this reason, it served the Hutterian cause well that a theologically trained Dax could debate with the Calvinist superintendent. Each side stood on different terrain, and used contrasting approaches in attempting to communicate its understanding of the nature of Christianity. The Calvinist superintendent worked on the basis of a rational intellectualism, founded on the Old and New Testaments, as the ultimate grounds for theology. Dax developed his position on the basis of the New Testament, interpreted in the light of Jesus, and reaching back to and understanding the Old Testament in view of the New.

Midway in the encounter, for example, the superintendent made the point that certain Old Testament practices were indeed changed in the New Testament, such as the offering of animal sacrifices. However, those areas in the Old Testament that the New Testament did not alter were still relevant in the New; since the Old Testament circumcision was for infants, and since in the New Testament there was no express command not to baptize infants, baptism applied to infants, especially since God's promised grace and mercy applied to children as well as to adults.

Dax's response suggests his radically different balance between the Old and New Testaments. For Christ, in establishing his New Testament, had in fact changed other highly significant aspects of the Christian faith: true Christians were no longer to rule like heathen rulers; Christians did not shed blood or go to war; Christians did not sue at law or demand personal vindication; Christians did not swear or take oaths. All of these aspects of the Christian way of life, and others besides, Dax was certain, could be substantiated from Scripture, and from examples taken out of the early Christian church tradition; indeed, Christ's new covenant was far superior and stronger than the old covenant of Israel, which predated Christ.[17]

## b. Divine Election and Christian Discipleship

On its most basic level the confrontation centered in the classic debate between the idea of Christian discipleship, based on freedom of the will

(Dax's affirmation), and the concept of God's election and grace, the great point of departure out of which the whole of Christian dogmatics is to be understood and interpreted (the superintendent's affirmation). In fact, every major point of doctrine—mission, baptism, the Lord's Supper, the church, the state, coercion, and marriage—takes on Anabaptist or Calvinist flesh, in accord with the underlying premise of either freedom or bondage of the will.

Although there was no full-fledged discussion on the nature of divine election, the idea quite naturally entered the discussion as part of the Calvinist affirmation of infant baptism; since, along with adults, the elect infants were in the covenant of grace, and had God's merit, they were to be included in baptism, the seal of the new birth. The discussion which ensued merits close attention, and in compressed form takes the following argument:

>   **Superintendent:** All who are in the covenant of God's grace should be baptized.
>   **Leonhard:** All who have *comprehended* the covenant of God's grace *through faith in Christ,* namely adults, should be baptized.
>   **Superintendent:** But children of believers should be baptized, for they have the Holy Spirit, and are in the covenant of God's grace.
>   **Leonhard:** Only if they *desire* it, and have received the Holy Spirit of *understanding and knowledge,* through faith in Christ, should they be baptized.

Dax's view that baptism was for those who through their own volition "obligated themselves to God" is based on the idea of Christian discipleship, and this the Calvinist superintendent could not accept. He explicitly denied this possibility, and shifted from Dax's discipleship motif to that of God's grace and mercy:

>   **Superintendent:** You err in supposing that baptism is only a seal by which we consent to die to the old man and promise to lead a Christian life which infants cannot yet promise; it is much more a seal of the grace of God and pardon for sins, which is as necessary for infants as for adults.
>   **Leonhard:** Do not grant too much power to the water, or I might say that you act like the heathen who honor Neptune, the water god. For us it is enough to know and believe that God has translated us into the kingdom of his beloved Son, in whom we have redemption through his blood, even the forgiveness of sins.[18]

At this juncture a basic difference between Calvinism and Anabaptism becomes evident. The Calvinists were, of course, concerned with Christian

# Illustrations

# The Story of the Hutterites

In the town hall of Zurich, on January 18, 1525, the City Council outlawed the emergent Anabaptist movement, giving the adherents eight days to rejoin the (Zwinglian) State Church. In December 1526, the Council added the death penalty as a possible punishment for those continuing in their "heresy." Felix Mantz became the first victim; George Blaurock—not a Zurich native—was banished from town on the same day, January 5, 1527.

The rise of Zurich Anabaptism occasioned the birth of the first known "free church" to arise from a Reformation setting—also the point of departure for the Hutterian movement.

Banished from Zurich, Blaurock began his missionary travels through Austria and northern Italy, establishing numerous fellowships on the southern slopes of the Alps. The village of Moos (Moso) [above] was the hometown of Jacob Hutter, who joined the movement during the Blaurock era. Hutter led many to tolerant Moravia, where he organized the brotherhood that now bears his name.

After being captured in nearby Gufidaun, (Gudon), George Blaurock was tried and executed in Klausen (Chiusa) [below] on September 6, 1529. In 1535 Hutter and his wife, Katharina, returning to South Tirol, were captured in Klausen, and kept in the episcopal castle Brandzell overlooking the city. Hutter was tried and executed in Innsbruck on February 25, 1536; his wife was executed two years later at Schöneck.

Nikolsburg (Mikulov) [above left], a city and domain on the main road between Vienna and Brno (German: Brünn), Moravia, became known as a haven of tolerance to the oppressed Anabaptists. By 1529 more than 12,000 refugees had found their way to Nikolsburg and vicinity.

Balthasar Hubmaier [above right] of Waldshut on the Rhine arrived in Nikolsburg in July 1526 and was for some time the leader of the large community. Hubmaier was executed in Vienna on March 10, 1528.

In 1528 a group of two hundred Anabaptists, the nonresistant "Stäbler," separated from the larger group at Nikolsburg (the "Schwertler", who justified defensive war as a Christian principle) and moved to Austerlitz [below]. On the road, the group pooled all its earthly possessions, and so gave birth to communitarian Anabaptism. The movement soon spread from Austerlitz to nearby Auspitz and Rossitz. The communitarian Anabaptists were reorganized by Jacob Hutter (1533-35), through a careful attention to Ordnung (corporate orderliness)—a major clue to the ongoing success of this brotherhood.

131

*Peter Riedemann, an early Hutterite leader (d. 1556), was imprisoned in the Castle of Marburg on the Lahn, 1540-42. During his incarceration he wrote a major part of his famous* Rechenschaft. *A handwritten copy of the* Rechenschaft *[below] is now located in South Dakota.*

*Peter Riedemann, working on his* Rechenschaft *while imprisoned in Marburg. An artist's conception by Ivan Moon.*

*The "New Mill" at the village of Neumühl (Nové Mlýny), Moravia [above left and right], the hub of the extensive Hutterian network of* Haushaben *during the Golden Years. Two cornerstones show the dates 1779 and 1751; an early cornerstone on the oldest part of the mill dates back to circa 1506.*

*The Great Chronicle of the Hutterites was begun by Kaspar Braitmichel in the 1560s at the Neumühl center. Vorsteher Peter Walpot, who lived here, was a capable and influential leader for thirty-five years (1542-78).*

134

*Damborschitz (Dambořice) [above left], and Gross-Seelowitz (Židlochovice) [above right], two sites of the more than one hundred Haushaben once existing in Moravia from 1528 to 1618.*

*Kitzbühel (Austrian Tirol) [below], the birthplace of Nikolaus Geyersbühler and way station for many on their trek to Moravia.*

*Mountain trail in Tirol: Hutterite and other Anabaptist missioners traveled trails like these (above) in search of new converts and to lead others to comparative freedom in Moravia.*

*The authorities placed soldiers on the bridges and ferries to question all travelers in order to single out the Anabaptists. Those caught were kept in the dungeon towers of castles like Kufstein on the Inn (below).*

*Restaurant Walderwirt [above left] in Wald (Tirol) in which Veit Uhrmacher was discovered to be an Anabaptist when he prayed before his meal. He was taken to the Mittersil Castle dungeons [above right], and from there to the fortress Hohensalzburg where he was held in prison from 1570 to 1576.*

*Hohensalzburg, built and enlarged between 1077 and 1519 by Salzburg's archbishops, remains the largest intact fortress in Europe. In its dungeons and cells Anabaptist prisoners and Hutterite missioners awaited their fate.*

137

*Urach, South Germany, home of Klaus and Margarete von Grafeneck, Schwenckfeldians who befriended Paul Glock during most of his nineteen-year imprisonment at Hohenwittlingen.*

*The ruins of Castle Hohenwittlingen, "home" of Paul Glock for almost nineteen years, and the Hohenwittlingen Bauerei (castle farm), where, on his word of honor, Glock was permitted at times to work and roam unfettered.*

138

*The Blautopf, source of the Blau River. Glock reports washing his hands in the Blautopf while running an errand as a trusted prisoner.*

*Hohenneuffen [above right], fifteen kilometers north of Hohenwittlingen, where Matthias Binder was incarcerated in 1573 before being transferred to Hohenwittlingen.*

*Leonhard Dax and five others were imprisoned at the Rheinhessen Castle of Alzey [below] for three months, 1567/68. Here, Dax presented his eloquent Hutterian Confession of Faith.*

*The invitation to the 1571 Frankenthal Debates, a planned Disputation among the established denominations, to which the South German Anabaptists were invited with guarantee of safe-conduct.*

*Frankenthal [below], where the Disputation was held. Among the participants was Leonhard Sommer, later imprisoned at Hohenwittlingen with Paul Glock.*

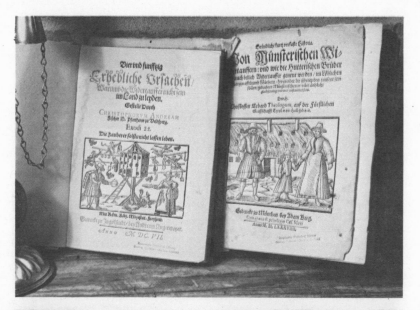

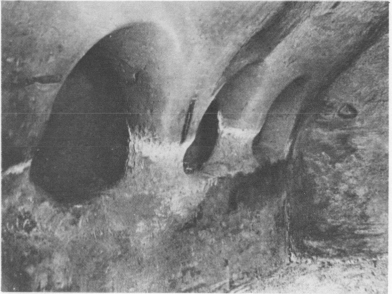

*Jesuit polemical volumes published in 1589 and 1607, by the priests Christoph Erhard and Christoph A. Fischer, containing a wealth of information (and much malicious misinformation!) about their Hutterite fellow countrymen.*

*Hutterian "Lochy"—subterranean passages and caves mostly in Moravia, but also found elsewhere, dug by Anabaptists as hiding places during recurring periods of severe persecution.*

The Thirty Years War wiped out the whole of the more than one hundred Moravian Haushaben. The majority of Hutterites died from the direct and indirect ravages of war. A few fled to Sabatisch (Sobotiste) (a Hutterian dwelling [above left] and Hutterian school [above right]) and Gross-Schützen (Velké Leváry). Here, a certain religious toleration continued into the eighteenth century (middle left, the straw-roofed house of potter Josef Hörndl at Gross-Schützen, and [middle right] a 1772 production manual for fire-retardant straw-roof construction).

A Hutterian Haushaben in Alwinz, Transylvania (Rumania) [below], existed from 1621 to 1767. It was made up of a Hutterite remnant which was joined by a small group of Lutherans expelled from Carinthia (Austria). In 1767 the Alwinz community was forced to flee to Wallachia, later into the Ukraine.

*The Hutterites became famous (1570s following) for their beautiful pottery, and even their archenemies purchased these beautiful Hutterian works of art, and willed them to their descendants.*

*The Market Regulations of Alba Julia (Rumania) refer specifically to the "New Christians" and their wares: pottery and cutlery.*

143

*In 1874 all Hutterites migrated from Russia to North America. They first established the Bon Homme Colony near Yankton, South Dakota. This sturdy building, constructed from limestone cut from the banks of the Missouri River, still serves the community today.*

*Today the Hutterites are located in 250 colonies in the Canadian and American Northwest, holding to their Tirolean dialect and Old World dress.*

ethics; it has even been suggested that Calvin developed his deep ethical concerns out of his contacts with the Anabaptists and their writings, and also by his marriage to Idelette de Bure, the widow of an Anabaptist.[19] However, for the Anabaptists the Christian life took on a dimension set apart from "morality" and "ethics," at least in the sense of the Kantian "ought," or in line with the Greek philosophical framework, accepted in part by the later Church Fathers. Obedience to Christ, with Christ's example itself the norm to be followed, set the whole question of how to live into the radically different framework of "Christian discipleship." Dax understood this fundamental difference, and avoided the pitfall of shifting the nature of his argument to the Calvinist basis. He—consciously or otherwise—remained within his own well-developed framework in presenting his own confession of faith.

But later in the discussion a turnabout in the application of the concept of divine election came when Dax applied it to support nonresistance and noncoercion, albeit in a manner which if applied to baptism, would hardly have strengthened his case there. But on the subject of the sword, it made sense. Dax climaxed a long, complicated dialogue about church and state with a reference to Acts 15; his refutation of the Calvinist position merits verbatim quotation:

> If you are an apostolic church and your foundation is well laid, then say openly that you do none of these things and, like the first church of the apostles, that you refrain from the uncleanness of idols, from fornication, from that which has been strangled, and from blood. For I say with Job that the sword is the wrath for misdeeds, that one may know there is judgment.
>
> Therefore, you Calvinists, because you consider the sword to be a handmaiden of your church, you forsake God and are not servants of Christ. Besides, you steal what is God's and give it to the power of men—this you can judge by the testimony of this scripture:
>
> First, "No one can come to me unless the Father draws him"— not the sword of the Calvinist church but the sword of the Spirit.
>
> Second, Paul says that faith is not granted to every man, and so the sword of your Calvinist church cannot give or take away faith in Christ, but it is a gift of God. If your Calvinist sword could give faith in Christ, you could do no better work than constantly to slay and kill heretics.
>
> Third, it is God that both wills and does the good, that he may have pleasure in you. Physical force cannot give and do it, but the Father in heaven.
>
> Fourth, those whom the Spirit of God impels are his children, not those whom dungeon, agony, and martyrdom impel.

Each of these four arguments relates to the doctrine of divine election, yet each can be reconciled with the idea of Christian discipleship. The point which follows is more problematic:

> Fifth, if it does not depend on the one who wills or runs, but on God's mercy, of what good is the use of the Calvinist sword here? For it is a matter of God's foreknowledge and election, and his mercy.[20]

Such a paradox was a greater threat to the Calvinist, who attempted an absolute and systematic resolution of biblical contradictions, than to the Anabaptist, who placed greater emphasis on obedience to Jesus, making a systematized dogmatics less crucial for the Anabaptist. Yet Dax was able in his own way to harmonize the ideas of divine election, mercy, and fore-knowledge, with his Anabaptist position on the freedom of the will. He capped the above argument by affirming the Anabaptist position that God's grace in Christ was a potential reality for all people, since Christ was an open door to eternal life for anyone who desired to enter.[21]

### c. On Restitution

A second idea arising out of Dax's encounter with Calvinism has to do with the concept of the restitution of the church, a theme long debated within scholarly circles: Did the Anabaptists consciously attempt to recreate a New Testament church, or did they see themselves as continuing God's true church which had always existed alongside the fallen state church? Or were they simply attempting to be true to the spirit of the New Testament?

For Dax, the question of restitution was a corollary of his view of the church and was based on a definite eschatological awareness. Throughout the encounter Dax talked in terms of the "first" or apostolic church and the "last" church; thus, in a real sense, he supported the theory of restitution. Dax affirmed, for example, his deep desire to "follow Christ's commandments as well as the practice and faith of the first apostolic church"[22] in pointing out to others the way of New Testament Christianity. Just as the first apostolic church was light to the world and the salt of the earth, so too was the last church of Christ; both were commissioned to reveal the truth.[23] Dax asserted that if this commission had been only for the first church and not for the last, then

> one would no longer have baptism, faith, Spirit, or gospel—in short, there would be no Christian church on earth, which would be false and wrong, no matter who says it.[24]

The idea of a continuity within the history of God's true church could perhaps be read into this statement by Dax on baptism:

> I confess and believe truly and honestly without wavering that in the Christian church and brotherhood there has always been a right, Christian, holy baptism as still exists today in our church, praise be to God.[25]

But his intention was obviously simply to affirm that true baptism had been established in apostolic times and existed as well within the Hutterian Brotherhood, and that the nature of true baptism was clearly presented in the writings of Christians from the New Testament and early apostolic times.

## d. The Church

The idea of Christian discipleship in Hutterianism found its fulfillment in the idea of the gathered church. At one point, when Dax was expressly asked to define the word "church," he gave an answer that is basic to the understanding of the brotherhood approach to Christianity:

> **Superintendent:** Then tell us, what does the word church *(ecclesia)* mean? Give us the answer to that and the basis of your assurance.
>
> **Leonhard:** According to its Hebrew and Greek content and meaning, I understand under the word ecclesia that it indicates the called-out and called-together gathering and community of Christ; these are the people who deny themselves and all things. And as many of these as depart from themselves and all things and come to our Lord, they are then incorporated and united with all the godly, like the limbs of one body, and brought together according to the word of Scripture.
>
> Also, I say that a church, or ecclesia, of Christ is a temple and dwelling place of God and the Holy Spirit, wherein God himself reigns with effective power. Such a church God has sanctified unto himself in the blood of Christ so that it may have no spot or wrinkle or anything like it, but be holy and blameless. Because it is written that the paths and highways (meaning in the church of Christ) will be called the holy way, no tainted man shall walk through them but the Lord himself will go with them on the way, and no lion or beast of prey shall enter therein. For on the outside are dogs, sorcerers, whoremongers and hypocrites, and all who do not live out the truth.
>
> Therefore no matter how many churches there are on earth, if they still consort with sin and abominations they are all churches of devils and a lodging for unclean birds and evil spirits. Let him comprehend it, who can, and he who has ears to hear, let him hear.
>
> I think you probably understand by now what I mean by the word *ecclesia catholica*, namely, that he who is made godly in faith in Christ

and sincerely lives correctly, is a member in the church of God and Christ, according to the testimony of the Scriptures.

Dax then accused the superintendent of accepting an unbiblical compromise on church membership:

> You willfully want to build an impure church, and have betrayers and children of Judas in your meetings, contrary to the evidence of all the writings of the saints which for all Christian churches command excommunication that evil may be expelled.[26]

### e. A Way of Life

The essential point, as already implied, is the Hutterian emphasis on acting in accordance with New Testament precept, and not only verbalizing about the Christian life. During a discourse on the nature of nonconformity, Dax charged the Calvinists with boasting of Christ with their mouths, yet at the same time performing heathen deeds. Later he went a step further; "One who does not live in Christ's truth cannot show me the truth." Another major focal point which Dax very naturally assumed to be essential for the fulfillment of Christian living was the idea of community of goods. When the superintendent asked, "Do you, Leonhard, believe that one who keeps his own possessions can be saved?" Dax answered:

> I believe that one who keeps and misuses his own possessions may well be damned. Furthermore, I say that he who voluntarily distributes his possessions according to the command of the Most High may well be saved.[27]

Christian discipleship, joined to Christian brotherhood, and expressed in a process of mutual sharing at all levels of human existence, merged into a way of life within the Hutterian movement, the "last" brotherhood-church which Leonhard Dax felt was one in essence with the "first" apostolic church.

### In Conclusion

Dax preserved a more complete account of his opponent's argument than did any other Hutterite who wrote a Rechenschaft. His sympathetic rendering of the superintendent's argument shows Dax's attempt to preserve the original intent of his opponent. The superintendent's position seems plausible, although at places Dax may well have underplayed those strictly Calvinistic tenets of predestination and divine election which his discussion partner put forth. At least we must question Dax's ability to capture the complete thought of the Calvinist superintendent; contact between Hutterites and Calvinists was too rare for that. To be noted, however, is Dax's sharpened awareness of the ramifications of Calvinism in the second encounter, most probably to be attributed to Dax's own reading of Calvinistic writings, such as the Heidelberg Catechism and the Second Helvetic Confession. He, in fact, seems consciously to have turned the Calvinistic argument of God's election in his favor, when he applied it so forcefully to the Christian view of the sword.

In his own carefully stated answers, we can be sure that Dax related his own views; the ideas which he expressed, however, were not only his, but those of the whole Brotherhood. The many existing manuscript copies of Dax's Rechenschaft and the inclusion of parts of it in the Great Article Book[28] show that Dax based his arguments squarely upon Hutterian tradition, and at the same time helped the Hutterian Brotherhood to perceive more keenly the unique formulation of the faith underlying that tradition. The Brotherhood's own evaluation of the Rechenschaft is found in the Great Chronicle, which says that Dax "answered powerfully with the whole of Scripture."[29]

The remark of a Calvinist scholar of a bygone generation about the meaning of the radical differences between Calvinism and Anabaptism serves well as a closing point for reflection (even though the Anabaptists would have strongly affirmed that their faith too was grounded in God's grace, as revealed in Christ):

> Whenever the questions of sin and salvation become acute, the problem of freedom or bondage of the will, of ethics or faith, again becomes central. And whenever the questions of sin and salvation are asked in the light of the Bible, the question whether Christian discipleship or faith in God's grace in Christ is the way to reconciliation and to justification before the Absolute must of necessity disturb man to the depths of his being.[30]

# Ch. 7

# Hutterian Encounter with the Polish Brethren

Poland was the first modern European country officially to sanction religious toleration. The newly established political confederation granted protection to all religious dissenters in 1573, including the Polish Brethren. In practice this freedom had come much earlier, with Lutherans, Calvinists, Bohemian Brethren, and Polish Brethren existing alongside the official Roman Church. The Polish Brethren who had been condemned by the Helvetic synod at Cracow in 1563 for their Antitrinitarian leanings, had by 1565 officially organized as an autonomous brotherhood. They enjoyed this toleration for less than a century, for in 1658 they were banished from the country. They dispersed to other parts of Europe and to America, preparing the soil for modern Unitarianism.[1]

## Peter Gonesius and the Founding of the Polish Brethren

The major roots of the Polish Brethren movement which differentiated them from other Protestant groups originated theologically, at least in part, in the teachings of Servetus, and structurally, also in part, in the congregational patterns of the Hutterites. Other major factors influencing the movement were Erasmian ideas and, in the 1550s and '60s, the radicalism of Italian dissenters who united with the Polish movement. But the Polish Brethren movement had even earlier roots, going back in history beyond Calvinism to the early Upper German spiritualistic radicalism of the 1520s, and the Low Country radicalism of the 1530s. The break-up of Münsterite

Anabaptism, for example, most certainly aided the spread of radical Christian thought into many corners of Europe, including Poland.

One man who combined Antitrinitarian doctrine with Hutterian ideas on style of life and religious practice was Peter Gonesius, a scholar and teacher in Padua during the same years when Servetus confronted Calvin in his famous debates. Although Servetus lost his life as a consequence, his ideas were furthered by disciples such as Gribaldi, who acquainted Gonesius with Antitrinitarian theology. On his way back to Poland in the mid-1550s, Gonesius visited the Hutterites, was favorably impressed, and incorporated into his Antitrinitarian theology the Anabaptist ideas of believers' (adult) baptism, nonresistance, and Christian community of goods. Fervently proclaiming his cause, Gonesius continued to win adherents to his faith until, in 1563, the movement was strong enough to be recognized as a definite religious body at variance with Calvinism, and was expelled from the Polish ecclesiastical circle of Calvinists.[2]

During the first years of creative ferment within the newly founded brotherhood, a marked structural instability and theological disunity plagued the Polish Brethren community, and some leaders began to look to the communal pattern of the well organized Hutterites as a possible answer to their problem. As early as 1562 there had been discussion between the Hutterites and refugee Antitrinitarians fleeing from Italy to Poland. Some had joined with the Hutterites in Moravia, and a few of these, as Hutterite emissaries, had returned to their native lands to seek converts among their kin. Again in 1566 Antitrinitarian emigrants from Italy brought stories of their encounters with the Hutterites to Poland. Doctrinal differences had prevented closer cooperation.[3]

However, in early 1567 a new type of contact began to take shape, when a delegation of five Polish Brethren, including Simon Ronemberg, an apothecary, and Lucas Mundas, an alderman of Wilno (Lithuania), visited the Hutterites. A year later, Mundas made a report of the visit to the Polish Brethren synod meeting at Pełsznica; he spoke warmly about his fellowship with the Hutterites and announced that a Hutterian delegation would soon be coming to Poland.[4]

Very soon the Hutterian pattern of community caught hold among a faction of the Polish Brethren led by Gregory Paul, and in 1569 this group transformed the middle of a forest near Sandomierz into a brotherhood community which they named Raków. Their goal was to establish a New Jerusalem, patterned after the first church, where the personal faith of each member combined with, and in turn was supported by, the transforming strength of the brotherhood. Unfortunately individualism was still too strong for the group to submit to the discipline needed to actualize this vision. When the Hutterian delegation, headed by Ludwig Dörker, arrived in September 1569, it was given a warm welcome. The Hutterites took a special interest in this communal experiment and proposed that four of its youths destined for the ministry should live among the Hutterites to learn a trade. This was in keeping with the Rakóvian belief that all members of a brotherhood, including the ministers, should develop some manual skill.[5]

During the next two years several Polish delegations visited the Hutterian Haushaben. In 1569 and again in early 1570 Simon Ronemberg led groups which spent some time with the Hutterites to study Hutterian organization and discipline. The community at Raków was still so unsettled that its members were considering abandoning believers' baptism until they could come to some agreement on it. They were consequently even open to the idea of uniting with the Hutterites.

## Reason and Obedience

The Hutterites, however, saw that reaching consensus would not be a simple matter. The two brotherhoods held divergent views on such vital issues as the form of baptism and the nature of Christ. The Polish Brethren, who had come to the Hutterites in the first place to learn about the process of brotherhood discipline, could not avoid trying to promote their own ideas. Such intellectual dialogue, integral to the Polish Brethren doctrine, was quite foreign to the well-established and anti-philosophical Hutterian thought of the 1560s. The Polish Brethren were offended when the Hutterites rejected their request for an open discussion on the nature of God, although they still regarded the Hutterites as a people of God who were, of all the churches, most in keeping with the Apostolic church. Needless to say, the Hutterites were also offended by the Polish Brethren request, and by their daring to criticize the printed Hutterian Brotherhood Rechenschaft, even wanting to improve on it.

The Polish Brethren were aware of their problems of disunity, and accepted the Hutterites' demand to discontinue the discussions of a possible union. A cordial parting of the two groups was accompanied by a Hutterian admonition that the theological arguments of the Polish Brethren would be more convincing if they could effect a solid Ordnung, so that their actions would be more in line with their words, a reprimand which was acknowledged and accepted in good faith.[6]

The next meeting of the two brotherhoods took place in mid-1570. A letter from the Hutterites to Poland opened up the way for the discussions, and three Polish delegates brought with them a letter to the Hutterites which introduced them as John Baptista (Swiecicki) and John the Italian from Raków, and Järish Müller from Olkusz. Müller's presence indicated a willingness among the Polish Brethren to continue communal living, which by this time had spread beyond Raków. The Polish Brethren of Olkusz were grateful for the renewal of spirit resulting from the Hutterian letter to them earlier that year. They believed the time was ripe for a renewed attempt at cooperation with the Hutterites, to learn from them the nature of Christian group discipline (the firm Gemeindeordnung of the Hutterites). In view of their still rather chaotic state of affairs, the Polish delegation was determined to find the key to the success of the Hutterites, and again affirmed the Hutterian Brotherhood to be a true people of God.

Although the May visit did not lead to closer relationships, the Hutterite Vorsteher, Peter Walpot, did not drop the matter. He wrote to a number of well-intentioned seekers, including John the Italian, underscoring his hope that the Poles would respond with a well-founded, renewed Christian life, and with the depth of love which surpasses all knowledge, made possible through Jesus Christ, who is Lord and Savior. Walpot addressed his message to all who desired divine justification and salvation.

Walpot reflected upon the encounter between the two brotherhoods. The hope engendered by the arrival of the Polish Brethren had turned into disappointment, for although they had come

> to converse with us, and so we thought, to accept or to learn about the charter of the church of the Lord, which had never correctly been effected among them . . . , but rather it turned out as if they desired to teach us or the church or to align us with their ways. This we, who are not built upon sand, could not do; namely, to adjust to such as have not completely repudiated the worldly and heathen life, having no baptism, true submission to God, nor Christian order and discipline which belongs to a people of God.

Walpot stated further that knowledge alone was not enough. The test of faith, he argued, was not in knowing many languages and possessing a so-called wisdom, but rather in tribulation, hard work, imprisonment, and chains. Since he believed the recipients of the letter to be more serious than some of the other Polish Brethren, he suggested for them the way of living which would include right living; for to know an answer intellectually fell short of the mark, as the five foolish virgins had exemplified, and would find only condemnation despite all excuses. Only by entering into the correct Christian pattern of life, he continued, would the Polish Brethren find the strength to endure the times of suffering and tribulation that would surely come; otherwise their end would only become a shame and mockery before their enemies. But Walpot hoped that God might motivate them to seek seriously his kingdom and righteousness, and to reach this kingdom in thought and life through the strength of Jesus Christ, who is both Lord and Savior.[7]

Not all the Polish Brethren, however, looked with favor upon the Hutterian pattern. During the spring or summer of 1570, a conservative Polish brother wrote a lengthy treatise against the Hutterian approach to community. The author betrays a deep bias against the Hutterites in his attempt to persuade the more radical Polish Brethren to give up their goal of establishing in Raków and elsewhere a Hutterian-type community. The treatise to some degree influenced the outcome of the Polish communal experiment, although it was probably less persuasive than other brotherhood factors. Indeed, at the same time when Raków was slowly developing into a major Polish Brethren intellectual center, the idea of a New Jerusalem community was slowly fading; intellectualism seemed to stand in the way of communal brotherhood. Still, the idea of communal living remained alive in thought and deed in at least one faction of the Polish Brethren, located chiefly at Śmigiel (Schmiegel). (The leader of a later generation, Socinus, still felt compelled to counter radical brethren who continued to promote the Hutterian idea of community within the Polish brotherhood.)

The author of the treatise claimed not to be opposed to a New Testament, apostolic church pattern; he was rather disputing the Hutterian methods of attempting to reestablish this original Jerusalem community. He listed his objections: the Hutterian hierarchy practiced what seemed to be despotic methods of leadership; large sums of money were supposedly on hand, contrary to Apostolic tradition; and the workers were exploited and used as slaves by the elders, who were actually hypocrites with only superficial piety. Instead of being "communists," they were "economists," the Polish author charged, and compared the Hutterian hierarchy with that of the Roman Church. He charged that Walpot wanted to be like the Pope, offering to his membership the Brotherhood Rechenschaft as the basis for life more often than he did the Bible.[8]

Certainly the treatise is far too harsh, and to a great extent based on hearsay evidence. The testimony of other Polish Brethren helps to balance the picture. The man who played the most important role in the Polish-Hutterian dialogue was Simon Ronemberg, mentioned above. Through his personal acquaintance with the Hutterian communities this "new Ezra" was able to mold the Raków settlement after the Hutterian pattern, and thereby slowly to clear up much of the chaos. Although the repeated contacts between the two brotherhoods did not lead to union, this fact did not keep the Poles who were led by the vision of Ronemberg, from imitating those Hutterian norms of communal life which they considered valid.

In Ronemberg's last known letter to the Hutterites, November 1, 1570, he acknowledged certain Hutterian traits as being praiseworthy, calling Walpot a "noble instrument of the living God," and a "Noah," the builder of an ark. Ronemberg desired further admonition from the Hutterites, but was not yet ready to concede to all the tenets of Hutterian faith. Were not the Polish Brethren also a true people of God, who had been taught by God, who possessed his Spirit and were ruled by him, even if they were only in the first stages of his will?

In his extended answer to Ronemberg, Walpot would not grant to the Polish Brethren even this modest claim. The document cuts to the heart of the fundamental issue separating the two brotherhoods. This time the bias is on the side of the Hutterites, although it is based on first-hand, yet limited, knowledge of the Polish Brethren, some of whom had lived with the Hutterites for a winter.[9]

Walpot's letter begins with a long introduction, presenting a synthesis of the Hutterian idea of Gelassenheit and discipleship, where Walpot spelled out his hopes and counsel:

> Deny, forsake, and abandon... yourselves and your self-will, body, and life, taking captive your reason under the obedience of Christ, so that you do not run in uncertainty, nor fight as one who merely beats the air, but rather tame your body and bring it into true servitude, and through self-restraint push through by the narrow gate and walk the narrow path leading to life, which few people find.[10]

Walpot then wished that God might grant unity of heart and spirit, made possible through Christ, the Lord and Savior, a unity which dwelt solely under his truth and honor, and which led to salvation. The cross was part of this way of life, and dared not be evaded by those who wanted to be true followers and disciples of Christ.

Slowly and with careful thought Walpot unfolded the problems of the past two years. He centered his complaint in the "empty words" of the Poles who spoke one way and acted otherwise. Furthermore Walpot felt that the Polish Brethren should give up private property and submit to the ways of the true people of God. The Polish Brethren, he maintained, had not even reached the first rung of the ladder in fulfilling the will of God, namely, submitting themselves and uniting with his people, the Hutterites.

Emphasizing the necessity for unity within God's people, Walpot pleaded for a change of heart in the Poles, that they, like Paul (Acts 9:17) and Cornelius (Acts 10:1-48), submit to the laying on of hands and to baptism, and unite with the true people and their leaders. But if they did not consider his word to be God's Word they were free to go their own way. Indeed, among the Hutterites everyone had joined of his own free will. Walpot granted that there might possibly be some hypocrites among them—God would take care of them—but God demanded that the church be pure, and that it be kept active through brotherly admonition. Each brother in the group was to exercise this duty which if need be could lead to disciplinary measures and even to the ban.

Walpot assured them that the Hutterites did not want to condemn anyone; a person's own evil deeds were in themselves self-condemnatory. Yet just as Noah saved his household in the ark and thereby condemned the world, so also the gathered believers who separated themselves from the world also condemned this world by their act of leaving it (Hebrews 11:7). In fear and trembling, with imperfect knowledge, and aware that even the church was imperfect, Walpot and his church were following Christ like the Apostle Paul (Philippians 3:12-19). In turn, he said, they were also being seized by God in Jesus Christ. While the Hutterian Brotherhood was open to correction—a continuous activity within the gathered membership—it stood upon the true foundation; such was not the case with the Polish Brethren, who possessed the gift of discernment but did not live up to what they knew was right; therefore, the Polish Brethren would henceforth fall under the Hutterian practice of avoidance since the true signs of Christianity were lacking among them: true submission in baptism, the new birth, and renunciation of the world, sin, the devil, and their own flesh and self-will. He rejected the Polish Brethren claim that God dwelt within their midst, for they cared more about self than their neighbor, and they still held to private property; love stemming from faith was not in evidence, and they did not exercise the Christian ban or brotherly admonition, which was essential for a people of God.

After recounting the wanderings and sufferings the Hutterites had passed through, and the possibility of suffering yet to come, Walpot stated that the Polish Brethren, when their time of suffering came, would also lay aside some of their high, human knowledge and cling solely to God. He pleaded that they pray for the necessary strength to grow, for the group at Raków was already helping other Polish Brethren by establishing a genuine community; indeed this would be the way in which they might come closer to the Hutterites. Although the Polish brotherhood had had the chance to become members of Christ's kingdom—and the Hutterites had gladly housed the various Poles as guests, as long as their eating and drinking remained moderate—still the Polish guests had shown no signs of improvement in conduct, and they even wanted to teach the Hutterites. Walpot warned them that they did not yet hold correct views concerning repentance, baptismal doctrine, the laying on of hands, the resurrection of the dead, and eternal judgment; hence the Hutterites had decided upon avoidance of the Polish Brethren.

Even so, Walpot hoped his admonition would be received as from a friend, for this was the way he too wished to be admonished. Keeping the door open for reconciliation, he urged them to respond with a change of heart, with the new birth, and with deeds corresponding to the Christian walk, accepting "the water of life" freely given to anyone who would partake, and participating in God's way of life by hearing evidence of proper fruit and the works of repentance.[11]

Walpot's epistle to Ronemberg is blunt and to the point. There was perhaps reason for the Hutterites to raise doubts about the Christian faith of their Catholic, Lutheran, and Zwinglian-Calvinist persecutors, but here was a group which shared the same convictions about a believers' church founded on adult baptism, which emphasized love, fellowship, and nonresistance, and which was even open to the idea of communal living. But still Walpot boldly asserted that he was the leader of the one church of God, outside of which there was no salvation:

> If you recognize and confess me to be the ark-builder, Noah, and if you are not hypocrites, tempters, stubborn, rebellious, and disobedient to the truth (one of which qualities must be at hand [among you]), why do you not gather in this ark, outside of which there will be no salvation?[12]

On the surface Walpot's stand appears to be intolerant, sharp and unbending. Yet considering the character of most sixteenth-century polemics, Walpot exercised toleration and tempered his harsh appraisal with a face-saving alternative. Another look at some of the ideas already alluded to will bear this out, for Walpot writes:

> All this I do not write to you, dear Simon, in order that you or anyone of yours should look to me or us and build upon us as human beings, far be it. If you do not recognize this as the truth and as the foundation of the apostles on which one must build, and hold our word to be God's Word (as it truly is), then let it alone, and continue in your own manner of life and station.
>
> I write you at your request (for the sake of my conscience and the

honor of God) to admonish you and warn you, and I do not speak in
order that you should give yourselves up to the Lord in his and our
church, and sign as members for my word's sake (although it is not my
word). It lies within each person's choice. If the Word of God and the
testimony of one's conscience do not lead to this end, nothing else will
help.

No one is compelled to do this, as you imagine, and if we knew of
anyone in our midst who only pretended freedom, but in his heart felt
otherwise, he should not have any continuance with us. And even if he
conceals it from us, God knows him, and will blot him out of the book
of his people and the members of his household, out of his book of life.

Then Walpot defined his concept of the nature of the church as a
voluntary group of believers who had experienced a new life, and who had
separated themselves from the worldly evils:

The Lord desires a new heart and spirit and a voluntary church
which of its own free will separates itself from all evil and all taint of sin
both within and without. And not alone this, but every faithful zealous
soul and friend of God is responsible, and obligated in the love of God
to testify against all evil, unrighteousness, works of darkness and ungodly life of the world and all unbelievers, also to reprove them and to
remind them of their evil ways, and to warn them on account of their
transgression, to use the sword of the spirit against them. If he does not
do so, he is a hypocrite before God and man.

Walpot then returned to the theme of Noah's ark and explained that
the Hutterites did not condemn anyone; in fact, they would have liked to
see all people redeemed. Furthermore, in line with the Apostle Paul,
Walpot suggested that

when Noah prepared the ark for the saving of his household and
through the ark condemned the world, so still today all those who
follow Christ and the church of believers (which bears the likeness of
the ark), condemn this world by going out from and separating from it
with the testimony that its works are evil and that if men do not repent
they will not become heirs of salvation.

He then made an appeal that the Polish Brethren put themselves on the
balance to see whether they were living up to the biblical norm of what
Christianity and the church should be.[13]

## Cultural Differences Separating
## the Two Brotherhoods

What differences finally thwarted the attempted uniting of the two
groups, in view of sincere efforts by each group to work with the other? One

important reason lay in the different social milieu of the two groups, and the different circumstances under which each group emerged as a brotherhood. On the one hand, the Hutterites were for the most part artisans and workmen, accustomed to obedience and subservience, low wages and simple food, and to association with others of their kind. The Hutterian communities met their needs and gave them the assurance that they were indeed the people of God, living according to scriptural precept.

The Polish Brethren, on the other hand, were composed primarily of landed gentry, although some former priests and clerics were to be found among them. Apart from those who had migrated to Poland from other lands, the Polish Brethren had not been compelled by persecution and poverty to flee to a "promised land" such as Moravia, for they enjoyed religious freedom at their doorstep. The type of religious motivation within the Polish brotherhood was consequently of a different quality from that of the Hutterites.

In contrast to the Hutterian emphasis upon a general unity of faith and life within its ranks, the Polish Brethren were a discrete group which engaged in endless intellectual discussions about the nature of ultimate reality, and debates engendered by differing views of Scripture. The Hutterian theocracy, within which a total acceptance of and strict obedience to the regulations of the community were presupposed, was therefore a difficult goal for the Poles, and one which might not have met their needs just as the Polish way of life might not have met the needs of the Hutterites. The Hutterites were a German minority group often located in the midst of a Slavic-speaking population which they generally bypassed as a mission field; their status as a minority group furthered the idea of a complete separation from the world. The Polish Brethren, on the contrary, found their mission within their midst at home. Uniting with the Hutterites would have granted them neither greater religious toleration nor better economic conditions. Rather, such a move would have cut the Polish Brethren off from their means of livelihood and, perhaps more important, would have cut them off from the Slavic-speaking population open to the brotherhood message.

Nevertheless the role that communal living played for at least a small group within the Polish brotherhood must not be minimized. In the communal pattern which he established at Raków, Ronemberg attempted to create some sort of order in the chaotic state of the Polish brotherhood. This chaotic state had resulted in part from their philosophical discussions on the nature of ultimate reality. The Polish Brethren continued to be seekers after the truth, whereas the Hutterites were sure that the truth could only be found in a practical way of surrender and obedient discipleship, as revealed in the time of Christ and the apostles. Therefore Ronemberg could ask for admonition, yet also feel able to provide some admonition by way of response.

The Hutterites also recognized the problems which continually haunted their own Brotherhood, but believed they possessed a built-in corrective to remedy such problems, namely, mutual admonition and church discipline, including the ban. Ronemberg, on the other hand, did not have this built-in corrective and found it necessary to deal with brethren who were strongly opposed to the communal ideal. Although he admitted that the Hutterian way was one valid option and pattern for Christianity, he also saw other possible means of fulfilling the New Testament demands, which in fact finally won out within the divergent factions of the Polish brotherhood, perhaps out of economic necessity.[14]

The Polish-Hutterian encounter came to an end in 1571 with Walpot's letter. Indeed the letter left the Polish Brethren with little choice, for the Hutterites had announced their practice of avoidance of the Poles:

> For this reason we had cause, and divine cause, as we should know—because you call yourselves our brothers though in fact you are not—to separate ourselves from you and to avoid you as Paul commands that if there is anyone who calls himself a brother and is covetous and brings another doctrine which does not conform to the sound words of our Lord Jesus Christ and the doctrine of godliness, and is admonished once and a second time, we should have nothing to do with him (1 Corinthians 5:9-13); . . . from such a one we should also not accept a greeting so long and until we observe a real conversion and profession.[15]

Two decades later, and again in the 1650s, contacts between the two brotherhoods were renewed, but the outcome was no more fruitful than the one which took place during the Walpot Era. In the 1650s, however, one Polish brother was won over to the Hutterian cause, Dr. Daniel Zwicker, who became a Hutterite missioner and proclaimed the cause of Christian community for many years. He finally went to the Netherlands to become a solitary defender of the truth, alone and perhaps forlorn in the last years of his life.[16]

In summary, it can be seen that Hutterianism exerted a strong influence upon the Polish brotherhood, especially in the doctrine of the church and the areas of social concern, despite certain underlying differences between the two groups: 1) Differing social milieux kept the two brotherhoods apart. 2) Community of goods did not spread within Polish circles in a way which would have met Hutterian requirements. 3) Doctrinal differences also contributed to the failure of the attempt at closer cooperation; as Walpot said, the Poles held "another doctrine."[17]

## Different Theological Approaches
## Separating the Two Brotherhoods

The nature of this "other doctrine" which separated the two groups needs further elaboration. We noted in Chapter Six, in juxtaposing Calvinism and Anabaptism, that both these approaches to Christianity seemed to take ethics seriously, yet each was at odds with the other in the area of dogmatics. Something of these theological differences between Anabaptism and Calvinism directly influenced the historical development of the Polish Brethren, who twenty years earlier had entered into the attempted union of these two movements through the efforts of Peter Gonesius and others.

The Polish Brethren had in a real sense begun with Calvin, and then receded from a total acceptance of his systematic theology. What ensued was a restless quest for truth on an intellectual basis, within an intellectual structure which had its source in Calvin—or better, in a reaction to Calvin. Consequently, the intellectual approach to truth became a tenacious disintegrating factor within the movement which blocked the way to a unified and disciplined brotherhood. To stand "in reaction to" rather than "in affirmation of" major blocks of one's heritage tends to undermine the unity of a movement. For within a voluntaristic, gathered brotherhood, the ordered life, where peace may reign, is only possible where unity of vision is a reality for all. And vision has its roots in heritage. No one can be coerced into such a unity. The Hutterites were the living example of this brotherly unity founded upon a growing tradition already approaching half-a-century; the Polish Brethren had a less unified foundation to conserve. The acceptance of theological diversity seems to have been an important part of their theological basis. Gonesius had attempted to bridge the Calvinist and Anabaptist ideologies but the pieces did not mesh and the Polish Brethren could not look back to a unified heritage which held together naturally. Peter Walpot very naturally sensed the disparity between the groups and found what he felt was the crux of the problem: The Poles were not taking their human thoughts and intellect captive into the obedience of Christ (2 Corinthians 10:5).

These two approaches to truth can in general terms be typologically classified as : 1) a historical approach which emphasizes man's ability to respond in obedience to God as a disciple of Christ (Erasmus, the Anabaptists) by covenanting together with other believers within a

brotherhood where God's Spirit is at work (the Anabaptists); 2) in contrast
to it, a formal theological approach which attempts rationally (Calvin) and
rationalistically (Servetus, the Polish Brethren, and the Socinians) to resolve
the questions of the nature of God, man, and the universe. The latter approach attempts systematically to define God, who himself alone effects salvation (Calvin), or intellectually attempts to reevaluate Calvin's view and
find better answers—but uses Calvin's methodology in doing so (the Polish
Brethren). The first approach rests on the belief that God is working in history, most intensely through his son Jesus, whose message is normative for
the art of living, and who is to be obeyed and followed in his person (the
way of the cross), as well as in his message and commandments (the Sermon
on the Mount, the Great Commandment, the Great Commission); it also
rests on the belief that God extends his mercy and grace through the witness
and mission of his church—but that to find salvation, man must respond.

It is the scientific and rationalistic approach (a fully coordinated system
of intellectual thought), in conflict with a simple obedience-to-Jesus approach (an existential response of obedience) which stood as opposites in the
1560s and '70s for the Polish Brethren and the Hutterites. From the Hutterian viewpoint the opposites were knowledge that begins with man, as
contrasted to knowledge which comes from God. The latter demands the
response of obedience. The former is not the place to begin in fulfilling life
as followers of Jesus, for those who make this their starting point tend to be
content to reflect intellectually and then simply to call the results of this
reflection "truth"; for since man cannot respond in that God does it all
(Calvin's view), the most man can do in coming to grips with salvation is to
attempt to define God and the nature of his mercy and justice. Although
the Polish Brethren were attempting to break away from Calvinism in this
sense, they continued to affirm a methodology which approached truth on
the same intellectual terms.

The Hutterites finally concluded that the Polish Brethren had fallen
into the dangerous position of wanting to theologize their way into truth
(beginning with man's own powers of cognition and reason), rather than to
respond initially through obedience to a man and his message which had
broken into history, which the Hutterites believed was clearly interpreted in
the New Testament and affirmed throughout the history of Christ's new
covenant.

It is a tribute to the Polish Brethren experiment that they kept the
pieces together as long as they did. Their century in Poland is the classic attempt at merging a rationalistically-oriented, quasi-Calvinistic theological
approach to truth with certain social structures and religious ideas (disciple-

ship and community) of a sixteenth-century Anabaptist brotherhood. Its successes and failures need further analysis and interpretation in order to answer the two questions—which structure can contain and carry a brotherhood movement through the generations, and which nucleus is compatible to that form of Christianity.

The main difference between the two brotherhoods lay therefore in two opposing views on the nature of truth. As noted above, the Polish Brethren were eternal seekers after truth, continually knocking, asking, and seeking. The message that George Schoman, one of the brethren who had visited the Hutterian Brotherhood, left for posterity in his testament written in the 1590s, expresses the nature of the Polish Brethren mentality:

> I have reached the true catholic faith by way of Catholicism, Lutheranism, Calvinism, and Anabaptism. If, in the future, an even purer church were to emerge, join it![18]

The Hutterites, on the other hand, certain that they had founded their Brotherhood upon God's Word in line with the pattern of the New Testament church, were concerned with preserving this essence of the early church as they interpreted it. Truth, once recognized, was for them by definition to be obeyed, and was never under any circumstances to be compromised.

# Ch. **8**

# Hutterian Encounter with the Swiss Brethren

The group of Anabaptists that originated in Zurich in 1525 referred to themselves as "Brethren," and thus, when they settled in Alsace, South Germany, or even Moravia, they were known among the Anabaptist groups as the "Swiss Brethren." The extensive literary legacy left by the pioneers of this group has permitted extensive research on early Anabaptism, from the 1520s to about 1540.[1]

The charter of the Swiss Brethren brotherhood is without doubt the Schleitheim Confession of Faith (1527), a document built upon the idea of brotherhood consensus as the means to realizing Christian faith. It provided the stability needed for the Anabaptist movement to continue beyond its first, tumultuous years of rapid spread. The Confession gave substance to the Anabaptist movement within Switzerland, Alsace, and South Germany, and also made a major contribution to the shape of Hutterian faith and practice. The sixteenth-century Hutterian codices are clear evidence that the Schleitheim Confession is firmly incorporated into Hutterian thought.[2]

After 1540, the Hutterian branch of Anabaptism continued to produce written accounts of its faith, adding its own testimony to the heritage it held in common with the Swiss Brethren. In contrast, the Swiss Brethren produced surprisingly few known documents after 1540. There was, to be sure, the colloquy at Frankenthal in 1571 between Calvinists and the Swiss Brethren, proof of the latter's ongoing vigor; but not much is known about the leaders or the activities of the members within the Swiss congregations. Present knowledge suggests isolated, semiautonomous groups spread thinly from Alsace to Moravia, rather than an integrated and unified brotherhood.

These widely scattered Brethren continued to consider themselves Swiss wherever they lived, although many were in fact of non-Swiss origins.[3]

Because of the scarcity of Swiss Brethren sources after 1540, research on Swiss Anabaptism must be based in large part on Hutterian documents. Aside from court records these documents are the main source of information about the second-generation Swiss and are a valuable source for the inner history of both the Swiss Brethren and the Hutterites. Even the account of the first Swiss Brethren baptismal service in Zollikon is found only in Hutterian documents. Presumably the lack of an overall organization accounts for the paucity of Swiss Brethren materials after the passing of classical Anabaptism, which, for the Swiss Brethren, came as early as the 1530s. During the 1550s and '60s some Swiss leaders possessed the writings of Michael Sattler and Melchior Rinck. The Swiss Brethren were still very much aware of their beginnings, but they apparently were unable to preserve their second-generation heritage in writing. Even known documents of book length are no longer extant.[4]

Such a picture suggests that during these years after 1540, the Swiss Brethren were coping with a precarious economic and religious existence. Many began looking to the firmly established Hutterites for help and support. Consequently, internal as well as external conditions occasioned a steady interaction between the Hutterites and Swiss Brethren throughout the sixteenth century.

## The Strength of Hutterian Organization

The small, solidly founded community of several hundred brethren, which Jacob Hutter left behind in 1536 when he was martyred, grew during the next two generations to a sizable brotherhood enclave containing some 20,000 souls.[5] This growth resulted in part from the ability of the Hutterian community to attract large segments of less well-organized brotherhoods such as the Gabrielites, Philippites, and even some Polish Brethren.[6] The Swiss Brethren, however, were the greatest source of converts flowing into ever-expanding Hutterian communities. Despite the crowded conditions, these newcomers were always welcomed, on the condition that they adapt themselves to Hutterian ways of faith and life.

The numerous Swiss Brethren congregations in the "promised land" of Moravia enjoyed many of the same political and economic privileges accorded the Hutterites. This made the influx of Swiss into the Hutterian fold all the more significant. During the 1570s there were at least fifteen, and possibly more than twenty, Swiss Brethren congregations in Moravia, as compared to over seventy large Hutterian communities. But while the number of Hutterian communities continued to grow until the 1620s, the number of known Swiss Brethren congregations in Moravia soon dropped sharply.[7]

The Great Chronicle of the Hutterites relates in general the more important parts of the story of the many individuals, families, and larger groups of Swiss Brethren who united with the Hutterian Brotherhood through the decades. In 1539, for instance, an unusually large number of Swiss Brethren joined the Hutterites. Seventeen years later a large faction of a Swiss Brethren congregation, including the leader, Lorenz Hueff, joined the Hutterites.[8]

During the first year of the Walpot Era, Farwendel, a Swiss Brethren elder at Kreuznach, Germany, was imprisoned for his faith at Ogersheim, near Worms. He suffered mental torment because he feared that in his coming encounter with the state-church clergy he would break down and deny his faith. He called to God, but found no peace. He believed that death was imminent. Then he recalled that a Hutterite missioner had earlier told him that he had not yet given up his self-will. When he reached the decision to join the Hutterites, he finally found peace. Three Hutterites, Ludwig Dörker, Claus Braidl, and Bastl Reusch, visited him in prison. He repented of his sharp words against the Hutterian teachings on war taxes, marital separation, the ban, and the special treatment accorded Hutterite ministers. When Farwendel was released from prison, he and a number of other Swiss from his area joined the Hutterites.[9]

In 1567 a group of Swiss Brethren in Moravia initiated an exchange of correspondence by writing a book of 160 pages to which the Hutterites responded in length. Paul Glock's dialogue with Leonhard Sommer five years later also provides welcome commentary on the nature of Swiss Anabaptism in the 1570s. A third encounter was an exchange of letters in 1577 between Walpot and the Swiss Brethren of Modenbach, the last such dialogue during the Walpot Era.

Contacts between the Swiss and the Hutterites continued beyond the Walpot Era. In the 1580s Swiss Brethren poured into the Hutterian communities. On October 9, 1586, because of a famine in their homelands, 402 persons arrived, and five days later, another 249. Three years later, Stoffel Schenckh, a Swiss Brethren minister at Rehag, in the Canton of Bern, and his congregation united with the Hutterites.[10]

The Hutterian chronicles mention only one instance of a Hutterite joining the Swiss Brethren: in the 1620s Thoman Wilhelm left the Hutterites to join the Swiss Brethren; the Great Chronicle laments that he "forsook the faith, transferred to the Swiss Brethren, and died outside."[11]

In developing the history and ideas in the Hutterian-Swiss encounters, we shall begin with the dialogue between Walpot and the Swiss Brethren congregation at Modenbach in 1577, which portrays Hutterian mission strategy for winning whole congregations. Then follows the account of the rather heated Hutterian-Swiss encounter in 1567, where the fundamental issues dividing the Hutterian Brotherhood from the Swiss are debated. Finally, the unusual personal encounter between Paul Glock and the Swiss brother, Leonhard Sommer, completes the presentation of the Hutterian-Swiss encounter in the Walpot Era.

## Peter Walpot and the Swiss Brethren of Modenbach

The dialogue between the Swiss and the Hutterites in 1577 throws light on the phenomenon of various Swiss Brethren congregations converting in toto to Hutterianism. It reveals clues to mission strategy. In this instance, the Swiss initiated the dialogue with a letter, no longer extant, to which Peter Walpot as Vorsteher of the whole Brotherhood replied. He acknowledged receipt of the letter, stating that he himself had read it, that it was then read aloud and discussed among the brethren, and that the Hutterian answer represented the understanding which had come out of the extended discussion. The Hutterian reply enables us to identify two basic Swiss concerns: the question of the nature of the church and a related point on the nature of marriage.

The Hutterian reply affirms that their Brotherhood is a people of God with a mission. As the body of Christ, led by Jesus himself, they were commissioned to search out, gather, and strengthen the scattered sheep, wherever they might be found. For the very essence of being God's people was based on the idea of community. Scattered individuals who lived in disunity could not enter into the fullness of the Christian faith, which was made possible solely through a life of sharing, in a true and untrammeled submission to God (Romans 1; 16; 2 Corinthians 8).

Community of goods, the Hutterites continued, was an important aspect of such Christian sharing and mutual love; the Hutterites were certain that the Swiss did not need to look far before seeing that there was sufficient evidence for this in Scripture. Repeating some of the same arguments written into their communication of 1567 to the Swiss, the Hutterites insisted that the nature of Christian community, as opposed to worldly individualism, could be compared to the transformation of grains of wheat into flour, and grapes into wine, resulting in the fulfillment of the Great Commandment of loving one's neighbor as oneself. Such community had to be based upon group unity which must be present within the church, if it was to be Christ's body. The Hutterites reminded the Swiss that community had been a reality for the disciples of Christ and that it included the bonds of love, which the world understood only in terms of bondage, as human halters and coercion. The world notwithstanding, the nature mankind received at birth was incapable of self-fulfillment except within community, for what one person lacked could be counterbalanced only by the complementary strengths of others. Indeed, there was no other path to salvation than that of obedience and discipleship within community, which led to peace of soul; it was this path which led to the realization of the kingdom of the Lord.

The Hutterites closed their epistle with the same invitation that they included in their salutation: that the Swiss Brethren at Modenbach consider uniting with the Hutterites and enter into the salvation and fulfillment of life which is defined in terms of God's kingdom. It was the invitation that was extended throughout the Walpot Era to all seekers of God's righteousness.[12]

## The Seven Articles of 1567

In 1567 the Hutterites gave extensive thought to a long letter, no longer extant, from the Swiss Brethren, who had requested a point-by-point reply. The Swiss authors had written on behalf of their entire brotherhood within and beyond Moravia, and raised the issues that they believed were the basis of why the Swiss Brethren and the Hutterites, although both were brotherhoods, continued to be at odds with one another.

In reply, Vorsteher Peter Walpot took time to compose a careful, 376-page missive. No doubt he followed the usual custom of first conferring with other brethren. A copy is still extant. After a word of greeting, Walpot interpreted the basic Hutterian confession of faith in line with the printed Brotherhood Rechenschaft, and then moved directly into an answer to each of the main questions raised and charges leveled by the Swiss. He expressed the hope that this encounter would move the Swiss Brethren to submit totally to Christ, in obedience to his will.

Because our knowledge of the Swiss Brethren after 1540 is so scant, the information about them in Walpot's epistle is most welcome, even though the Hutterian bias is obvious. His discussion of all seven articles reveals the similarities as well as fundamental differences between the Swiss and the Hutterites.

## The Introduction

The Hutterites noted having received the Swiss Brethren epistle, stated that they had carefully read and analyzed it, and acknowledged that the Swiss Brethren wanted to work toward greater unity with the Hutterites. Both brotherhoods were in agreement that since God was not divided, neither should the Body of Christ be cut apart; hence it was good to work at the problems separating them even if the Swiss Brethren demonstrated in their letter a lack of good faith by leveling hearsay charges against the Hutterites.

The Hutterites denied the charges. They pointed out that if they were as evil as the Swiss made them out to be, God would not have granted them such great increase but would certainly have rooted them out. On the other hand, the Hutterites accused the Swiss Brethren for creating schism upon schism. In the eyes of the Hutterites, this added up to a faith in word only, devoid of its full expression which included love in deed and truth (John 17).

The Hutterites traced this problem of disunity as follows: In the early history of the Austerlitz Brethren, the Gabrielites, the Philippites, and the Swiss Brethren, there soon appeared group divisions with reciprocal excommunications. Leaders would also be banned, and yet in some cases would be permitted to remain in office during the time they were banned. All this, the Hutterites felt, was pure mockery before God. Often one faction would argue against the other for a whole night without reaching a solution. The crux of the issue was the absolute necessity for any and all Christian brotherhoods to establish Christian discipleship within an ordered brotherhood. The Swiss were by-passing this central issue, preferring rather to push on to other articles for discussion, as if these other articles were the principal impediments to closer cooperation. But unless the roots were firmly embedded, the means and the end could not be called holy (Romans 11:16). Where this beginning point of disciplined order was missing, human reason could not build what only the Lord himself could erect (Isaiah 8; Matthew 22; Psalm 127). On any other foundation, the builders only struggled in vain and in the last analysis became a mockery (Genesis 11). The Hutterites hoped that the wise might listen and improve in their ways (James 1:5).[13]

This opening section is of the utmost importance for understanding the Hutterian view of the Swiss: the lack of order among them led to continual disunity; and the strength of the Hutterites was their *Ordnung*, which they maintained by constant vigilance.[14]

**Article One: Concerning Community of Goods**

Whereas the nature of baptism was the obvious point of doctrine separating the Hutterites from the established churches, the nature of community was the major point of doctrinal disagreement between the Hutterites and the Swiss Brethren. Hence the Swiss quite naturally began with the theme of community. In their communication, the Swiss had attempted to substantiate on scriptural and other grounds that because all Christians are free in Christ they do not need to give up temporal goods or live in community; they can earn their own livelihood, raise their own children, and give to the church as often and as much as they deem correct.

To this the Hutterites replied with a seventy-page apologia on the communal way of life. The argument opens as follows:

> We must answer . . . that the word *gemainschaft* (fellowship or community), or *gemainsame* (common or together), comes from the word *gemain* (commonality; congregation, brotherhood, those who are united in a common cause) and that therefore those who are called *gemainschaftig* (sharers in community), have conjointly the use of those things they hold in common. This is seen in nature: when a father in the world has many children, they have equal rights to his goods; one has the same as another, and they may enjoy or share it together. [15]

We note that in their defense of community the Hutterian answer to the Swiss Brethren went well beyond the arguments of Acts 2 and 4. Jesus himself had set the prime example of community by establishing a common purse with his disciples. Jesus also noted that the rich could enter God's kingdom only with great difficulty (Matthew 19). The Old Testament too emphasized caring for the needs of the poor brother (Deuteronomy 15). God had instituted the Year of Jubilee (Exodus 16), when there was to be equality, and Jesus established this year as a perpetual reality. They even saw in the animal world examples of mutual sharing. Private ownership, a manifestation of the temporal ways of the world, worked against brotherhood unity, which needed as its base a Christian community as established by Jesus.

The Hutterites also interpreted the Lord's Supper to signify the communion of brethren, using the ancient metaphor of individual grains and grapes being transformed into bread and wine. This transformation formed the basis of Christian fellowship, and of course any untransformed grains or grapes were carefully removed from the flour and wine.

A long section in Article One lists the incidents that illustrated the depth of disunity among the Swiss Brethren caused by a lack of community. Some children within the Swiss Brotherhood were in the service of heathen, some women were serving in inns, and Swiss children in the Low Countries had to beg at times while others were living well. There was the example in Moravia of Tiopolt's father-in-law, a wealthy man who had given hardly more than two guilders during his lifetime for the poor brethren within his brotherhood. Tiopolt himself had a good business in swine at Eibenschitz. Other rich members such as Hans Beckh of Oberwisternitz and Michael Schneider of Unterwisternitz could bask in their wealth while some of their brethren had to live in the forest in dearth and destitution. A needy saddler of Eibenschitz was neglected. Indeed, the Hutterites charged the Swiss with being no better than the other groups who had called themselves brethren, such as the Spittelmaier group, the Mennonites, the Austerlitz Brethren, the Sabbatarians, the Gabrielites, and the Philippites, all of whom had been founded upon the dead letter.[16]

The next section of Article One answers specific Swiss charges against previous Hutterian events where problems had surfaced. Charged with using coercive practices in mission work, the Hutterites countered that this was not so: Converts were indeed required to give up all their possessions, but they were carefully instructed as to the financial implications before making their final decision about joining.

After citing Scripture passages which they believed supported the idea of Christian community of goods, the Hutterites concluded Article One with the idea that Christian love and unity, integral in the Christian faith, could be fulfilled only within the confines of close brotherhood sharing. Such a community of believers, they said, had been established by God in New Testament times, had continued up to the time of Augustine, had been reinstated by the Hutterites, and would endure as long as God would have his community endure; any Swiss Brethren who could fit into such a community were heartily welcomed into the Hutterian Brotherhood.[17]

## Article Two: Concerning Those
## Who Forsook the Hutterites

That their way of life was not suited for everyone, the Hutterites quite readily admitted. God, they said, gave to mankind the liberty to choose through his Word; hence salvation was effected without coercion. Salvation therefore was not for everyone, since there were individuals who chose not to become children of God. Furthermore, they believed that even among those who seemingly had chosen the godly path, there were individuals who were either hypocrites (Acts 5), or who at some point lapsed from their original covenant. The question of how to treat the latter is the topic of Article Two, the original title itself giving a clue to the Hutterian-Swiss tension: "Concerning Those Who Go Away from Us with Empty Hands." What happens to possessions which have been given to the church?

In coming to terms with the problem, the Hutterites found in their search of Scripture no biblical evidence that gifts presented to the church were later returned to unfaithful members. Hence, those who left went empty-handed. But at the time of baptism into the community, the economic implications of membership were explicitly taught to each candidate, as were also the other aspects of the Hutterian charter: how the Lord had established the Brotherhood in which an individual would have no personal property, and that if for any reason he later deviated from the truth and left, nothing would be returned to him. The Hutterites in their communication added parenthetically that there were far more who entered the Brotherhood empty-handed than otherwise, having left all their possessions behind. Furthermore, wealth improperly accumulated was never accepted into the Brotherhood treasury, nor was wealth accepted from anyone not becoming a member.

The Hutterites, however, knew that the Swiss themselves accepted money from their own members to meet the needs of the ailing and poor, money which they did not return to the donor when he left the brotherhood, even if he left in dire need. One such case concerned a girl named Anna who had moved into the castle at Bamberg at Stoda, believing she would find genuine community within the Swiss brotherhood. She had brought with her some money and a few other possessions, including her bedding. Later, disappointed in her experiences with the Swiss Brethren, Anna decided to leave and requested that she be allowed to take her bedding with her, but the request was refused. Another instance was the case of the Dutch Jan Kierschner who spent some time among the Swiss and received twenty-eight talers from them to support his family. When he turned to the Hutterian faith, the Swiss demanded the money back, a request which the Hutterites felt was simply not biblical. The Hutterites, on the other hand, allowed the few persons who forsook the Hutterian faith to take bedding and clothing with them.[18]

## Article Three: Concerning Servants of the Word and All Who Have Special Tasks in the Church

In view of the basic Hutterian idea of equality among all brethren, a certain long-standing custom of the Hutterites seemed highly incongruous to their non-Hutterite neighbors; i.e., the Hutterite leaders were granted special privileges not accorded other members, such as better food, special rooms, and better means of travel. This was one of the charges the Swiss Brethren made against the Hutterites in 1567.

The Hutterian defense did not deny the charge, but explained how the practice had come about, that it was biblical (1 Timothy 5:17), and that the total Brotherhood itself had initiated such favored treatment and desired to have the practice continue. As in New Testament times, God had in the last days again chosen for himself a people, wherein there was to be order and discipline, and within which peace dwelt. To fulfill this quality, the whole Hutterian Brotherhood chose servants to provide the needed leadership. The task of these leaders had been clearly established throughout the history of God's people, and the Hutterite servants of the church were to follow in the footsteps of previous saints of God. True, the leaders were vulnerable human beings, but what they could not accomplish in their human frailty, God could still fulfill out of his strength, as had been amply demonstrated in the lives of a great host of brethren who became Christian martyrs.

The Hutterites then outlined for the Swiss the nature of brotherhood leadership. The description is an unusually solid example of Hutterian reasoning and deserves a close reading:

> We [the Servants] should pasture the flock of Christ, that is, his Body and Bride, in all good things, instruct them in godliness, act compassionately, behave in a seemly way, offer a helping hand to the young in faith—correcting their mistakes, bearing with their shortcomings, and setting them right as much as possible in love and according to God's will. We should treat them in a fatherly, brotherly, warmhearted way, inspiring trust. We are deeply confident that all of God's children who have passed away in our time and those who are still alive, having a true and holy discernment, will witness to this on our behalf before God and all people, indeed before the Lord himself, in That Day, and before his whole congregation.. . .
>
> We have specified or chosen nothing for ourselves in the community to this day in eating, drinking, clothing, or such things; but we have accepted, used, and enjoyed what the Brotherhood gave us out of their own love, according to their poverty and their decision. When we were asked to move, we moved; when we were asked to stay, we stayed. Even as we are bound to correct and help them for the Lord's sake, we are [beholden] to the other brothers who serve the temporal needs. No one takes honor for himself; but we wait to be told what we should do, and accept what is granted by the community.[19]

The Hutterites believed that the task of leadership set down in these terms was biblical (1 Corinthians 9).

The Hutterites noted that Swiss leaders had also enjoyed the same privileges when they charged to their alms fund the cost of travel to Strassburg for their conference on original sin. On this and other occasions they spent many hundred guilders in public inns.

The Hutterites believed that their policy of leadership was effectively meeting the needs of the Hutterian Brotherhood. For the leaders were giving to each member according to his need—the sick, the healthy, the workers, the youth, the children—so that no one lacked in food, drink, or clothing. This same policy was extended to all newcomers who entered the communities. The reason why each minister had a private room was that it served as an office where the needs of the people could be cared for through planning and counseling.[20]

### Article Four: Concerning Marital Separation between Believers and Unbelievers

The question of the nature of marriage was a constantly recurring issue, as a result of the highly successful Hutterian mission program. There were cases where only one spouse moved to Moravia to join the Hutterites. This of course precipitated a family crisis, ending in separation of the spouses. In the late 1570s the Hutterites noted this problem as needing basic attention and included it as one of the five fundamental themes of the Great Article Book. In 1568 Leonhard Dax explained the Hutterian position on marriage and separation in his Rechenschaft given at Alzey.[21]

In 1567 the Swiss Brethren also charged the Hutterites with breaking up marriage by accepting into the Brotherhood one marriage partner only. To this charge the Hutterites responded at length in Article Four, adding some charges of their own. The Hutterites, recalling the straits of the church during the early Christian era when Christians were called God-robbers and child-murderers, could only affirm that the world could remain the world if it so desired, but the church was to be faithful to its heritage. When a person converted to a godly way of living, but the spouse remained recalcitrant and bitter, then there was justification for separating rather than compromising, for separation was in such cases the only means of obeying God more than man (Acts 5:29). Yet they wanted the Swiss to know that mixed marriages were definitely permitted within the Hutterian Brotherhood, for non-Hutterite spouses lived with the Hutterite spouses, sometimes for long periods of time. Only when it became apparent that more harm resulted than good was there cause for disciplinary action on the part of the Brotherhood (2 Corinthians 13). If the unbeliever was won in this manner, it was well and good, otherwise the Brotherhood was free before God, and without guilt.

Children were also taken into consideration in the problem of mixed marriages. Through proper discipline and training they were to be taught in the fear of God and kept from the ways of arrogance, evil, and carnality (Genesis 8; Proverbs 23). If the unbelieving spouse did not stand in the way of such training, a mixed marriage was permitted; for through the diligence of the believer, the children could find salvation (Ecclesiasticus 1; 4). The Hutterites noted in detail their views on rearing children:

> If believers are not permitted to raise their children as they desire, but rather must tolerate having their children mix with the heathen children, sticking feathers in their hats, going dancing or into the houses of idolatry, and growing up just like the world, become obdurate, not caring any more for the believers; then, if they come and ask for advice, complaining that they can no longer live with their spouse in good conscience, ... you [Swiss Brethren] would nevertheless say you had done your duty faithfully by keeping them together.... Oh, you of little understanding!
> Look at the tanner's wife at Oberwisternitz, who had an ungodly evil husband who hit her nine times in one day. When she came to complain to your people as a member and sought counsel, she was sent home without any other judgment.... Ought you not to have exercised a judgment?

The effect of ungodly wives upon the rearing of children was also noted in graphic detail:

> With time, one sees clearly how it turns out. They allow the children their own way, out of carnal love. They run around with others on the streets, even go gambling. They go to the "temple," go dancing, and are found wherever anything impertinent is in the making, according to the ways of youth. They stick feathers on their hats, carry weapons, and all this before their father's eyes. If he wants to have peace in the house, he dare not utter a peep. He has the name of the head of the household, but the unbelieving wife and the children rule. In addition their wives often have their children taken into the "house of idolatry" and puddle-bathed with infant baptism. And the father is supposedly a brother! He looks through his fingers or helps himself out with excuses as best he can. That settles the matter and he remains unpunished, just as before. And like others of his brethren, he finally takes comfort in the fact: "Oh, I am not the only one; my brothers must bear it even more! I am bound to my wife, cannot and dare not become separated." So it goes.... Through this so-called freedom [of lukewarmness (Revelation 3)] in which you take comfort, you rise so high in knowledge (which we consider inappropriate) that you are no longer

shocked even if your children do not follow after you—it is enough that they are raised in the flesh.[22]

Another incident that the Swiss Brethren charged against the Hutterites concerned a woman whom they permitted to visit her banned husband so that she could fulfill her relationship to him as a wife, but when she returned, she was not considered as a sister. Although this incident was not known to the Hutterite brethren who were responding to the Swiss, they could only hope that the husband and wife had not been treated as the Swiss described the situation, but rather that the wife's disciplining had been due to other causes.

The charge was also made that the Hutterites had narrow bedrooms, and that this led to immorality. The Hutterites acknowledged the close conditions in many Haushaben but disavowed the truth of the second charge. Hutterian bedrooms, we have already noted, were indeed often little more than beds in a large room, with cloth partitions as the only means of separating the various married couples. The Hutterites explained that although the practice of having such small bedrooms was not ideal, it was a temporary solution to the problem of providing housing for the constant flow of immigrants into the Brotherhood. Single men and women, it was underscored, were carefully separated, and all means were used to maintain good order throughout all the Haushaben. The Hutterites commended the matter to God, knowing that those with godly hearts did not stoop to such carnality as had been implied in the Swiss charge. They also granted, however, that for the wanton and loose-minded individuals, no amount of precautions would insure order and discipline.

Another Swiss charge, that the Hutterites took wives away from their spouses and in effect led them into captivity, gave rise to a Hutterian admonition that the Swiss look at themselves to see whether the wrong types of freedom were not rampant in their midst, causing their own downfall; it even seemed as if the Swiss at times were more concerned with keeping an individual from joining the Hutterian Brotherhood than they were about that person's religious welfare.

Given such attitudes and actions, the Hutterites could only interpret the Swiss concern for a greater unity between the two brotherhoods as paradoxical in the light of their negative criticism, which even accused the Hutterites of acting against God. On the other hand, the Hutterites had never criticized the Swiss in this manner, but rather prayed that God might enlighten them. Furthermore they said they were with great hesitation including the examples of various failings within the Swiss brotherhood, and did so now only because the Swiss had openly and maliciously criticized the Hutterites.

Three of these examples tell something of the Hutterian concern. There was one Hutterite woman who, before joining the Brotherhood, had lived for seven years with a man at Harrgart. She had never promised to marry him, nor did the Swiss unite them in marriage, yet the Swiss considered both as members during this time, allowing the two to dwell together. Although the Swiss had disciplined the man, they never banned him. The woman was baptized into the Swiss Brotherhood after which point the two still remained together. This came as a direct testimony of the woman herself.

Another incident took place in the Netherlands. Jan Nelusen, a charcoal burner, had made Katarina from Hullert pregnant. Although the Swiss had banned him, they neither separated the two nor united them in marriage but continued to consider her as a sister even while she continued to live with him as before.

A third case was that of a courtier at the Castle of Landtskron who raped a girl during the absence of his wife. The girl's sister Susanna spoke to the man about his actions. He was said to have answered approximately: "Oh, if you had been with me in her place, I would have done the same to you." Such actions could only be defined as carnal boldness and were a disgrace in the eyes of the Hutterites. What was worse from the Hutterian view was that the Swiss still held the man as a brother.

The Hutterites noted furthermore that few single persons who converted to Hutterianism from among the Swiss Brethren had been found without impurity in their lives. Although such impurity also happened at times among the Hutterites—there were always weeds growing next to good wheat—individuals were held accountable for their acts, and disciplined. Such action was apparently not a part of the Swiss Brethren discipline, however, for from the reports of incoming individuals there was little admonition about such sins. There were even youth who had grown up among the Swiss Brethren who confessed that they had never heard that such looseness was wrong. Consequently they had continued such actions while among the Swiss.

Therefore the Hutterites in all honesty could only conclude that the Swiss lacked Christian discipline, as exemplified in Christ and the early church: the dying to the old self and the lusts thereof, a renewed spirit lived out in true righteousness and holiness, and the outworking of love as exemplified in the original Jerusalem community.

As for marriage, the Hutterites maintained that wives were subject to their husbands; the husband as the stronger member functioned as head, and the wife as the weaker member lived for his honor, leading the way to God (Ephesians 5; 1 Peter 3). In this way she could also share with her husband in the grace of the Lord and become saved. Yet both partners were to take human weakness into account (1 Corinthians 7) and not react in an unreasonable manner against the spouse.

The Hutterites considered these tenets of Christian living essential to brotherhood. Not everyone had the same gifts. The divine Word effected belief and bound and led the godly to the point where their souls could find rest and be kept unspotted. To this end they must live in a brotherhood and community patterned after the Apostolic church. Since the Swiss also favored a voluntary fellowship, the Hutterites felt they ought to fulfill it correctly. But without order it would have little effect.

Returning to the theme of marriage and marital separation, the Hutterites affirmed that separation of partners was not unscriptural if, out of reasons of conscience, after repeated attempts to bring the unbeliever to repent, a believer found it necessary to leave the unbelieving spouse. Such separation, the Hutterites believed, was in line with the teachings of Christ.

But the Hutterites professed having experienced few such cases; they generally permitted mixed marriage, for it was only natural even in mixed marriages that the unbelieving partner loved the believer and desired to remain with the spouse until death. Where this did not lead to positive ends, however, the believer was obliged to obey God (Matthew 11:25 ff.; Luke 16:13) and with all seriousness resist weakness. The goal was, of course, marriage in the Lord, with the partners in his will and to his honor. Such a marriage was truly blessed by God.

It must, of course, be admitted that we have here only a Hutterian interpretation of the Swiss Brethren charges. Since the original letter as well as the Swiss reply to Walpot's charges are presumably forever lost, it is impossible to compare the tone of letters. As far as is known, the Swiss had no opportunity to reply to the charges of those from within their midst, some no doubt disgruntled, who had left with the intention of joining the Hutterites. It would be unfair not to note that the Swiss presumably could also have returned an apologia, countering the Hutterian charges. In fact, the Hutterite missioner Paul Glock, for one, took exception to some of the charges made in the Seven Articles, admonishing Walpot to be careful in evaluating the complaints of Hutterite converts from the Swiss. Indeed, the Hutterites might well have taken more to heart their own proverb which forms the epilogue to this very article: "Do not find fault before you investigate; first consider, and then reprove" (Ecclesiasticus 11:7).[23]

## Article Five: Concerning Children and Youth

The place of children in the gathered believers church needed a radical redefinition by both the Hutterites and the Swiss Brethren. The latter had heard many secondhand reports about the Hutterian philosophy of education; now it was time for the Hutterites to respond first-hand with a fuller picture of the Hutterian school system, their views on the upbringing of children, and how Hutterite youth were won to the Christian faith. The Hutterites presented first their biblical interpretation of how to raise children in the fear of the Lord and then the significance of this for the Hutterian situation.

The Hutterites believed that God desired to bless both child and adult. Of course children in their state of innocence were saved. However, when did they come to the point of knowing how to differentiate between good and evil, the process of passing from the state of ignorance into the state of understanding? A daily program of biblical instruction was presupposed, both to lead Hutterite children to that point of being able to differentiate between good and evil, as well as to lead the believing youth into a deeper faith (Romans 10:17). To implement this goal, an orderly context was needed, for God, who "arranged all things by measure and number and weight," operated within an ordered situation (Wisdom of Solomon 11:20). The Hutterian philosophy of education also included the ideas of protecting children from the ways of evil, breaking them of their selfish ways, and continuously implanting into them elements of godly living.

Such a teaching program, the Hutterites believed, had always been a part of the brotherhood pattern, where children were raised with a discipline and protected from sins. This was most certainly in line with Old Testament practice, where the command was given that children were to be taught diligently, with discipline (Deuteronomy 6; 11; Proverbs 13; Ecclesiastes 7; 30); it was also New Testament precept (Ephesians 6; Colossians 3). The Hutterites desired to remain within this pattern which they believed had been maintained by the godly throughout history.

For their school teachers, the Hutterites selected personnel who held no favorites, whose talents lay in the keeping and training of children, and who generally served well in the teaching function. Even the unbelievers from the world bore witness to the effectiveness of the Hutterian school system. Some of the nobility sent their children into Hutterian schools to be given good instruction and protected from the evils which they would otherwise experience on the streets. The Hutterian schools were known far and wide, it was noted, even attracting children from other lands, some of whom did not understand German. They remained all winter, and when they went home, it was only for a short reunion with their families, after which they again returned to school.

The Hutterites compared their system of education to the work of a tailor, who had good cloth and wanted to make it into a garment but was ill-taught in the art of cutting it. He did not consider it a disgrace to give the cloth to someone who could cut it out better. Such was the case for the children of believers, who gladly entrusted their children to the care of specialists. For if unbelievers took advantage of the educational opportunity accorded the children in Hutterian schools, believers had all the more reason to support the program.[24]

Hutterite parents, contrary to Swiss rumor, were permitted to see their children at any time, as long as it did not interfere with the work schedules of the Brotherhood. Furthermore, many parents were glad to be relieved of the daily tasks and problems within the family, happy that their children were well cared for both day and night, each according to his or her needs, whether healthy or sick. Each school was run by as many sisters as were found to be needed to carry on the program adequately. Of course there was sickness but sickness was universal. If it pleased God to keep the children healthy, he protected them. If he desired to take them in their innocence through death, this too was within his power. For God knew what was best for all mortals. Some died at a young age, some in old age (Romans 5; Wisdom of Solomon 14).

The Hutterites loved their children and attempted to maintain the best conditions possible within the schools. They denied the Swiss charges that Hutterian schools were pitiful places; the many visitors of all classes lauded the entire system, including the method of discipline. The children were of course taught to honor their parents even after they grew up. That the children had no money of their own proved to be no problem in that the Brotherhood provided all their physical needs.

The Hutterites were not at all pleased with the Swiss Brethren idea that a child ought to learn and experience something about the world, working among its people in order to better adapt themselves in their faith within the world. They noted that some Swiss Brethren ministers, such as Bühle and Feyachs, even allowed their children to enter heathen schools which practiced only wordly foolishness. Some Swiss children were allowed to work in the services of the "world people." For some this was not a financial necessity, but for others it was the only way to meet expenses, since other Swiss Brethren did not take them into their services. Indeed, such a procedure demonstrated how little regard the Swiss had for their children's salvation. For children were much more influenced by their environment than older people, not being able to differentiate between their left and right, as to good and evil (Jonah 4; Deuteronomy 1). In the same manner that they were led, they also learned and acted. For a child was just as apt to grasp for tinkling bells as for the good apple. Therefore the same Swiss, who demanded direct scriptural reference from the Hutterites to support the communal way of child upbringing, themselves permitted or even commanded their own children to be sent into the world in order to grow and be taught in heathen schools. There were children who went to dances, entered state churches, and participated in many types of worldly activities for which the Hutterites could find no biblical precedent. True, many Swiss were dismayed at the consequences of such liberties, but neither the parents nor their brotherhood had the power to carry through with a correct discipline. Even the heathen could judge such undisciplined disobedience as unbecoming and abominable.

The Hutterites acknowledged that an infant inherited through his natural birth the tendency to unrighteousness. Yet given their views on freedom of the will, they were of the opinion that if godly people dealt correctly with the children, not being too soft or too hard with them, then insubordinate children would carry their own judgment—along with Esau of Old Testament days—unless they returned later in repentance to a godly life.[25]

The protection of children played a large role in the Hutterian philosophy of education. We have come to sense something of the nature of this protectionism, which placed the responsibility of child-raising upon the parents during the first few years, then directly upon the shoulders of the Brotherhood when the children entered the kindergarten at the age of two or three. The Hutterites sometimes referred to the biblical reference that children do not bear the guilt of their parents (Ezekiel 18:20). One cannot help but believe that the Hutterian system of the nurture of children allowed, to a greater degree than within the small family pattern, certain children to rise above the sometimes scarred background of some of their parents.

### Article Six: Concerning Taxes

The printed Brotherhood Rechenschaft of the Hutterites, also known to the Swiss Brethren, clearly laid down the Hutterian position against payment of war taxes, a position against which the Swiss reacted. Although the Hutterites saw no need to repeat the same arguments, they did see one aspect of the question posed by the Swiss which merited further clarification, namely, how it was possible to take exception to the payment of war taxes, when the punishment of evildoers—even the shedding of blood—was the legitimate function of the magistracy.

The Hutterites affirmed at the outset that without exception the magistracy was ordained by God (Romans 13; Wisdom of Solomon 6) especially for people who walked outside of Christ's divine law. Herein lay the duty of the magistracy: to hinder bloodshed and to protect the rights of all people. Furthermore, in order to carry out its function of insuring order and discipline, it could justifiably demand the payment of taxes.

The godly, on the other hand, lived on the basis of another norm, the law of the Spirit (Romans 8; 1 Corinthians 9). This however did not abrogate natural law for the Christian, except for the aspects that violated the Christian conscience. However, God himself limited the law of the magistracy. For God was the Highest Power, Lord over both natural and spiritual law (Wisdom of Solomon 1; Daniel 4; 5).

But what were the limits of magisterial power? The Hutterites believed that this was set forth in God's original ordering of creation. Every magistrate was to remain in the region where God placed him to rule, effecting a common peace for all citizens, yet not transcending those bounds with warfare nor looking with jealous eyes to the lands of other princes. To those magistrates who transcended their rightful bounds, taxes could rightfully be denied. The Hutterites cited history as a witness to the consequences when princes and kings violated the natural laws of creation. God allowed them to be overthrown with horrible rage, sometimes even by a still more ungodly people. This was where the Turks were possibly fitting into God's history.

The Hutterites, although not quite sure of the facts, believed that earlier in their history the Swiss Brethren had held to a similar position of not paying war taxes, not even for war against the Turks. Then at a later point, the Swiss decided to make the question of war tax payments an individual matter, which opened the door to a basic shift in Swiss practice. Finally members were advised to give hangman's taxes, and at least one Swiss member, Herman, an old tailor from Kertdorf, was actually banned for sixteen years because of his convictions against the payment of "blood taxes." On the other hand, Ludwig Drächsler of Kertdorf was not banned when he willingly paid taxes for a war against the emperor.

The Swiss, in their communication to the Hutterites, also had affirmed that if taxes were used for such ungodliness as fornication, adultery, gambling, drinking, and gluttony, then the taxes should not be paid. The Hutterites replied that on this basis alone war taxes should not be paid, for there was never a war which did not include these and greater evils.

One last Swiss argument for payment of war taxes was founded on their interpretation of the writings of Michael Sattler. The Hutterites could not accept this view, based upon Sattler's having confessed that if war were correct, he would rather fight against would-be Christians than against the Turks, for Turks were "Turks" according to the flesh, whereas would-be Christians were "Turks" according to the spirit who murdered true Christians. Since Sattler had not given credence to either warring party, the Hutterites reasoned, he must have taught still less that one should give war taxes against the Turks.

The Hutterites could not go along with the obvious inconsistency they perceived between refusing to bear arms and at the same time giving money willingly to help others bear arms. For the very nature of godly people did not allow participating in such wrong doings, either in direct physical action, or in financial support. It was God and God alone who "wrought desolation in the earth." (Psalm 46:8).[26]

### Article Seven: Concerning Avoidance

The last article was a final Hutterian attempt to communicate to the Swiss Brethren what were the basic issues separating the two brotherhoods. To do this the Hutterites first noted what Christianity meant for them.

True Christianity is not founded upon great formulations about faith, nor upon the depths of great knowledge (2 Peter 2:20; 2 Corinthians 13:5; Titus 1:1; Jude 1:3). Instead, genuine Christianity results whenever the true love of God pours forth in faith. It results in a Christian quality of life, empowered by the Holy Spirit, a quality and power given to all believers who are members of Christ's body, the church. Such Christianity is fulfilled only when a people of Christ submits to God in righteousness, dies to the old life, and is renewed in the Holy Spirit. Church discipline is the tool effecting a godly life (Matthew 18:15-20), which stands in absolute enmity with evil and injustice (Romans 6; Ephesians 1; 4; John 3; 16; 2 Peter 1; Galatians 5; 6). The end result is a true community ruled by God which dwells in peace and unity.[27]

But in the eyes of the Hutterites, the Swiss Brethren were not a unified brotherhood, and consequently, in view of their constant splintering and a slow but sure drifting away from their original vision, exercising no Christian discipline, the Hutterites could simply not accept them as a genuine people of God. Three and even four splinter groups resulted from disagreement on even just one small article of doctrine, each banning the other. They were admitting merchants into their midst. Some of them wore protective armor, which was but a short step to using weapons of revenge. Even one of their own ministers, Galus of Odenkirchen, had written disparagingly of the changes within the Swiss Brotherhood, that "whoever has lost a Swiss in or among the world can never find him again."[28] As a consequence, even though the Swiss still considered themselves to be a people of Christ which had died to the world and sin, the Hutterites considered them a people which drank deeply of the world, entered into strife, and did not care for the needs of their brethren. They even accused the Swiss of sounding Lutheran at one point—doing evil that good might come (Romans 3:8). Furthermore, for the Swiss to affirm, "I have prayed to the Lord, and he has forgiven me," was not sufficient; Matthew 18:15-20 and 1 John described it differently; a brother who had sinned was to be punished.

In their communication to the Hutterites, the Swiss were seemingly searching for means of closer cooperation with the Hutterites. But the Hutterites could not understand such a desire when the Swiss at the very same moment were castigating the Hutterites in the manner of the world, becoming so worked up that some of their brethren even turned to fighting with their fists. In the presence of some Hutterites, Christof of Pausram, a Swiss leader at Nikolsburg, had exercised such a fighting spirit and derision. The Hutterites likened all this to an impatient sick person in bed who cries for help, and then when help is offered, refuses it, only to lament later that no one wanted to come and help.

The salt had indeed lost its savor among the Swiss, the Hutterites felt, and present realities needed to be faced. The Swiss were simply not true followers of Christ. The world remained the world, and the Hutterites avoided it; since the Swiss leaders were part of this world, the Hutterites were therefore to avoid them in eating, drinking, working, buying and selling.[29]

## The Conclusion

In their final paragraphs the Hutterites appended a last "speech" for the benefit of those Swiss seekers who heretofore had been ignorant of the facts about the Hutterites. It was hoped that clarity would result from the issues presented in the Seven Articles, so that no one could say he was uninformed, and that some would be saved.[30]

The expectations of the Hutterites were hardly fulfilled, as can be seen in the Great Chronicle entry for 1567:

[The Swiss Brethren] paid little or no attention to our answer, nor did they have it read to their brethren or congregations, so that it must be evidence of judgment to them on That Day rather than to a witness of improvement. A copy of our reply is still extant.[31]

We may legitimately ask to what degree the Hutterites were fair in their sometimes harsh appraisal of the Swiss Brethren. Fortunately, there is an in-group Hutterian criticism of this very document, written six years later, the details of which are presented below.

## Dialogue Between a Hutterite and a Swiss Brother

One episode in the long prison experience of Paul Glock was his encounter with a Swiss Brethren prisoner, Leonhard Sommer. Sommer, a mason by trade, came from Necklinsberg (near Asperglen) in Württemberg. For some four or five years he had lived among the Swiss Brethren in Moravia, and it was probably for this reason that he was known to the Hutterites. Sommer was active in winning others to the Anabaptist cause. He also openly criticized the established church, convinced that Protestant church practices stemmed from the devil. Because of his Anabaptist beliefs and activities, he was imprisoned in Württemberg, at Winaden (Winnenden) during the 1550s, and at Esslingen in the early 1560s.[32]

Sommer was married, but had not been able to convince his wife to change her faith. Although he did not judge her for her beliefs, he felt compelled to separate himself from the Protestants and to move into another religious environment, for it bothered him, after leaving the church services Sunday after Sunday, to see preacher and congregation alike engage in acts of pride, dancing, gambling, drunkenness, and gluttony.

In 1571 Sommer attended the renowned Frankenthal Disputation. According to the printed Protocoll of that event, he played a minor role, speaking only once about the relationship between the Old and New Testaments. Sommer also wrote a hymn which survives, to be discussed below. Around February 1573, Sommer experienced the fate of many Anabaptists: imprisonment from which only death some eleven months later would free him.

The encounter between Glock and Sommer was not a happy one, mainly because Glock believed that Sommer held the Hutterites in contempt and slandered them. Nevertheless, Glock recognized the kinship between the two brotherhoods, which impelled him to press for further discussion with Sommer.[33]

In a series of three letters to Peter Walpot, our only source of knowledge about this dialogue, Glock recounted a rather wide range of issues that were discussed. Although the two met but rarely during the ten or eleven months Sommer was imprisoned in Hohenwittlingen, they did manage to share views about the nature of Christianity. Unfortunately, the picture is one-sided, since Sommer appears to the reader only through the eyes of a Hutterite. Yet Glock's letters are at least an attempt at objectivity, and in the end he even warned his own Brotherhood not to criticize the Swiss without just and proven cause, a mistake sometimes made in the past, for the Swiss were not as bad as their reputation among the Hutterites. In the give-and-take of these discussions both the weaknesses and strengths of the Swiss position emerged, even as did those of Glock's own views.

Because differences in beliefs were intensified by personal affront, the account of the dialogue will be presented largely as Glock recorded it for Walpot, with no attempt to separate the narrative from the issues discussed.

One issue that haunted Glock was the question whether thieves, upon repentance, were obliged to return the stolen goods. Sommer said yes; Glock, tied to a system where this in some cases would have been difficult to carry out, thought carefully and searched the New Testament for an answer, but found no passages where Christ demanded that converts return stolen goods. He presented his thinking on the subject in detail to Walpot, and asked him for correction if he was wrong or if he did not understand the problems involved, so that he could discuss the subject with Sommer more in line with Hutterian beliefs.

Sommer could give a quick answer to this problem because the economic structure of the Swiss Brethren was based on individual earnings. The Hutterites on the other hand considered even a merchant's gain as robbery and would have found it difficult to require new converts to return such profits to the original owner. Even so, it should be noted that Glock's position does not necessarily reflect a typical Hutterian view of theft. No other known source speaks to the problem, and Glock himself was not sure of his position.

Glock became so involved in the issue that he finally wrote a note to Sommer expressing willingness to learn from a non-Hutterite brother. The note begins:

> Dear Leonhard, I remember our conversation about evildoers, and the more I reflect, the more I marvel that you, who are considered to be such a wise man by your brotherhood, are not better able to state whether it is a sin or not. Now I am moved to ask you further, that I may arrive at a more correct understanding, in case I have erred. . . .[34]

Then follow Glock's reflections on the matter. Sommer, he claimed, had changed his mind about the need to return stolen goods, and supposedly told Glock the subject ought not to have been broached in the first place and that he no longer held to his position. However, upon receiving the note, Sommer turned against Glock so harshly that Glock could hardly sleep for two nights on account of the vexation this caused, even among the castle corps of magistrates and their servants.

Glock had also lent Sommer the printed Brotherhood Rechenschaft but Sommer considered its contents as merely human invention, not based upon the gospel. He especially condemned the Hutterian rearing of children, saying that Glock could not prove from Scripture that children should be taken from parents and placed into schools. In a separate report to Moravia which no longer exists Glock listed other matters about which Sommer had "scolded and raved." Glock then summed up Sommer's attitude: "He has a thoroughly bitter heart full of gall, with many lies which he has picked up."

In an attempt to resolve the disagreements, Glock asked Sommer to write down all the harsh charges which he held against Glock, for which he would supply pen and paper if necessary, and Glock would send them to the Hutterites—or Sommer could even have the Swiss Brethren take up the argument, and send their answer to the Hutterites—in order that truth might finally emerge. Glock challenged Sommer that if the latter were the zealot and witness of God as he boasted, he would write. If the charges were correct, Sommer's criticisms would be a just punishment, disgrace, and humiliation upon Glock before God; if the charges were mendacious, they would bring punishment on Sommer, either on earth or in eternity. If Sommer refused to write, he would deserve to be labeled a lazy, disrespectful slanderer.

Sommer refused to write. A maid at the prison, one of the many who had learned about the dispute, judged that Glock must therefore have been more upright than Sommer. He supposedly rejected the challenge on the ground that he could see well enough how Glock had been led astray. Glock considered this a slanderous remark which he would not accept. He told Walpot that slander was Sommer's main talent, adding: "Whatever is being said defaming our faith I shall not accept in faith. On that you can depend!"

Glock's letter of April 1573 shows that he was an able debater. He could hold his own, not only against the ministers and doctors of Scripture of the established church, but also—probably too forcibly—against brethren of a different cast. Sommer, who was soon to succumb to his malady, may already have been suffering physically, for he proved no match for Glock.

At Glock's request Walpot wrote to Sommer, sending him a copy of the lengthy Hutterian answer to the Swiss Brethren, composed in 1567. The book, with a letter, arrived in the early spring of 1574, but Leonhard Sommer had died during the preceding Christmas season. Meanwhile, Glock had had further discussion with Sommer, this time on more positive, brotherly terms, with controlled tempers. This time, Glock seemed willing to listen and learn from Sommer, as can be seen from some of the questions Glock raised about certain Hutterian practices.

He wrote to Walpot about these concerns. He began his letter by saying that he had read the book of articles, and that it was a good report. Had he known that Walpot and the brothers had written a whole book about the alleged disorders of the Swiss Brethren, he would not have taken such great pains in thinking through the whole problem. Now he wanted to report new developments in the encounter under eight points.

First of all, Glock had spoken with Sommer about the Hutterian stand on marital separation and the causes which led to it. If the problem arose simply because an individual was lazy, or sluggish in his Christian walk, his case was presented to the Brotherhood for his own welfare. Such admonition often sufficed in correcting the weakness, but there were also other types of cases. Glock gave as an example the hypothetical case of a young sister who lives with an unbelieving husband.

The husband has the infant baptized. This happens once or twice, even though the sister disapproves. The third time the sister becomes pregnant, she leaves her husband, because infant baptism in her eyes is an abomination before God. Sommer replied that infant baptism did not hurt the child. Glock answered that Sommer was only indirectly correct; for as the children grew up, people would point out that they had already been baptized, and the children were thus led to believe they were already saved, in this manner being led astray.

Second, Sommer had reproached the Hutterites for their requirement that Hutterite converts sell all their possessions and move to Moravia. He believed that the Christian was justified in living within a non-communal economic system, in order to meet the needs of the many poor brethren living out in the world.

Third, Sommer had reproached the Hutterites for not returning the possessions of those who decided to leave the Brotherhood. Glock replied that many individuals had entered without a penny and that the property was needed for the support of the children and the infirm.

Fourth, Sommer thought it unjust that the Hutterites took the small children from their parents and put them into schools. Glock answered that the Swiss made idols of their children, not wanting to be separated from them, and asked:

> My dear man, where is the one heart, one soul, and one purse among you if you do not trust one another [as to the care of children]? Oh, the unholy brotherhood that they are![35]

Fifth, the Hutterites, according to Sommer, were raising their children so badly that while running errands they could not even deliver wine across the roads without being corrupted by it. When Glock said he had never experienced such a case, Sommer replied that it had happened during the 1540s. Glock answered that if once upon a time it had taken place, and improvement followed, what more could one ask; was it still to be held over one's head as a reproach?

Sixth, Sommer had criticized the practice of giving the ministers and the Diener der Notdurft better meals than the rest of the brethren. Glock answered that the people owed it to the leaders and showed him biblical references (probably 1 Timothy 5:17) to prove his point.

Seventh, the question of Leonhard Sailer's (Lanzenstiel's) morals had been raised.

Finally, Sommer charged the Hutterites with changing their position in the course of Glock's fifteen years of confinement. Glock admitted that Sommer had reproached the Swiss for the still greater degree of change within their brotherhood: there was no more persecution; some members were even dissolute, lazy and indolent; they had lost their first enthusiasm and love, and had thus become like the world. Glock attributed some of Sommer's remarks to his having had to endure persecution and imprisonment while other Swiss were not suffering.

Earlier in their discussions, Sommer and Glock had compared notes on the Incarnation, the former believing that Christ had not taken his flesh and blood from Mary. When Glock asked where Christ's flesh and blood came from, Sommer answered that it was inappropriate to discuss the incarnation in greater detail.

Sommer, according to Glock, did not accept the idea of original sin. Instead, he believed that sin arose as a consequence of law and effected itself only within the individual himself. This interpretation did not satisfy Glock, who we may assume held the current Hutterian view that original sin had indeed been a reality before Christ, but that Christ had changed this by reconciling all men to himself through his death. Consequently, in order to share again in Christ's redemption, a child needed to be born anew and submit to baptism only after he had come of age.

Glock related additional themes at random to Walpot. For example, to Sommer's questions about what the Hutterites would do had there been no passages in Acts referring to community of goods, Glock replied that they would then have had to share in the Swiss Brethren's chaotic congregational pattern. Glock, interestingly enough, did not follow other Hutterite apologists who attempted to prove that the communal system was a way, or at least an ideal, to be found in both the Old and New Testament eras. He simply presented Acts 2 and 4 as adequate reason for the Hutterian position. To this he added that if the Swiss could not respect Scripture, they could not be better than the world which also took from Scripture whatever it desired and closed its eyes to the rest.

The topic of merchandising was also discussed. The Hutterites firmly maintained that it was wrong to buy goods for the express purpose of resale. Sommer had related that in the Netherlands where much cheese was made, many Brethren could be found who did nothing but buy and sell foodstuffs. Glock was quick to pick up a chance remark of Sommer's that some Brethren in the Low Countries, questioning the ethics of merchandising, desired to change to other vocations. Sommer explained that the Swiss Brethren gave their members the freedom to continue in such vocations, provided, of course, that they would not cheat anyone. This Glock could not accept as being compatible with true Christianity. He cited Christ's act of expelling the merchants from the temple as reason enough for believing that all merchandising should be driven out from the house of God.

On the subject of paying taxes, Sommer had granted that taxes could be paid for mass, for the sextons, priests, and bell ringers. Even war taxes might be paid. Glock thought it improper to pay church taxes, which only went to false prophets, and war taxes, and added that the reason why the Swiss could remain so long in their lands was because they paid these very taxes, thereby making no distinction between what was pure and impure.

The two men also had compared ideas on prayer. Glock believed that the Christian should ask God to move the hearts and souls of the magistrates that they remain attentive to the physical needs of prisoners. For God held the hearts of all men in his hand and could move them like a river of water. Glock made it a practice to pray that God might move the magistrates' hearts positively, for strength to bear whatever might come, but above all, that God's good will might result. Sommer considered Glock's prayer pagan; only heathen prayed for temporal matters.

Glock's confrontation with Sommer raised still one more problem. Sommer had asked him whether the Hutterites also included three speakers in one worship service as did the Swiss Brethren, the second and third witnessing that the first and second had spoken according to the truth; Sommer produced biblical evidence to support his case. Glock could only answer that as far as he knew there was only one speaker in Hutterian services, a procedure which seemed better to him than two or three speaking in confusion. Glock later made a study of the theme, and noting the possible biblical precedent for the Swiss form of worship, he asked Walpot to exegete the pertinent passages (probably 2 Corinthians 13:1, and Acts 20:30), which point to the probability of worship services with more than one speaker.

Some statements Sommer made while under cross-examination in 1562 supplement Glock's account about the nature of Swiss worship patterns. The Swiss congregations in Württemberg had no bishops, and did not meet at the same place for their services, undoubtedly because of the constant danger of official harassment and imprisonment. They had no set pattern for their meetings, for the course of the service was determined by an inner conviction or concern within individual Brethren, which would lead them to speak out. Whoever felt called to speak would do so.[36]

## Significance of the Dialogue

Gradually the attitudes and views of Leonhard Sommer emerge from Glock's report. His comments indicate an idealization of the faith of an earlier Swiss generation, to which he still longingly looked back as the time of true Christianity under tribulation. Glock reflects none of this attitude. He seemed able to master each new situation as it arose, for he rarely sounded that note of despair which seemed to be the constant refrain with Sommer. The relationship between physical, mental, and spiritual well-being, and the ability to enjoy life will probably remain an open question. Yet during the Walpot Era, at least, the Hutterites were often, and Glock almost always, able to recognize the reality of the three score and ten years of this life and the joy which could come through godly living within a trusting brotherhood. Glock wanted to continue in life wherever he was, whether in prison or at home in the community, and to a large extent he found life satisfying, even if he needed to stretch the limits of the Brotherhood a bit in his fellowship with sympathetic non-Hutterites such as the Grafenecks who had taken Glock into their sphere of concern. Sommer, one of the last of a generation, was perhaps anticipating a martyr's death and truly saw a real change taking place among the Swiss Brethren—the rise of a new generation which would no longer fit into the former pattern of a martyr's life. Glock, not sharing Sommer's pessimism, remained confident about his

Brotherhood's steadfastness and about Walpot's ability in leading and preserving the Brotherhood.

Change within the two brotherhoods must have influenced the lives
and thoughts of Leonhard Sommer and Paul Glock. The will to live, which
Glock affirmed with vigor, seemed weaker in Sommer when the two
prisoners discussed the appropriateness of making demands upon the
magistracy. This very point, so sharply discussed by Glock and Sommer,
substantiates in large part two dissimilar attitudes as presented above about
martyrdom. Glock reported that Sommer called him a beggar for having
the audacity to demand from the magistracy whatever he felt he needed—
food, clothing, blankets, and other supplies—and said begging was a sin. If
the magistracy doled out goods without being asked, the goods could be accepted, but if it gave nothing, Sommer insisted, the Christian in need
should request assistance from his brotherhood. Glock, on the other hand,
maintained that as long as the magistrates kept an innocent Christian under
lock and key, they had the responsibility to fulfill the prisoner's needs, and
the prisoner in turn was responsible to make his needs known. If the
magistracy did not grant the necessities, divine judgment upon them would
be that much greater. Glock was confident that his position was correct, for
otherwise his Brotherhood would have counseled him differently.

In an ironic twist at the end of the Glock-Sommer episode, Glock mentioned that Sommer himself finally needed to beg for a maid, when, in dire
illness during the last fourteen days of his life, he could no longer help
himself. Glock was almost ready to interpret this as a divine punishment.

In the aftermath of these highly emotional encounters, some of which
portrayed a very humanly vulnerable Paul Glock, Glock had time to
evaluate the questions Sommer had raised. Adverse change during the
fifteen years of Glock's imprisonment might well have entered the brotherhoods: Sommer might have been right about his own brotherhood, and
even about the Hutterites. Glock consequently admonished Walpot to ap-
point strong leaders who knew how to lead orderly lives. For only with solid
leadership among the ministers, Diener der Notdurft, and those in charge
of the schools and households could order be maintained. He advised
Walpot about those individuals who came to the Hutterian communities
from another people, calling themselves brethren but reporting negatively
about their previous brotherhood. The Hutterites should not believe such
stories uncritically but should write the complaints down and send them to
the brethren in question to find out the facts. Walpot was also to inquire
why the individual had left, in order to judge the situation with better dis-
cretion.

Glock also wished to underscore that he was not worried about Walpot's procedure in handling the Swiss Brethren in 1567, for there had been reason for being critical. Yet at the same time, Glock warned that the Hutterites should not unjustly slander such groups as the Swiss Brethren, for such so-called brethren would then have all the more reason to slander the Hutterites. We note that since Glock had talked with Sommer, he was able to compare what he knew about the Swiss Brethren with the Hutterian critique as found in the book of Seven Articles. Thus Glock could pinpoint areas where the Hutterites did not quite understand the Swiss, and he therefore courteously admonished Walpot to tread carefully in making just such a judgment as could be found in the 1567 answer to the Swiss.[37]

One more word remains to be said about Leonhard Sommer, for he did not go down in Swiss Brethren history completely unknown and forgotten. One Swiss Anabaptist codex, rare, and not yet thoroughly studied, includes a hymn written by Sommer during his months in prison in Hohenwittlingen.[38]

In the poem, one notes the semi-pietistic mood, characteristic of the later Swiss Brethren, which stands in contrast to a more outgoing Hutterianism of the 1570s. Vestiges of an earlier Swiss Anabaptism are still evident, although the original Anabaptist idea of Gelassenheit has faded into an almost fatalistic resignation. A strong, offensive yieldedness to God was still a central reality for the Hutterites during the Walpot Era, tied of course to a community of goods and to a mutual yieldedness, one to another.

The poem also indicates a "martyr theology." But Sommer's longing for bygone days sets him apart from the martyrs of the 1520s. He was perhaps not a typical Swiss Anabaptist of his era. Indeed, he himself admitted that the "new generation" had fallen below the norms set by classic Anabaptism. Yet his witness is important in defining the nature of Swiss Anabaptism during the 1570s, an era which has lain largely in darkness. As a bridge between the first and second generations of the Swiss Anabaptists, Sommer held onto remnants of the first, but also displayed characteristics of a new generation which was slowly transforming itself into a type of pietism.[39]

# Ch.9

# Sixteenth-Century
# Hutterian Anabaptism
## --The Historical Question

Between 1528, when communal Anabaptism was born on the road to Austerlitz, and 1578, the year Peter Walpot died, lay a half-century of Hutterian history. It remains in this last chapter to interpret the Walpot Era within the larger setting of sixteenth-century Hutterianism, building and enlarging upon Chapter One, which sets Hutterianism within the broader perspective of Upper German Anabaptism of the 1520s and 30s. We want to note, through the history of ideas, the evolution of the original impetus into a strong second-generation manifestation of the original vision.

Although Jacob Hutter was not the first to dream the idea which later came to be known as Hutterianism, he brought unity and substance to the communal idea of brotherhood. During a span of three years, from 1533 to 1536, Hutter led the communal movement at Auspitz with a strong sense of divine calling and implemented an orderliness, that granted the Brotherhood a unity which has carried the movement through 450 years.

But Hutter was also an activist who dared to protest against injustice meted out by civil and ecclesiastical authorities. This note carried throughout sixteenth-century Hutterian history and is an important clue to the tenacity of the movement. Paul Glock exemplifies this fighting spirit, with his emphasis on obedience to God, and its sometimes necessary corollary, a defiant and conscious opposition to the world. Hans Arbeiter, Leonhard Dax, and many other missioners also were witnesses to both the obedience and the defiance which defines the relationship of the Christian to the two realms, the kingdom of God and the kingdoms and powers of the world. This spirit, given to the movement by Hutter, created a healthy self-affirmation which is still evident in twentieth-century Hutterianism.

In 1535, when violent persecution set in throughout Moravia, the Hutterian movement seemed doomed, for the Haushaben were forcibly broken up and the brethren dispersed. It is amazing that the movement did not die. That it held on was due in part to the fighting spirit of Jacob Hutter, who encouraged others to cling to their convictions; it was also due in part to another aspect of their faith in God's kingdom: the "tending of the gardens." The Hutterian concern to care for God's creation, the earth, made the brethren economically useful to the nobles; hence the nobles soon not only tolerated them again, but welcomed them back. Keeping the garden helped the Hutterites through many threatening times in their long history.[1]

## The Birth of the Hutterian Idea:
## The Legacy of Jacob Hutter

During these early years of consolidation amid social and political ferment, brotherhood *Ordnung* developed as a fundamental part of the idea of communal life. And although many Anabaptists stemmed from the spiritualistically inclined mission of Hans Hut and Hans Denck and their followers, they soon exchanged their quasi-individualistic views of Christianity for the stronger Anabaptist pattern of brotherhood unity and consensus. This transformation is most strikingly evident in the life and writings of Peter Riedemann. In his *Gmünden Rechenschaft*, Riedemann expresses the typical early spiritualistic interpretations of God's kingdom, the key to which is the Spirit of God working within the individual. This interpretation indicates a loosely organized Anabaptism, the only form possible in the face of the ruthlessness of the imperial policy of persecution. In fact a fuller development of God's kingdom on earth, as Hutter understood it, would have been impossible to achieve throughout much of Europe. Consequently Riedemann's early views of Anabaptism lack the strong, social vehicle necessary to carry a brotherhood movement.[2]

But Hutter did not build upon the spiritualistic idea of Austrian Anabaptism; in Moravia another option became viable, namely, the establishment of God's kingdom in the present world. This conviction, though not the form, stems from the Anabaptist conference at Schleitheim in 1527, and from the first Zurich Anabaptists, Conrad Grebel and Felix Mantz, who as early as 1524 recognized the historical realization of such a kingdom of God among the early Christians—a visible brotherhood of peace and love, a gathered church, conscious of the opposing reality of the world.[3] Hutter must have caught something of this brotherhood vision in

his Tirolean days through the work of George Blaurock, and then again at
Auspitz, where he found in embryonic form the Schleitheim concept of
peace and nonconformist living.[4]

Hutter died too soon to develop fully his views about God's kingdom
on earth, but it is evident existentially in his careful attention to establishing
a firm brotherhood Ordnung. Indeed, all the points of a kingdom-of-God
Christianity, as developed at Schleitheim, were integral to Hutterianism
from its inception.

## A Written Confession of Faith:
## The Legacy of Peter Riedemann

It is highly significant that the spiritualistic Peter Riedemann of the
1520s and 30s adopted the Schleitheim idea upon joining the Hutterites.
While in prison in Hesse in 1540-42 he found the time to write out a new
confession of faith which represented the brotherhood experience of all
Hutterites. The *Rechenschaft* centered in a vision, but a vision in large part
fulfilled; it was not the wishful thinking of an idealistic dream. It radiates
the experience of an already established group, and could not have been
written in its final form without the backing of the group, which confirmed
what Riedemann had written by publishing it as Part Two of the official
Brotherhood charter and confession of faith.[5]

Riedemann's *Confession of Faith* is a biblical vision of faith and life in
broad, bold sweeps, couched in seven parts. The two-kingdoms idea, basic
to the entire work, can be seen in the title of the opening section, "How
God Desires to Have a People Whom He Himself Has Separated from the
World and Chosen to Be His Bride." The second section is on the theme of
how the "House of the Lord Should Be Built Up in Christ," reminiscent of
Riedemann's earlier "How the House of God Is to Be Built, and What the
House of God Is."[6] But whereas the formulation of 1529 deals with a
spiritual house, defined in large part by the inner, individual aspects of effecting discipleship, the second formulation, 1541, is a new concrete for-
mula for the building up of the disciple within the *Gemeinde*.[7] The other
sections of the Confession further define Gemeinde and contrast it with
general society. The Confession ends on the same dualistic note with which
it begins.

Riedemann's Confession of 1541 is the most perfectly balanced
expression of Anabaptist faith to emerge during the sixteenth century and
deserves greater scholarly attention than it has received heretofore.[8] The
careful ordering of life on all levels is found in both the content and

development of the hundred-page confession. The author bases the necessity for such orderliness in all phases of life on God's way of acting in creation, as witnessed to in the Old Covenant and reestablished in the New Covenant in Christ, which will continue through all time.

## The Brotherhood Charter

No confession of faith in itself was enough to carry the Hutterian movement. The Brotherhood asked Riedemann to complement his *Confession of Faith* with a practical work, which became the official charter of the Hutterian Brotherhood. This verbalization of their socioeconomic as well as political-theological life was written after Riedemann returned to Moravia in 1542. It is now Part One of the Brotherhood *Rechenschaft*, and is composed of ninety short chapters generally of one or two pages each.[9] The growth of the Hutterian movement necessitated such a detailed charter which would permit a unity of life and spirit in all of the somewhat isolated communities scattered throughout Moravia and Slovakia. The Charter, based upon a definite concept of faith, was the foundation upon which Brotherhood fulfillment could take place, especially after the 1540s, during the "good years" when Brotherhood expansion and consolidation was not impeded by persecution. This unique Hutterian Charter also permitted a new level of relating to other non-Hutterian brotherhoods, in mission and in admonition.

Peter Riedemann, a spiritual giant among the Hutterites, died in 1556. His vision of existential Christianity will remain definitive as long as the original Hutterian idea, actualized within brotherhood, remains.

## Faith and Mission: The Legacy of Leonhard Dax

Fortunately for the Hutterian Brotherhood, shortly after Riedemann's death, Leonhard Dax converted to Hutterianism; his gifts were also highly useful for the new generation, in a new phase of the mission program. For it was Dax who developed the definitive Hutterian teaching on missions in the 1560s and 70s. Dax applied the Brotherhood *Rechenschaft* to the various mission fronts wherever Hutterite missioners ran into conflict with the established church. But whereas Dax drew together the Hutterian documents which related to the established churches (Catholic, Lutheran, and Calvinist), Peter Walpot addressed himself to the encounters with other brotherhoods (the Swiss and Polish Brethren). Most of these documents have already been noted, including the general "Noble Lessons and

Instructions" written with the Catholics in view; Dax's prison confession of faith of 1567/68 written with the Calvinists in mind; and a general writing, Dax's "Refutation" of 1561, relating to a Lutheran setting. The anonymous (but presumably in part the work of Dax) "Charges and Allegations" opens up another aspect of mission: protest and defiance. It begins with a dialogue between the world and the church, which Dax used in his "Refutation," and then launches out in an unusually strong and bitter invective.

This new Hutterian approach to missions was the result of a new attitude of the established churches toward heretics. Execution was no longer the only possible penalty, for the established church now attempted to convert heretics by lengthy and patient dialogue. Hence, the Hutterites had to understand the differences between their own beliefs and that of their antagonists. This new formulation was also needed to effect a unified mission message, and indeed, the main works, including "Noble Lessons," "Refutation," and that part of "Charges and Allegations" which is entitled "Concordance," were basically apologetic in nature, composed for seekers who came out of the established church milieu. However, these doctrinal writings also served the home front, for a way of life which was totally separate from the world demanded an apologetic reasoning process for the in-group, to validate its life pattern and also to define polemically its problems with the world. With the various other brotherhoods which the Hutterites encountered, differences were in large part sociological, and the Hutterites—generally correctly—based their criticism upon the lack of Ordnung within many of the groups, a disunity which militated against brotherhood consensus and peace. The Hutterites believed firmly that Ordnung—one important manifestation of God's Spirit at work—was essential to a strong kingdom of God in this present world.

## Vorsteher Peter Walpot: Brotherhood Coordinator

Leonhard Dax, who died in 1574, was the last creative Hutterite "theologian" of the century; his counterpart and needed complement was Peter Walpot, who defined for Hutterianism the sociological and economic questions of the nature of community, and combined them with an existential definition of Christianity.

Neither Dax nor Walpot was a prophet as Hutter had been. Nor was it their task to formulate a synthesis of the Hutterian idea, which Riedemann had performed so well. However, both Dax and Walpot were creative spokesmen who met the Brotherhood needs of their generation. Dax was the best Hutterite polemicist of his time. Walpot was the organizational genius, the implementer of social and economic ideas. As a team of authors, these brethren united their efforts in producing a large work entitled the Great Article Book (described below) presumably compiled in 1577 by Walpot, who made extensive use of Dax's literary legacy.

In 1578, the year Peter Walpot died, the Hutterites were still to a great extent in possession of their original vision, whereas the Swiss Brethren, as noted above, had lost something of theirs. What was it that allowed one group to contain much of its original Christian expression for so many decades but prevented another group from continuing its original program and substance?

The disintegrating factor, lack of Ordnung, correctly noted by the Hutterites as a major weakness among the Swiss Brethren, certainly undermined the original Swiss vision. But the wearing-down tactics of almost all magistrates (with the exception of those in Moravia), who harassed and persecuted the Swiss Brethren year-in, year-out, exerted an even greater demoralizing power upon the loosely organized Swiss Brethren movement, resulting in the loss of vitality and the development of quietism.

The Hutterites had avoided both these pitfalls. Through the labors of Jacob Hutter they had early reached consensus about the basic nature of Christian society, including Christian community founded upon total sharing of goods. Their confession of faith was set in the 1540s by Peter Riedemann, in the one and only volume the Hutterites found worthy of printing during the sixteenth century. The Brotherhood then continued to enjoy the fruits of a firm and incisive leadership under their third great Vorsteher, Peter Walpot, whose influence spanned the four decades of 1540-78. These three men provided the solid leadership a movement must have in order to remain stable and healthy.[10] Moravian toleration provided the social and economic base for the growth of Christian community.

But part of the original Hutterian vision was the outward look. The Hutterites continued to excel in service to the nobles and witness to the world. Decade after decade they carried on successful mission, and met its challenge well. They taught beggars, orphans, and newly arrived converts about hygiene, about working together, and indeed, about the whole Hutterian way of life which by the time of the Golden Years had already become a solid heritage upon which to build.

The missioners also provided the Brotherhood with a growing tradition of suffering mixed with victory, where God demonstrated his power in the face of the whole world. The list of martyrs grew; so did the number of tales and exciting experiences of returning missioners. One senses the eagerness of the Hutterites, waiting to hear the inspiring tales which the missioners told about their trying circumstances. The Hutterian story of the Walpot Era is not complete without this mission perspective. But mission also provided the Brotherhood with new expressions of the meaning of faith; the large dogmatic works produced in the 1560s were built largely upon a "theology in action" which resulted from encounters with the world.

It was doubtless their growing awareness of the power of the written word that led the Hutterites to compose in the 1570s a simplified yet comprehensive answer to the world, this time with a full-blown polemical dimension added to the apologetic note found in the earlier Hutterian writings. Hutterian thought patterns during the late Walpot Era center in this new level of thought, captured in two large documents: the Great Article Book and "Charges and Allegations."

## The Great Article Book: The Second-Generation Simplification of Idea

During the first generation of the Hutterian movement, the memory of Jacob Hutter lived on in the minds of all Hutterites. They were conscious of a heritage in the making, and their archives were gathering correspondence, prison confessions, and various Brotherhood documents. But the early history of Hutterianism remained unwritten even during the time of Riedemann and into the Walpot Era. The printed *Confession* and charter carried the movement through the 1540s and 50s, serving well in maintaining order and granting direction within an ever-expanding Brotherhood. But after forty years, the need for a different approach to their heritage became evident. The original members of the movement were dying of old age, and with them that knowledge which was so strong in the minds of these older brethren was also in danger of dying out. A new level of Hutterian literature was needed, to meet the needs of a second generation of brethren who at best had dim memories of Hutterian origins. The new question being asked was, how can a movement perpetuate itself?

It is here that Peter Walpot made his great contribution. Highly gifted as an organizer, he helped to consolidate Hutterian life and thinking on an entirely new level. Walpot established a new center at Neumühl.[11] Here the several levels of Hutterian life and organization merged, the cultural, the communal, the socioeconomic, and the educational, all within the context of God's kingdom, separate from the world.

The aging brother, Kaspar Braitmichel, was appointed to organize the correspondence and documents, and establish an official chronicle so that the heritage of the Hutterites would not be lost;[12] an awareness of their history as a part of the ongoing history of the New Covenant was necessary for the preservation and promotion of the spirit of unity. This brotherhood spirit of unity was constantly threatened, and was therefore constantly and victoriously worked at. Because the Hutterites believed that fulfillment of the kingdom of God was contingent upon a careful attending to the (political) business of kingdom building, whether spiritual, economic, or social, they worked on all these levels under the outstanding leadership of Walpot. The outcome was a continuation of the Golden Years throughout the rest of the century.

The Hutterian spirit of unity, which centered in the Brotherhood Rechenschaft, also needed renewed attention in the 1570s in view of the proliferating number of confessions of faith originating with missioners imprisoned during the mid-century decades. New questions were being asked, the answers to which were to be found scattered among a score of written confessions. These documents provided the Brotherhood with information about the essential points in Hutterianism which were significant in both the mission program for seekers as well as in defense of the faith in the encounter with the world and its prisons. Yet the scatteredness of these answers in itself was confusing. Upon analyzing the documents that were gathering, the Hutterites identified five themes that continued to surface within the confessions and needed constant defending, and therefore seemed basic to the idea of Hutterianism. Four of these issues were basic to the preservation of the Brotherhood: believers' baptism, the Lord's Supper, community of goods, and the relationship of church and state. A fifth issue arose from the mission program: the question of existing marriages between Hutterite converts and their non-Hutterite spouses.

The Great Article Book became the synthesizer and simplifier, in a format which all brethren could understand—five articles, around which the fundamental Hutterian truths were built. This approach stands in direct contrast to John Calvin's monumental system of dogmatics, which could hardly be understood by the average church member. Since the Hutterites were not intellectually oriented, a simpler vehicle was needed to carry their faith and beliefs. Within this new, composite confession could be seen the thought of the more profound Dax, Arbeiter, and Glock, as well as that of less articulate brethren such as Uhrmacher, Geyersbühler, and Klampferer. The ideas of the Great Article Book were therefore comprehensible rather than bewildering to the members of the Hutterian Haushaben, whether they were members of long-standing or recent converts. The writing of such a composite work was made possible, it should be noted, by the rich archival resources of the Neumühl center.

This book-length document has both beauty and depth. Its beauty does not consist in a balanced polished prose, but rather in its mood, mirroring a brotherhood which both affirmed itself, and was not afraid to accost critically the whole world. Written in simple biblical language, it bears witness that Christianity is a way of life where mind and action relate integrally and where both are colored by the message and acts of Jesus and fulfilled in the spirit of Jesus, who lives on in the community gathered in his name.

The Great Article Book of the Hutterites reflects a new level within Hutterian history, which also parallels general European history of the 1570s and 80s: the age of confessionalism, and of a beginning orthodoxy. By sifting through the correspondence and confessions of faith, and integrating them historically in the Great Chronicle and systematically in the Great Article Book, the Brotherhood found its "orthodox" position; by placing themselves in historical perspective they could contrast themselves to other religious movements. By the 1570s, the truth as interpreted by all the Reformation movements was fully developed into a system, whether Lutheran, Calvinist, or Anabaptist. The Five Articles of the Great Article Book were the Hutterian synthesis of this era.[13]

The title of the Great Article Book in English translation reads: "A Beautiful, Joyful Book Containing a Number of the Main Articles of Our Christian Faith, Made by Compiling Much Godly Evidence; Also How the World has Perverted [The Christian Faith], and Lives and Strives Against It."[14] The work is prefaced with a Hutterian adage which incisively sets the mood of the whole work:

> It is absolutely crazy and fundamentally wrong that a physician, a shoemaker, a weaver, and every artisan may each defend his vocation, but a Christian dare not express the grounds of his religion, or justify the same.[15]

The introduction emphasizes the idea of brotherhood by noting the comprehensive unity which the writers of the Bible delineated for God's people. There is to be

> one body, one Spirit, one hope of our calling, one Lord, one faith, one baptism, one God and Father of us all, who exists above all of us, through all of us, and in all of us. There is only one way; one truth; one life; one teaching of Christ; one gospel; one table of the Lord; one door; one gate; one shepherd; one head; one master; one Christian church; one fellowship of saints; one people [gathered] from all peoples; one heart, one soul; and one mind with Christ.[16]

The typical Hutterian pattern of exegesis is developed throughout the volume: a protracted analysis of Scripture from Genesis to Revelation within each of the articles is followed by the polemical rejoinder, and concluded with documentation from church history.

Since the work appeared anonymously, there has been some question among scholars as to its author. However, there is in existence in Canada a later codex which names Walpot as author, and gives 1577 as the date for the writing.[17] Walpot was almost certainly the final compiler and editor of this collective work. The basic ideas in the volume are also found in the written testimonies of individual missioners (as noted throughout the previous chapters) and are here simply arranged in a definitive brotherhood formulation of Hutterian beliefs. The Great Article Book consequently merits a place alongside of the printed Brotherhood Rechenschaft of the 1540s. Although not printed until 1967, it was copied many times, and served the Brotherhood in many forms.[18]

The high point of the volume comes in the fourth article, in a passage collocating two realities which for the Hutterites defy correlation—two kingdoms, which differ as much as day and night:

> Christians and the world are as different as heaven and earth. The world is world and remains the world and acts like the world, and all the world is one world. Christians, however, are called out of the world and are required no longer to conform to the world (John 15:19; 2 Corinthians 6:11 ff.; Revelation 18; Romans 12:2), no longer to be its consort (Ephesians 5:3 ff.), no longer to walk in its disorderly confusion (1 Peter 4:2 ff.), no longer to pull its yoke (2 Corinthians 6:11 ff.).
>
> Worldlings live according to the flesh, which rules them. They believe no one is around to observe; therefore they need the sword in their realm. Christians live according to the Spirit, which rules them. They believe the Lord observes, that he is attentive; therefore they do not need the sword among themselves.
>
> The Christians' victory is "the faith which overcomes the world" (1 John 5:4). The world's victory is the sword with which it conquers.
>
> To Christians an inner joy is given; they have joy in their hearts, holding to the unity in the Spirit through the bond of peace (Ephesians 4:3). The world has no peace; by sword and coercion alone it attempts to keep outward peace.
>
> The Christian is patient, as the apostle writes: "Since therefore Christ suffered ... arm yourselves likewise with the same mind" (1 Peter 4:1). The world arms itself for the sake of revenge; it fights. The Christian is the most faithful who can suffer everything for the sake of God. The world considers most dutiful the one who can defend himself with the sword against everyone else.
>
> To sum up: Friendship with the world is enmity with God (James 4:4), and whoever desires to be a friend of the world is an enemy of God.

If being a Christian could be effected with words and an empty name, if Christendom could regulate itself as it desired, if what is pleasing to it were also pleasing to Christ, and if the cross were to be borne solely by means of the broadsword, then the magistracy and its subjects, yea, most of the world, would be Christian. However, since man must be born anew (John 3:7), and must die in baptism to his old life (Romans 6:3 ff.), and rise again with Christ to a new life and Christian ways, that cannot be the case.[19]

Here a rugged Christian dualism is posed in the sharpest possible manner, a clue to the tenacity of the Hutterian movement, even under the extreme testing of persecution and martyrdom. Discipleship is made possible through the process called the new birth (John 3), which demands leaving the realm of general society and entering quite a different kingdom, ruled by Christ's Spirit, where peace reigns. The notion that such peace could be fulfilled at all within the realm of the world is absolutely rejected. It can only be fulfilled through life in the Spirit of Christ.[20]

## "Charges and Allegations of the World": The Hutterian World View During the Walpot Era

The radical dualism of the Hutterites which defined their mission strategy also fashioned their witness to the secular authorities. And in the same manner that the composite Hutterian view of faith was drawn up in a simplified form from fifty years of Hutterian witness and affirmation in the Great Article Book, so also one Hutterite brother drew from the same half century of suffering and persecution to compose a bitter rebuttal to those individuals and rulers who were intent on destroying the Brotherhood. The book-length document is entitled: "Charges and Allegations of the Blind, Perverse World and All Ungodly People, Who Constantly Agitate Against the Devout Witnesses of God and His Truth, and Blaspheme Against the Truth in Them, Thereby Bringing upon Themselves Eternal Perdition (Revelation 15)."[21]

The work, composed toward the end of the Walpot Era,[22] is a Hutterian answer to the world's hostility, in the form of an incisive apologia, coupled with a prophetic message of judgment.

At first sight, "Charges and Allegations" seems to be a rambling, endless joining together of hundreds of quotations from Scripture. Yet upon closer scrutiny, an organic wholeness becomes evident in the development of its two distinct parts. After the refutation of thirty accusations by the world, the author concentrates on one basic demand that the world places upon the Hutterian Brotherhood: to recant.

A writer, in using Scripture, opens his eyes to those parts of the Bible which speak to his situation and times. The author of "Charges and Allegations" took a careful look at the Old Testament passages portraying God's wrath poured out upon the wicked world, and concluded that once again a righteous God would ultimately punish those who committed obvious sins during the decadence of the sixteenth century.

There is another important reason for this prophetic dissent. The Hutterites were a Christian version of the Old Testament "people of God," separate from other peoples and separate from the world. It was their firm conviction that the prophetic remnant of Isaiah, culminating in the New Covenant remnant of God, was again realized in Zurich Anabaptism of 1525 and was brought to its original purity within Hutterian Anabaptism in Moravia. Within this promised land the elect and separate people of God again underwent persecution as Scripture promised, because they adopted a biblical, theocratic organization, founded upon Christian discipleship within a disciplined brotherhood. As a German-speaking minority group in a Slavic culture, the Hutterites could identify more readily with the Old Testament people of God than could other churches or brotherhoods whose members were not cultural foreigners to their society. The Hutterites had also been able to develop a program of mission where seekers were invited to share in a unique kingdom of God experience. Now, at a point in history where their mission was at low ebb, they found biblical precedent for the reverse side of the mission message: "We have given you a chance, you have not responded. God's judgment will fall upon you: Woe, woe, thrice woe!"

The Hutterites were still sparing no effort in carrying the mandate of mission throughout Europe. Yet a new type of literary activity was taking form, this time created in quietude and reflection, a difference which distinguishes this material from the earlier writings noted in above chapters, which had arisen out of the white heat of conflict when Hutterite missioners were struggling for their very existence. The new level of writing was a concerted effort to do battle with the enemy, via Christian apologetics (the Great Article Book) and via the polemical channels of communication ("Charges and Allegations").

The defiant mood of "Charges and Allegations" is evident from the outset. The power which the beast of evil is able to unleash against the godly (Revelation 12), the Hutterites believed, was now being unleashed in an attempt to wreak havoc among the people of God. Consequently the godly, who at times are to keep quiet, are also at times commanded to speak out; Christians must be bold to answer where truth is blasphemed and scorned. The author intends to carry through with this commission, maintaining a spirit of friendliness, although also promising to mix in a goodly dosage of salt, as Paul himself suggests (Colossians 4:6).[23]

Thirty "dialogues" between the people of God and the world compose the first part of the writing which holds forth a positive redemptive note. The author, however, makes clear that true Christianity is not a surrender to the world either through compromise or through living in an individual ivory tower of quietistic pietism. Instead, the sharp Hutterian prophetic utterances found in "Charges and Allegations" even breathe an air of superiority, suggesting that the people of God indeed have the upper hand in their relationship to the world, and that life in the present world is an important part of God's kingdom which needs defending.

Part Two of the document begins with an extended, pointed polemic against the world which, as interpreted by the Hutterites, says to God's people:

> Desist from your error and your sectarianism....If you were devout you would have remained in your own land....You want to fathom the Godhead much too deeply and be far too holy. It is not so serious; one can still find redemption....After all, we also believe in God; you could well come to the church too and take the sacrament, and eat it with any interpretation you wish; keep your own faith in your hearts. Don't be so obstinate, but do as other people who also call themselves brethren, ... who still follow us; they are not as headstrong and stubborn as you. They pay war taxes and hangmen's fees. They live separately in their own little homes, and not together in a swarm like you.... Soon a king will be raised up to fight against us as they did in Münster.... You are called Hutterites. You think your faith is the only right one. Yet it is a new faith; ours is centuries old.... You call us all ungodly and sinners and claim to be better than we. Are we to tolerate that? You must rather all be burned! You are seducing the people. It is we who will teach you to believe![24]

In reply the Hutterites assert that words cannot express what the devil does among his children of the world, trying with lies and fabrications to break the people of God away from divine truth; the whole world is full of lies and guile, as shown throughout Scripture.[25]

Then follows a detailed analysis of the contemporary situation, the pressures placed upon the Brotherhood by the world: In the face of the ever-present danger that the Hutterian community might be torn apart by outside forces the Hutterites resolve never to abandon Christian community, where there is one heart and soul among all the faithful people of God. They reject the demand of the world to halt their program of mission, for to keep silent about Christian faith would amount to pure hypocrisy, and would be denying the Lord God. "Oh you crafty and poisonous and treacherous serpents," the Hutterites cry, "depart from us with your deceit! For you shall not succeed—so help us God—in deceiving us."[26]

Neither will the Hutterites submit to the demand that they attend services of the established churches, which for them would be nothing more than trampling the Son of Man underfoot and crucifying him again by worshiping anew the greatest of all enemies of truth, the devil. Indeed, the Hutterites confess they had been led out of the "idol temples" where the "bread-god" is consumed, the practices of which in truth deny God, and lead to damnation.

At this point the Hutterite author continues with a prayer that God may act on behalf of his people, and continue to sustain them:

> Oh my God, preserve us, Thy people. . . . Drive that evil spirit and devil, the fear of men, far from us, that fear of Thee may be and remain with us forever. Oh, Thou sovereign Lord, our mighty King, give us courageous hearts to struggle and to fight for Thy Truth until death. . . . Care for Thy people whom Thou hast loved from the beginning of the world—that portion which Thou hast made holy. . . . Be Thyself a fiery wall and surround us. . . . Remember Thy covenant and promise which Thou hast established with Abraham, Isaac, and Jacob, and with his seed unto all eternity. Let Thy power and might be seen, that Thou alone art a God of Thy people and supreme in all lands. Those who afflict Zion must be disgraced and driven back. . . . And if Thou art chastening us now, Thou wilt not deliver us over to death, but rather grant at the same time a gracious way out of the temptation. Faithful Father, be highly praised, extolled, and glorified in all eternity. Amen.[27]

Then the world is again allowed to speak, a world which leads the devout, and even their children, into prison: "Aye, away with the heretics and fanatics. . . . Aye, how miserable you folks are, exposing yourselves to danger." The Hutterites, the world says, only bring such hardships upon themselves, and let themselves be led astray that God may have pity upon them. If they desire to exemplify a good life, they should show pity upon their non-Hutterite relatives, who must be ashamed of them. All the Hutterites accomplish is to cause society worry and pain. Therefore they should protect their lives by recanting, and join society, for all of society believes in God, and the Hutterites too should follow established, centuries-old ecclesiastical precedent.

The world continues to speak out: Life is not so serious. The Hutterites desire to live holy lives without sin, whereas God in his mercy knows that all are poor sinners, having sent his Son for this very reason; since no one can live without sin, the Hutterites are only demonstrating the hypocrisy of those in the temple who also pretended to be righteous. The only answer for these blockheads is: "If you refuse to obey, you will be stretched on the rack. You will be so cruelly tortured that you will have pity on yourselves, and then you will be put on the rubbish heap and burned!"

To this outburst, the Hutterites plead: "Oh my God, how many lies and how much blasphemy must the godly listen to? It is enough to break one's heart." Still the Hutterites know that such persecution will continue, even until the end of the world. Furthermore, the Brotherhood is determined not to allow the rampaging of the world to discourage the devout, for God's way wins out over all the powers of the world.

Despite the charges of the "Pope and his crowd" against the Hutterites, the latter believe it is rather those of the world who "are the true dogs of hell, who incessantly bark and yelp, and incite and stir up the magistracy and temporal power with lies and treachery to make them attack the godly." Maligning words are spread abroad and heeded by the world. As a result, gruesome mandates are proclaimed. The godly are outlawed and banned. They are legitimate and common prey, to be robbed, captured, and murdered by everyone. The godly dare not be given food or shelter, dare not buy or sell or work. They are spied upon, sought out in high mountains and forests, and in clefts and caves. They are hunted day and night like wild animals. Informers are sent out who act as if they also seek devoutness; they spy upon the godly, then go and bring judges and constables. The time had come, the Hutterites were certain, when God was going to act against an unrepentant, wretched world—especially the people in the German lands, whom the Hutterites had faithfully admonished, but who had not responded:

> Thus woe to the world and to all who spill innocent blood, who persecute, banish, slaughter, and murder the devout witnesses of God who have been sent unto their salvation before the great day of the Lord. . . . Thus woe to you, O German lands! For God will require from you the innocent blood of his messengers and witnesses, . . . which is even now clearly seen.
>
> Thus woe to the world, and especially the German nation. For the blood of the devout witnesses of God has been found in you, for the greatest of sins is to grasp at the apple of God's eye. You have refused to recognize the time of your affliction, when God sent his witnesses and messengers to you and faithfully let you be warned to amend your ways and meet your God before his fierce anger comes upon you. How often has he wanted to gather you as a hen gathers her chicks under her wing, but you refused. . . . For the day of the Lord approaches. . . .

Wickedness has grown into a rod, and not one disgraceful deed will escape. Thus take note! The Lord will again come out of His dwelling place and punish the iniquity of the inhabitants of the earth (Isaiah 26).[28]

We note, in way of interpretation, that by the time of the 1570s the Hutterites had experienced the consolidation of Protestant forces, and the countering strategy of the Catholics, eventuating in open and bitter conflict between these two Christian churches. Hence, the ever graver political situation in itself was one of the strong signs of the times. The Hutterites with their sense of history and awareness that sin is finally found out—not only for individuals, but for churches and nations as well—were able to utter a prophetic message suitable to the times. They perhaps were anticipating the outbreak of the Thirty Years' War fought among Christians, which would leave Germany a shambles, most of the population to perish from warring and pestilence. *Corpus christianum,* the Hutterites believed, had forsaken its New Testament mandate to be the reconciling Body of Christ. It had betrayed its Master, whom it was to follow in love and peace and unity. If the world only knew that the time was so near, and that it was only God's Word that kept the devout who trusted in God: This is the message which surfaces at the end of "Charges and Allegations," where the Hutterite author makes a final pronouncement of woe upon those who made up the world, those sinners and ungodly people who do not grant a listening ear to God's voice. God would punish them, avenging the blood of his missioner-witnesses:

Oh you wicked and dissolute world! God will someday teach the mockers to confess that he is Lord, and he will talk with them in his wrath and will terrify them with his fury.... These people believe this life to be an amusing game, and that our way of living is to be compared to a fair or circus, where one pursues gain and benefit,...profiting from all sorts of evil (Wisdom of Solomon 15a).[29]

For the Hutterites, the fulfillment of life lay in another sphere, in the reality of God's Word, which preserves his people. The quotation from the Wisdom of Solomon, which the Hutterite author presents near the end of his "Charges and Allegations," serves well as a final pledge of Hutterian allegiance:

For the creation, serving thee who has made it, exerts itself to punish the unrighteous, and in kindness relaxes on behalf of those who trust in thee. Therefore at that time also, changed into all forms, it served thy all-nourishing bounty according to the desire of those who had need, so that thy sons, whom thou didst love, O Lord, might learn that it is not the production of crops that feeds man, but that thy word preserves those who trust in thee. (16:24-26, RSV)[30]

## The Cultural Blooming of Hutterianism

The consolidation of the whole communal movement on its several levels which took place during the era of Peter Walpot fostered new heights in cultural and kingdom fulfillment. Jacob Hutter, the principal first-generation representative, helped create and implement the Hutterian idea. After the original creative impulse of the 1530s, there was a transition from the individual literary creativity of the 1540s, 50s, and 60s, symbolized by Peter Riedemann and Leonhard Dax, to that of communal works in the 1570s, symbolized by Peter Walpot.

In the first phase of this transition, Riedemann spelled out the vision, the charter of Hutterianism, in his Rechenschaft of 1541/42. Then Dax, applying this vision, developed a concept of missions vis-à-vis the Lutherans, Calvinists, and the Catholics. In the second phase of the transition, Walpot structured and coordinated the growing movement. For after Dax (d. 1574) came the needed process of simplification. The last years of the Walpot Era found the expression of Hutterian ideas firmly established, leaving no need for further creative thought in the area of doctrine. There was simply the continuing need of brotherhood unity through consensus.

When the Walpot Era came to an end, the Hutterites continued to build upon the solidly laid foundation of Hutter, Riedemann, Dax, and Walpot. And since they were enjoying a real measure of success as a brotherhood, they saw no reason to tamper with what God himself had established for his people.

Although the Hutterian tenets of faith were set during the Walpot Era, creativity of thought did not stop with Walpot. However the contributions of original thought that emerged after this era were not concerned with religious beliefs, but with social and cultural matters. There was a continuing need for new Brotherhood codes (Ordnungen). Some of these had been made for Walpot's time; the old general code dates from the 1550s, and other specific codes were created in the 1560s. The peak of this new phase of firming up the internal Brotherhood structure, needed because of rapid expansion into a multiplicity of crafts and vocations, came in the decades after Walpot's death, and found a new synthesis in the general code of 1612, which set the system in a way still felt in modern Hutterianism. Finally in the mid-seventeenth century, Andreas Ehrenpreis compiled most of these codes, and added some of his own in a volume that compares in significance to the Great Chronicle, the Great Article Book, and the Brotherhood Rechenschaft (Riedemann's Charter and Confession of Faith).[31]

After the crisis of the Thirty Years' War which devastated Moravia in the 1620s and literally wiped out the Moravian Haushaben, the new Brotherhood center developed at Sabatisch, Slovakia.[32] Ehrenpreis was the outstanding seventeenth-century Vorsteher, who organized and consolidated the new center, including the archives and library. There was a new flurry of activity in copying old manuscripts and binding them into volumes which would stand the wear of time. Isaac Dreller is the most famous craftsman of his era. He both copied and bound codices, many of which are still extant. This work was essential for Hutterian continuity after the destruction of the Neumühl center, when the Hutterian historical heritage was in danger of being lost.

The Ehrenpreis Era was consequently a time of regathering and consolidation. The historical literary fragments had to be found and reassembled. Fortunately, most literary pieces were found,[33] brought together, and assembled into various groupings; the chronicles, epistles, confessions of faith, hymns, Brotherhood codes, doctrinal works, catechisms, and manuscripts copied from published books. Ehrenpreis added still another category, Hutterian sermons.[34] Life was precarious in Slovakia, and for the sake of a widely scattered Brotherhood, such consolidation of heritage was indispensable. The only way to pass on their heritage was to preserve their written works, for this was the only way to remember. As to the future, they were confident that God was leading history, in spite of the fact that after the Thirty Years' War only a remnant of the original Brotherhood remained.[35]

The greatest crisis for Hutterianism came in the eighteenth century when Slovakian and Transylvanian religious toleration ended. Earlier, in 1621, a handful of brethren had settled in Alwinz, Transylvania, where a small Haushaben was established. The crucial factor there was the great Hutterian legacy of books. For when Carinthian Lutherans who had fled Austria in 1755 came into contact with the Hutterites and began reading the Hutterian works, they felt at one with the Hutterites and in 1762 joined the Brotherhood, by now a remnant which had all but died out.[36] This new impetus once again saved the Hutterian idea, although it did not come into full bloom because of hardships which led a handful of steadfast Hutterites at Alwinz and Sabatisch still further eastward into the Ukraine. When these Hutterites moved to the New World, many of them again reorganized communally on the basis of their written heritage; their ideas and history were still intact. Books had remained their most precious heritage, and they carefully packed their written heritage and took it wherever they migrated.

Johannes Waldner was the great Vorsteher who helped save the Hutterian movement both in Rumania and the Ukraine, in part by reestablishing the tradition of chronicling Hutterian history—in itself a sign of religious renewal and firm dedication. The Vorsteher whose efforts helped to reestablish the Hutterian pattern of life in North America was Elias Walter, who also saw the worth of the Hutterian legacy, republishing Riedemann's Brotherhood Rechenschaft (1902) and Ehrenpreis's *Sendbrief* (1920). He also published for the first time the songs and hymns of the Hutterites (1914) and the Great Chronicle (1923). This was also a time of reestablishing various Hutterian archives by recopying the old codices with renewed vigor.[37]

The great twentieth-century manifestation of renewal, however, came in 1920 with the birth of the brotherhood called the Society of Brothers. Eberhard Arnold, the towering spiritual founder and leader of the movement, also sensed the need for a heritage, and in his search came upon Hutterian literature at Wolfenbüttel, Germany. When he found out to his surprise that the Hutterites still existed, he journeyed to the New World, where Elias Walter ordained him as a Hutterite minister. Arnold returned to what came to be known as the New Hutterites. Now in its second generation, the Society has also emanated a vitality which is reminiscent of the way of life witnessed to by such brethren as Hutter, Riedemann, Walpot, Ehrenpreis, Johannes Waldner, and Elias Walter. But among those twenty-thousand Hutterites who still hold tenaciously to a continuity of idea and vision which goes back to their point of origin in 1528, there is also promise of renewal, as they once again are taking their long heritage seriously and as they—for the first time since their Golden Years—are approaching numerically the size they had reached four hundred years earlier.[38]

What special quality has kept the Hutterian spirit alive these four centuries, when all other communal groups enjoyed but a short-lived, fleeting moment in the annals of history? Although ultimately such a question cannot be answered scientifically, the Hutterites would attribute their endurance in no small measure to their fearless obedience as a people of God to the norms and example of Christ and the apostolic church. Hutterian Gelassenheit, a total yieldedness to God's Spirit and way of life, lay at the basis throughout these centuries. Such yieldedness was the Hutterian backbone from their beginning, a commitment to God, who reigned in the midst of his people. We can only add to this explanation of Hutterian continuity that the Hutterian story speaks for itself as to its strengths and weak-nesses. Granting the human imperfection which surfaced from time to time, other patterns which Christianity has formed in history have less effectively contained the original nucleus which can best be defined as the kingdom of God, already established here upon earth, imperfectly, to be sure, yet visible and definable.

There are few Christian groups which have taken faith in the reality of God's kingdom seriously on this level. And few of these have realized the biblical concept to such a degree as did the Hutterites. Also from the standpoint of New Testament discipleship, the sixteenth-century Hutterites have demonstrated an amazing resilience from generation to generation, surpassing the Swiss Brethren and Low Country Mennonites in their ability to maintain, well past the first generation, an authentic Anabaptism which was prepared to take the whole world to task. The Swiss Brethren soon gave up in their mission to the world in this respect. The Dutch and North German groups joined with the world in many areas of life. For decades the Hutterites did neither. They remained instead a powerful Christian nucleus, opening themselves to world mission and mutual sharing to any and all newcomers—whether ragged and penniless, or moneyed—who would simply affirm an openness to this new way of life. One tends to agree with the verdict of the sixteenth-century Hutterite chronicler: "And so it was a remarkable affair.... Indeed, it is an amazing work of God, whoever thinks about it."[39]

# Abbreviations

## I. Published Sources

ARG: *Archiv für Reformationsgeschichte*.

Beck: Josef Beck, ed., *Die Geschichts-Bücher der Wiedertäufer in Oester-reich-Ungarn, 1526-1785*, Vienna, 1883.

Bossert: *Herzogtum Württemberg*, Quellen zur Geschichte der Wie-dertäufer, Vol. I (Quellen und Forschungen zur Reformations-geschichte, Vol. XIII), Leipzig, 1930.

Brotherhood Rechenschaft: *Rechenschaft unserer Religion, Lehr und Glaubens, von den Brüdern, so man die Hutterischen nennt, aus-gangen durch Peter Rideman* (First edition, ca. 1542; Second, 1565; Modern edition, Ashton Keynes, Wilts, England, 1938; Eng., 1950, 1970).

Great Article Book: "Ein schön lustig Büchlein...." In Robert Friedmann, ed., *Glaubenszeugnisse oberdeutscher Taufgesinnter II*, Quellen zur Geschichte der Täufer, XII, Gütersloh, 1967, 59-317.

Great Chronicle: ="Z," see below.

KGB: *Das Klein-Geschichtsbuch der Hutterischen Brüder*, ed., A. J. F. Zieglschmid, Philadelphia, 1947.

*LdHBr: Die Lieder der Hutterischen Brüder*, Scottdale, Pa., 1914.

*ME: Mennonite Encyclopedia*.

*ML: Mennonitisches Lexikon*.

*MQR: Mennonite Quarterly Review*.

Wiswedel: Wilhelm Wiswedel, *Bilder und Führergestalten aus dem Täufertum*, 3 vols., Kassel, 1928-52.

Z: A. J. F. Zieglschmid, ed., *Die älteste Chronik der Hutterischen Brüder*, Ithaca, New York, 1943.

## II. Archives and Libraries Cited in This Volume

Alba Iulia: Bibliotheca Documentara Batthyaneum, Alba Iulia, Rumania.

Amsterdam: Bibliotheek der Vereenigde Doopsgezinde Gemeente, Amsterdam, now in the Universiteitsbibliotheek, Amsterdam.

Bratislava "B": Archiv mesta Bratislavy, Bratislava.

Bratislava "C": Slovenská Akademia Vied, Bratislava.

Brno: Státni Archiv, Brno, ČSSR.

Budapest: University Library, Budapest.

Esztergom: Bibliotheca Ecclesiae Metropolitanae Strigoniensis (Föszékesegyházi könyvtár), Esztergom, Hungary.

Goshen: Mennonite Historical Library, Goshen College, Goshen, Indiana.

Olomouc: Státní vĕdecká knihovna, Olomouc, ČSSR.

Prague: University Library, Prague.

Society of Brothers: Society of Brothers, Rifton, New York.

Wolfenbüttel: Bibliotheca Augustiana der Braunschweigischen Landesbibliothek, Wolfenbüttel, Germany.

# Notes

*Preface*

    1 Codex Geiser, located in the Emmenthal (Switzerland), contains a work by Hans Schnell, one of the very few extant Swiss Brethren testimonials from the 1560s. It is significant that most of the historical documentation for the Swiss Brethren during the Walpot Era is outgroup in its nature, whether Hutterian (see Chapter VIII for a fuller interpretation) or Calvinistic (e.g., the printed protocol of the Frankenthal Colloquy of 1571).

    2 "Second-generation," as used in this volume, simply refers to that era of Hutterian history which began about 1555/60, some thirty years after the birth of Anabaptism.

*Chapter 1*

    1 Such diverse Catholic movements as the Benedictine (sixth century), the Cluny (tenth century), the Cistercian (twelfth century), the Franciscan and Dominican (thirteenth century), all contained elements of a counter-cultural brotherhood movement. See the recent work, Kenneth Ronald Davis, *Anabaptism and Asceticism* (Scottdale, Pa., 1974), esp. 293-97.

    2 Luther's attempt early in the Reformation to effect a "true church" is well known, as is also his ultimate solution to the problem, centering in the establishing of *Notbischöfe*. See John S. Oyer, *Lutheran Reformers Against Anabaptists* (The Hague, 1964); John H. Yoder, *Täufertum und Reformation in der Schweiz* (Karlsruhe, 1962) and *Täufertum und Reformation im Gespräch* (Zurich, 1968); and for the latest interpretive volume on Calvin, Uwe Plath, *Calvin und Basel in den Jahren 1552-1556* (Zurich, 1974).

    3 See George H. Williams, *The Radical Reformation* (Philadelphia, 1962). Other significant forces from within the Roman Catholic Church itself were of course also at work and dare not be minimized in any fuller interpretive account of Anabaptist origins.

    4 See Ernst Troeltsch, *Die Soziallehren der christlichen Kirchen und Gruppen* (Tübingen, 1912; Eng., London, 1931); and Johannes Kühn, *Toleranz und Offenbarung* (Leipzig, 1923).

    5 Such documents as Conrad Grebel's letter to Thomas Müntzer, 1524, the Schleitheim Confession of 1527, and the writings of Menno Simons witness to these ideas. Two recent volumes on the subject are James M. Stayer, *Anabaptists and the Sword* (Lawrence, Kan., 1972) and Robert Friedmann, *The Theology of Anabaptism* (Scottdale, Pa., 1973).

    6 See Stayer; and Gottfried Seebass, *Müntzers Erbe: Werk, Leben und Theologie des Hans Hut* (Gütersloh, 1974).

    7 See Walter Klaassen, "The Nature of the Anabaptist Protest," *MQR*, XLV (1971), 291-311.

    8 See Yoder (1968), 204-05; Heinold Fast, *Der linke Flügel der Reformation* (Bremen, 1962), pp. XIX-XXII; and Friedmann, *Theology*, Part Two.

    9 A. J. F. Zieglschmid, ed., *Die älteste Chronik der Hutterischen Brüder* (Ithaca, N.Y., 1943) (hereafter "*Z*"), 432-33.

    10 Z 436. Sebastian Franck is the most objective early sixteenth-century non-Anabaptist reporter. See his *Chronica, Zeytbuch vnd Geschychtbibel* (1531).

*Chapter 2*

    1 Cod. Hab. 16 (Bratislava B), fol. 34r-34v.

    2 Z, 45-47, published in English translation in George H. Williams and Angel M. Mergel (ed.), *Spiritual and Anabaptist Writers* (Philadelphia, 1957), 42-44. See also Fritz Blanke, *Brüder in Christo* (Zurich, 1955; Eng., Scottdale, Pa., 1961), Chapters I and II, for the historical unfolding of the Anabaptist idea in Zurich. In order to understand the historical unfolding of the Reformation it is important to note that the two main Reformers, Luther and Zwingli, both retained the old ecclesiological structure of corpus christianum, but thereby were

compelled to change their earlier views of the Christian faith and be content with a compromise theological position qualitatively different from what they originally believed and hoped the renewed church ought to become. The Anabaptists reversed this process by changing the traditional ecclesiological structure in order to retain and fulfill their vision of biblical Christianity, a biblical Christian ideal which, during the early years, was a common *Leitmotiv* of Luther, Zwingli, and the Anabaptists alike.

3  See *ME* and *ML* for articles on Blaurock, Walpot, and Reublin.

4  A story based on oral history that I heard in Austria in May 1971 while visiting the Castle of Mittersill, Tirol.

5  *ME*, III, 883-86. But see Zeman (1969), 179, for a more guarded appraisal (2000-6000 baptized members).

6  Stayer, 167-87, effectively develops the story of the encounters between the Schwertler—who believed in defensive war—and the nonviolent Stäbler, which ultimately forced the Stäbler to emigrate to Austerlitz, Moravia. See also Zeman (1969), 192-95, 222-24.

7  Hab. 16 (Bratislava B), fol. 40r.

8  Z, 56.

9  Z, 89-140; Zeman (1969), 222-29 and *passim*.

10  Z, 141-49; Beck, 117.

11  Z, 151-53; also in Harry Emerson Fosdick, *Great Voices of the Reformation, an Anthology* (New York: Random House, [1952]), 303-7.

12  Z, 156-58.

13  Beck, 105-201; Z, 158-340.

14  Z, p. VII; Beck, 245.

15  Z, 56. Walpot was ten or eleven years of age, and not eight when he witnessed Blaurock's martyrdom. The entry in the Great Chronicle was added at a later date by a hand other than Hauprecht Zapff, the Brotherhood chronicler, and is probably determined by the falsely dated martyrdom of Blaurock found therein. (There are still Walpots [Walbots] living in South Tirol in the Grödnertal [Val Gardena]).

16  Beck, 153, 195.

17  When Walpot died, he was about sixty years of age. See Z, 499; Beck, 271.

18  Z, 499; Beck, 271.

19  "Eine dogmatische Hauptschrift der huterischen Täufergemeinden in Mähren," *ARG*, XXVIII (1931), 104.

20  See *LdHBr*, 186-87. The acrostic is "PETER W." Sailer also dedicated hymns to other brethren. See *LdHBr*, 188, 209.

21  Hab. 5 (Bratislava B), fol. 32r, 38v-39r.

22  *Ibid.*, fol. 40r.

23  *Ibid.*, fol. 37r-42v; Z, 265-67, 616.

24  *LdHBr*, 740-41.

25  See Beck, 245.

26  See Adolf Mais, "Das Hausbuch von Neumühl 1558-1610, das älteste Grundbuch der huterischen Brüder," *Jahrbuch der Gesellschaft für die Geschichte des Protestantismus in Oesterreich* (1964), 66-88. English, *MQR*, XLVIII (1974), 215-36.

27  Potsherds are discovered annually during the spring plowing behind the village school in Neumühl (Nové Mlýny).

28  Z, 435-36.

29  Z, 435. See also Frantisek Hrubý, *Die Wiedertäufer in Mähren* (Leipzig: M. Heinsius Nachfolger, 1935), who develops Hutterian social and economic history from out-group sources for the years 1528-1628 ff.

30  Cod. G-10-49-87 (Brno), fol. 29r-36v.

31  *Ibid.*, fol. 51r-64v.

32  *Ibid.*, fol. 107r-114v.

33  This codex of Gemeindeordnungen was lost around 1940, although two of Beck's

transcriptions of the whole volume are extant, one in Brno (G-10-49-87), and one at the Mennonite Historical Library, Goshen, Indiana. The Society of Brothers (Rifton, N.Y.) also has a number of codices which include Hutterian Ordnungen. See Friedmann, *Schriften*, 81-82.

34 "Von der Kinderzucht, und was die Geschrift darvon sagt," Cod. Hab. 5, fol. 210r-232v. See Chapter V, where the "Handbüchlein" is described.

35 Peter Rideman, *Rechenschaft unserer Religion, Lehr und Glaubens, von den Brüdern, so man die Hutterischen nennt, ausgangen durch Peter Rideman* (Ashton Keynes, Wilts, England, 1938; Eng., Rifton, N.Y., 1970), 247. The more usual spelling of "Rideman" is Riedemann.

36 Cod. III-96 (Alba Iulia), fol. 54r, 54v, 57r, 58r, 59v, 60r and *passim*. Eng., Harold S. Bender (ed.), "A Hutterian School Discipline of 1578 and Peter Scherer's Address of 1568 to the Schoolmasters," *MQR*, V (1931), 231-44.

37 *Ibid.*, fol. 55v-56r. Quote from Bender, 241-42 (slightly revised).

38 *Ibid.*, fol. 60v.

39 Cod. III-96, fol. 42r-52v, includes the Schulordnung of 1568. This Ordnung is different from the 1578 Ordnung found in M-365 (Olomouc), which is also found in Cod. III-96, fol. 62v-80r. See also Cod. III-96, fol. 49v, 54r, and 62v-93r.

40 Z, 429-30.

41 *Ibid.*

42 G-10-49-87, fol. 106v-107r.

43 Z, 466.

44 Z, 478-81.

45 Z, 495-97.

46 "A Treatise not Against that Apostolic Community, formerly in Jerusalem and described and commended by the New Testament, which should exist among the true followers of Christ, but against such as has been recommended by one of the numerous sects which multiplied from the teaching of Jesus after his Ascension, known as the 'Communists' in Moravia. *Extra quam*—they say—*non est salus*," *Transactions of the Unitarian Historical Society*, XII (1957), No. 3, 90-104.

47 *Ibid.*, 92.

48 *Ibid.*, 90, 92, 99.

49 See Zeman (1969), 262-69.

50 Henry A. DeWind, "A Sixteenth Century Description of Religious Sects in Austerlitz, Moravia," *MQR*, XXIX (1955), 44-53.

51 Hans J. Hillerbrand, *The Reformation: A Narrative History Related by Contemporary Observers and Participants* (New York, 1964), 272. For the original, see Bossert, 1105-8.

52 *Ibid.*

53 *Ibid.*

54 *Ibid.*, 272-73. The elder may have been Wendel Holba (Müller), who died in Stignitz in 1587. See Z, 549.

55 Z, 436-37. For a well-researched, but somewhat unsympathetic, interpretive work on the theme of Anabaptist social history, see Claus-Peter Clasen, *Anabaptism, a Social History, 1525-1618* (Ithaca, 1972).

**Chapter 3**

1 Z, 433.

2 Z, 458-59; Friedmann, *Hutterite Studies* (Goshen, Ind., 1961), 73; Beck, 255-56 and passim.

3 Z, 422; Bossert, 367. See also "Steinabrunn," *ME* and *ML*.

4 Christoph Erhard, *Gründliche kurz verfaste Historia* . . . (1588), fol. ciii$^v$ -ciiii$^r$ .

5 Cod. III-150 (Esztergom), fol. 288r. Only in tolerant Moravia could meetings be held with tacit consent of the manorial lords, but here the services were generally closed to outsiders, in line with the Hutterian interpretation of Scripture.

6 See Gerhard Neumann, "Nach und von Mähren. Aus der Täuferge-schichte des 16. und 17. Jahrhunderts," *ARG*, XLVIII (1957), 89-90; Bossert, 677, 874, 499, 179, 709; Wiswedel, III, 116; Wiswedel, "Die alten Täufergemeinden und ihr missionarisches Wesen," *ARG*, XL (1943), 183-200; XLI (1948), 115-32.

7 Z, 462-66.

8 Hans Joachim Hillerbrand, "Ein täuferisches Missionszeugnis aus dem 16. Jahrhundert," *Zeitschrift für Kirchengeschichte*, LXXI (1960), 326-27.

9 Lk. 18:18 ff.

10 *Ibid.*, 324-27. Hillerbrand states that "die Reformatoren an Mission gewiss nicht weniger interessiert waren als die Täufer." This is open to question, and is by no means the case, e.g., for the superintendent at Alzey, who questioned Leonhard Dax about the nature of mission. See below, Chapter VI. Also that a "martyr-theology" is more typical in later Anabaptism than earlier can hardly be maintained for Hutterian Anabaptism of the Walpot Era, in light of the liturgy in the farewell service: "So ist vnser begeeren / vnd biten auch gar schon, / das ir wolt got den herren / fier vns anrieffen thuen / vnd biten zu aller zeit, / das er vns wol behieten vor laidt / vnd vns mit seinem geiste / tröst, das wir werden erfreidt." Wolkan, *Die Lieder der Wiedertäufer* (Berlin, 1903), 208. Of course, upon facing death, the clear note of victory was seen, where Hutterite martyrs continued to demonstrate the depth of their faith, even unto physical death. But the Hutterian will to live out a full life on earth dare not be minimized.

11 Bossert, 410.

12 *Ibid.*, 411.

13 *Ibid.*, 412.

14 See below, Chapter IV.

15 Analyzed below in Chapters VI and IX.

16 The style of this document accords with Dax's "Refutation." Internal evidence points to Dax's authorship. A copy of this document is in Cod. III-107 (Alba Iulia).

17 *Ibid.*, fol. 57r.

18 *Ibid.*, fol. 81v-94v.

19 See Clasen, *Die Wiedertäufer im Herzogtum Württemberg und in benachbarten Herrschaften* (Stuttgart, 1965), 180-86.

20 *Ibid.*, 184. See *Ibid.*, Chapter II and *passim* for an excellent analysis of Hutterian mission activity in and around Württemberg, with a detailed and solid sociological analysis of the social milieu of the Hutterian converts as contrasted to those of other Anabaptist groups.

21 Christoph Andreas Fischer, *Der Hutterischen Widertauffer Taubenkobel* ... (1607), fol. B-i. See also Johann Loserth, *Der Communismus der Mährischen Wiedertäufer im 16. und 17. Jahrhundert* (Wien, 1895), 229, n. 1.

22 Clasen, 61.

23 Neumann, 89-90; Bossert, 511.

24 The following is a summation and paraphrase, in prose, of the original document which is in verse. See Wolkan, *Lieder*, 206-9; *LdHBr*, 650-52.

25 The song ends at this point.

26 "Wie die brueder des worts / so in die Landt gezogen / vor der gemein vrlaub nemen," Cod. III-139 (Esztergom), fol. 125r-132v. See Robert Friedmann, *Die Schriften der huterischen Täufergemeinschaften* ... (Wien, 1965), 56, 163-64; Loserth, *Communismus*, 228 ff.

27 Cod. III-139, fol. 126v.

28 *Ibid.*, fol. 131r-132v; Loserth, *Communismus*, 228-31.

29 See my "Newly Discovered Codices of the Hutterites," *MQR*, XLI (1968), 151; Gottfried Seebass, "A Recently Discovered Hutterite Codex of 1573," *MQR* XLVIII (1974), 257; *ME*, II, 826-34; *ML*, II, 353-63.

30 Robert Friedmann, "Claus Felbinger's Confession of 1560," *MQR*, XXIX (1955), 142-43.

31 The most extensive interpretive study of Anabaptist mission in general heretofore published is Wolfgang Schäufele, *Das Missionarische Bewusstsein und Wirken der Täufer* (Neukirchen-Vluyn, 1966), which includes the Hutterites within its scope.

### Chapter 4

1 Hab. 2 (Bratislava B), fol. 255v-256v; Beck, 240, 249; Z, 412, 423, 459-76.

2 Z, 344-46, 408, 412, 462-66, 552-53.

3 See my "Nikolaus Geyersbühler, Hutterite Missioner to Tirol," *MQR*, XLIII (1969), 283-92, an adaptation of this section with extensive footnoting. The Confession of Faith is found in Codex 305 (Bratislava C), and G-10-49-27 (Brno).

4 See *ME*, II, 512; *ML*, II, 111.

5 Z, 423-24.

6 Beck, 255-56. See also Wiswedel, II, 170-74, for an account of the episode. See also *ME*, II, 603; *ML*, II, 190-91.

7 Z, 481-82; Beck, 256; Cod. 798 (Brno), fol. 222r.

8 Cod. 798, fol. 222r-223v.

9 *Ibid.*, fol. 222v-223r.

10 *Ibid.*, fol. 223r-223v; Beck, 256.

11 Cod. 798, fol. 223v.

12 *Ibid.*, fol. 224r-230v.

13 Z, 481-84.

14 Cod. III-107 (Alba Iulia), fol. 236v; Cod. Hab. 17 (Bratislava B), fol. 403r; Z, 481, 484.

15 *LdHBr*, 725-26 (stanzas 36 and 37), with no attempt to preserve the original meter.

16 Beck, 255-56. The date that Beck suggests, 1587, is incorrect; see Z, 495, 520, 546.

17 Z, 384, 408, 426-29; Wiswedel, III, 88-95; *ME*, I, 145; *ML*, I, 80-81. Christian Hege, in his *Täufer in der Kurpfalz* (Frankfurt a. M., 1908), 81-82, wrongly speaks about two imprisonments (see also "Arbeiter," *ME* and *ML*).

18 Possibly G. Cassander, *De baptismo infantium, Testimonia veterum Ecclesiast. scriptorum .. De origine Anabaptist. sectae, de auctoritate consensus Ecclesiae cathol. traditionis Praefationes duae etc.* (1563).

19 Cod. Hab. 5 (Bratislava B), fol. 284r-315v, where Arbeiter relates the complete story, from which the above account is taken, as well as the doctrinal section below.

20 *Ibid.*, fol. 311r. See also fol. 306.

21 *Ibid.*, fol. 310r.

22 *Ibid.*

23 *Ibid.*, 310r-310v.

24 *Ibid.*, fol. 303r-303v. See also 310v-311r.

25 *Ibid.*, fol. 303v; 306r-307r.

26 *Ibid.*, fol. 290v-291v, 292v, 298r-301r.

27 The plural usage of the word "church" ("in den rechten Kirchen Christi") in Arbeiter's statements is significant. Universality among the Hutterites was not to be found in one all-encompassing organization, or within the confines of a political monolith; it emerged out of the idea of a chain of congregations, each in itself a true church of Christ. This view preserves both the idea of universality for the church, and its localized character as a gathered community of likeminded brethren.

28 Hab. 5, fol. 287v-288v, 294r-298v, 302r-305v, 308r.

29 For an excellent interpretation of the nature of the conflict between Anabaptism and the church-state monolith, as viewed in sixteenth-century terms, see Walter Klaassen, "The Nature of the Anabaptist Protest," *MQR*, XLV (1971), 291-311.

30 Cod. Hab. 5, fol. 287r. The term "apostle" was synonymous with "missioner" for the Hutterites. See Beck, p. XVI.

31 The Hutterites differentiated between Christian mission and human seduction: calling others to be godly was not seducing anyone, for the world—the majority of the people of

society—would never yield to the communal way of life. Leonhard Dax responded in this same manner in 1567, while in the prison at Alzey.

32 This parallels Luther's earlier position, that the proclaimed Word would bring everything to pass.

33 Arbeiter ought to have known the meaning behind this illustration, in view of his own vocation as thresher!

34 Cod. Hab. 5, fol. 286v-287r, 289r-289v, 293r-293v, 307r-308v, 312r-313v.

35 *Ibid.*, fol. 315r. See also Z, 476.

*Chapter 5*

1 "Prozess / wie es soll gehalten werden mit den Widertäuffern / Durch etliche Gelerten– so zu Wormbs versamlet gewesen / gestellt," Worms (n.d.), copy in the Stadtbibliothek, Worms. The document is also in Bossert, 161-69, based on a manuscript entitled "Bedenken der wiederteufer halber." The editorial changes found in Bossert, however, are not found in the printed *Prozess*. Nikolaus Paulus, *Protestantismus und Toleranz im 16. Jahrhundert* (1911), 339, notes a copy located in the Münchner Hof- und Staatsbibliothek. Whether this is the same edition as the copy at Worms needs further researching.

2 *Prozess*, fol. B ij r .

3 *Ibid.*, Aiij r -Aiiij r .

4 See *ME*, IV, 643.

5 "Hantbiechl wider den process der zu Worms am Rein wider die Brüder, so man die Hutterischen nennt, ausgegangen ist, welches war im 1557 jar dessen sich dann Philippus Melanchton und Johannes Barenthius selbst andre mehr aus ihren mittel unterschrieben haben," in the Archives of the Society of Brothers, Rifton, New York (Cod. EAH-155, fol. 1-151). Two modern manuscripts from around 1900 are at the Mennonite Historical Library, Goshen College, Goshen, Indiana. See Friedmann, *Schriften*, 80, 144; *ME*, II, 645-46.

6 See Wiswedel, III, 171-83; *MQR*, XXIX (1955), 212-31; Paul Gross, *The Defence Against the Prozess at Worms on the Rhine in the Year 1557* (n.p., n.d.).

7 Bossert, 275-94, 295-334.

8 Beck, 261. Sources for the Klampferer episode are: Beck, 261-64; Z, 471-74; and Marx Klampferer's Account, Cod. 798 (Brno), fol. 231v-248v, from which the following narrative is taken.

9 See Chapter II; *ME*, IV, 607; *ML*, IV, 229.

10 The Hutterites often complemented the arguments based upon *sola fide* theology with such passages as 1 Cor. 13; Rom. 8; 12:1-2; Gal. 5:16-24, etc., defining the Christian faith, even in Pauline terms, in a manner contrasting to that of both the Lutherans (who here brand the Hutterites as "Jesuits") and the Catholics (who at times saw the Hutterites as "Lutherans").

11 Cod. 798, fol. 248v.

12 *KGB*, 104. See Friedmann, *Schriften*, 106, 116. Materials missing in Bossert (334-478, 1048-1103, and passim) are supplemented from codices Hab. 13 and 17 (Bratislava B); Cod. III-90 (Alba Iulia); Cod. 587 (Brno); Cod. 305 (Bratislava C); Beck, 269, 270, 274; Z, 484-94. Epistles to Glock are found in Cod. III-107 (Alba Iulia), fol. 230r-242v, 243r-246v. See also Wiswedel, III, 27-34. Bossert, 435, incorrectly lists Glock's epistle of September 6, 1574, as being addressed to Wendel Müller; it was addressed to Walpot (See Cod. Hab. 17, fol. 317v, 318v, 320v-321v). The epistle ascribed to both Glock (No. 20) and Binder (No. 4) by Friedmann, *Schriften*, 116, 106, is written by Glock, in the name of both men. But the "19th" letter in Friedmann, *Schriften*, 116, is written by Binder, and not Glock, although in the name of both (Cod. Hab. 17, fol. 329v). The articles on Glock and Binder (*ME, ML*) need correction at places, in light of the account presented below.

13 *LdHBr*, 726-27; *ME*, II, 525-26; *ML*, II, 123-24.

14 Bossert, 123-24, 171-72, 187. The Great Chronicle describes Glock's early months of imprisonment, Z, 485.

15 Cod. III, 90, fol. 315r-316r; Bossert, 1065-78.

16  Klaus von Grafeneck, his wife, Margarethe, and daughter Christine played an important role throughout the prison years of Glock. The Grafeneck family is an important clue as to how Glock was able to begin correspondence with his brethren, despite prison bars.

17  For an analysis of Glock's thought, see the section below entitled "The Faith of Paul Glock."

18  Waal, who had earlier been a Swiss Brethren minister, converted to Hutterianism, and became a Hutterite minister in 1561. See Z, 399, 407, 505.

19  Bossert, 250-51; 1049-81; *LdHBr*, 729.

20  Bossert, 1087-88; *LdHBr*, 734.

21  *LdHBr*, 712, 733-34; Bossert, 1088-92.

22  Bossert, 1092-93. The Stuttgart "Bedenken und Ordnung ... " of 1584, stemming from the 1571 documents, commanded that Anabaptist leaders who had not baptized or stirred up the people, upon capture, should be fed "mit schlechter Speis, als suppen, brei, wasser und brot allein, das er plössig (Kaum) darbei pleiben könte, zu erhalten und mit gemachten und lieferung nit als ein pfründer zu versehen, sonder es mit ime dahin zu richten, das er spüren möge, es seie seine halsstarrigkeit und irtumbs halb ein straf. ... " *Ibid.*, 572.

23  See Ethelbert Stauffer, "The Anabaptist Theology of Martyrdom," *MQR*, XIX (1945), 179-214; "Martyrdom, Theology of," *ME*, III, 519-21.

24  Z, 485; *LdHBr*, 710-11; Bossert, 1092-95.

25  Bossert, 1096-98; *LdHBr*, 712.

26  Bossert, 1097-98, 1100-1, 335-36, 339-43, 350.

27  Bossert, 346-50.

28  Bossert, 350-59. At this point in the account, Glock entered into a discussion with the Swiss brother, Leonhard Sommer, the details of which are presented in Chapter VIII.

29  Hab. 17. fol. 305v-308v, 320v-321v.

30  Hab. 17, 322r; Wiswedel, III, 40-42; Z, 429, 459; Bossert, 369-76, 414, 416-17; Hab. 13, fol. 398v-411v; Cod. III, 107 (Alba Iulia), fol. 243r-246v.

31  Cod. Hab. 17, fol. 322r-330r; *LdHBr*, 721-23. See also pp. 713-14, and 729-30 Å, where the other two poems mentioned above are published. Another letter by Glock, most likely written in late February 1576, is found only partially preserved in Cod. III-90 (Alba Iulia), fol. 416r-428v.

32  Cod. III-107, fol. 238r-242v.

33  The idea of the two kingdoms, a common Anabaptist view, is developed in Robert Friedmann, "The Doctrine of the Two Worlds," *The Recovery of the Anabaptist Vision* (Scottdale, Pa., 1957), Guy F. Hershberger, ed., 105-18.

34  It was in this letter that Walpot inquired whether Glock or Binder knew the circumstances of Veit Uhrmacher, mentioning that he had sent two brethren to investigate. See Chapter IV.

35  Cod. III-107, fol. 230r-237v; Cod. Hab. 17, 337v-402r, 405r.

36  Z, 494-95, 520, 539.

37  Bossert, 1089, 1093-94, 1098; Cod. Hab. 17, fol. 314r-314v.

38  Bossert, 1050-52, 1054, 351-52.

39  Bossert, 357, 1094-95.

40  Bossert, 1089, 363; Cod. III-90, fol. 315v-316r.

41  See Chapter VI and IX for the background and significance of Dax.

42  The Hutterites were not opposed to a missioner's breaking out of prison. We noted how Veit Uhrmacher broke out of the Salzburg prison fortress in 1576 (see Chapter IV), although he had never promised not to break out. The closest parallel to the situation of Paul Glock from earlier Hutterian history is the case of Peter Riedemann, imprisoned at Wolkersdorf, Hesse, to whom the Brotherhood sent a communication in 1542, later summarized in the Great Chronicle: "Weil Im Gott die gfencknus het geringert / vnd zum tail ein offne thür gezaigt / Die gmain aber sein zu grosser not bedürfft / So wer der Eltesten vnd der gantzen Gmain willen Rath vnd mainung / Wouerr er ein vnbefleckten abschaidt möcht machen / so

solt er vnd sein mitgefangner auffs beldest zu der Gmain kommen." (Z, 228). Riedemann was able to make an escape, to become, at the request of the whole Brotherhood, co-Vorsteher with Leonhard Lanzenstil. We do not know how Riedemann broke out of prison, nor whether or not he broke any confidences with prison officials by breaking out. It is possible that once the Brotherhood called him as co-Vorsteher, he took this calling to mean that God would never again lead him as a missioner to the land of Hesse; hence he could, in good conscience, promise not to return. (See *ME*, IV, 327; and Robert Friedmann, "Peter Riedemann: Early Anabaptist Leader," *MQR*, XLIV, (1970), 5-44.

We can, however, assume that Walpot's letter to Glock, communicating the Brotherhood sentiment about escaping prison, contained the same proviso as that which in 1542 had been sent to Riedemann, namely, that Glock should escape only if "ein vnbefleckten abschaidt" were possible, i.e., only on terms of a properly executed exit from prison, in good conscience. When Glock affirmed he could not follow through with such an escape, it seems that Walpot was satisfied, although there is evidence that from time to time there were some brethren who were still hoping that Glock could escape.

43 Cod. Hab. 17, fol. 312v-314r, 337r-337v, 315r-315v; Bossert, 353-54, 1062, 335, 1100, 348-49.

44 Cod. Hab. 17, fol. 320v-321v, 322v, 328r, 338v-339v, 400r-402r; Bossert, 1077, 1079, 349-50.

45 Bossert, 1057-61.

46 Bossert, 358-59, 355-56; Cod. Hab. 17, fol. 314v-315r.

47 Bossert, 356.

48 Bossert, 579-81.

49 Bossert, 652-58.

50 Cod. Hab. 17, fol. 304.

51 *KGB*, 104.

52 *Lehrbuch der Dogmengeschichte* (1910[4]), III, 773.

53 *LdHBr*, 712, here translated without regard to the verse.

*Chapter 6*

1 Published in English translation in Arthur C. Cochrane (ed.), *Reformed Confessions of the 16th Century* (Philadelphia, 1966), 220 ff., 305 ff.

2 See *ME*, II, 21; Manfred Krebs (ed.), *Baden und Pfalz*, Quellen zur Geschichte der Täufer, IV (Gütersloh, 1951), 181, 197, 198.

3 "Reffutation vnd grindtliche widerlegung etlicher lesterungen der gottlosen wider die gemeindt Christy, damit sie die warhait villen verdächtig machen. Allen guethertzigen zum trost geschriben durch Leonhard Taxen, Anno 1561. Gestelt auff 26 artickhel, die sie wider uns, die Huetterischen Brüeder einfüerren. ("Refutation and a Thorough Rebuttal of Numerous Blasphemies of the Ungodly Against the Church of Christ, Through Which They Make the Truth Suspect to Many. Written by Leonhard Dax for the Comfort of All Good-hearted People. A.D. 1561. Written in 26 Articles with Which the Hutterian Brethren are Accused."). Cod. EAH-80 (Society of Brothers), fol. 104v-139v.

4 See Chapter V (Notes 1-7).

5 See Chapter III (Notes 16-18).

6 See Chapter IX (Notes 21-22).

7 Dr. Jarold K. Zeman (Acadia University), upon reading an earlier draft of this book speculated that Leonhard Dax conceivably would come into question as the discussion partner of the Czech brother, Peter Herbert, in the Colloquy of 1565. Zeman was unable to trace the name (Martinus Behem) given to the Anabaptist who debated with Herbert. If Zeman is right, Dax represented Hutterianism on still another (fourth) front: the Bohemian Brethren. See Zeman (1969), 259-62, 346-49.

8 Z, 346-48; Cod. Hab. 5 (Bratislava B), fol. 233v-234r, 282v-283r.

9 Z, 404-5, 411, 422.

10 Dax is the logical transcriber of the one extant Hutterian Latin codex, a transcription of Herman von Kerssenbrock's *Historia Anabaptistarum*. . . . See Friedmann, *Schriften*, 18.

11 Cod. Hab. 5, fol. 283v.

12 Cod. III-128 (Esztergom), fol. 33v-34r. See fol. 31r-36r.

13 Cod. III-107 (Alba Iulia), fol. 327r-334v.

14 Cod. Hab. 5, fol. 283r.

15 *Ibid.*, fol. 283v; Z, 474.

16 Cod. Hab. 5, fol. 233r-283v. The complete Rechenschaft in English translation is published in the *MQR*, XLIX (1975), 293-334.

17 *Ibid.*, fol. 263v-264r.

18 *Ibid.*, fol. 267r-268v.

19 See *ME*, I, 495-97; *ML*, I, 300-01, 314-17.

20 Cod. Hab. 5, fol. 277v-278v.

21 *Ibid.*, fol. 278v.

22 *Ibid.*, fol. 235v.

23 *Ibid.*, fol. 236r.

24 *Ibid.*, fol. 240r-240v.

25 *Ibid.*, fol. 257v-258r.

26 *Ibid.*, fol. 270v-271v, 273v.

27 *Ibid.*, fol. 246v.

28 E.g., Dax writes: "O ich wolte, Got, dz sollicher künig vil auff erden weren, die durch dz bluet Cristi zue künigen vnd priestern vor Got gemacht wärent . . ." (*Ibid.*, fol. 279r); a quotation from Dax in the Great Article Book reads almost verbatim: "O, ich wolte, Gott, das solcher amvatter vnd künig vil auff erden weren, die durch das bluet Christi zu künigen und priestern von Gott gemacht werden." (Friedmann, *Glaubenszeugnisse oberdeutscher Taufgesinnter*, II [Gütersloh, 1967], 278). Compare fol. 278v-279r with the whole section, No. 77, of the Great Article Book (pp. 277-78).

29 Z, 424.

30 Franz Bäschlin, "Die bernischen Täuferdisputationen," ms. in the Archives of the Mennonite Church, p. 32.

### Chapter 7

1 Erich Hassinger, *Religiöse Toleranz im 16. Jahrhundert* (Basel/Stuttgart, 1966), 22; *The Cambridge History of Poland* (Cambridge, 1950), I 322-47; Stanislaw Kot, "Polish Brethren and the Problem of Communism in the XVIth Century," *Transactions of the Unitarian Historical Society*, XI (1956), No. 2, 53; George H. Williams, *The Radical Reformation* (Philadelphia, 1962), 639-69, 733-63.

2 Kot, *op. cit.*, 39-40; Kot, *Socinianism in Poland: The Social and Political Ideas of the Polish Antitrinitarians in the Sixteenth and Seventeenth Centuries* (Boston, 1957), 16-22; Earl Morse Wilbur, *A History of Unitarianism, Socinianism and its Antecedents* (Cambridge, 1945), 286-90. The best monograph on our era is that of George Huntston Williams, "Anabaptism and Spiritualism in the Kingdom of Poland and the Grand Duchy of Lithuania: An Obscure Phase of the Pre-History of Socinianism," Ludwika Chmaja, ed., *Studia Nad Arianizmen* (Warsaw, 1959), 215-62, esp. 228 ff. Williams underestimates, however, the similarities between the Hutterites and other Upper German Anabaptists, as well as the differences between Upper German and Low Country Anabaptism (see pp. 218-19).

Although a rationalistic foundation could already be noted in the 1560s among the Antitrinitarian Polish Brethren, their faith was more biblical than creedal in its orientation, and perhaps more Ante- than Anti-Trinitarian in its confession of faith. See George H. Williams, *The Radical Reformation* (Philadelphia, 1962), 319-20. Therefore, what seemed to be a similar biblical frame of reference allowed the Polish and Hutterian brotherhoods to consider a possible uniting; "theology" *per se*, although a definite factor separating the two groups, did not as directly stand in the way to unity as did the question of how the Christian expression of life may find fulfillment, i.e., the question of fulfilling Christian community.

3 Theodor Wotschke, *Geschichte der Reformation in Polen* (Leipzig, 1911), 224; see also Kot, *Socinianism*, 26-28, for an extended quotation on the types of personalities and doctrines to be found within the group.

4 Wotschke, 224; Kot, "Polish Brethren," 42; Kot, *Socinianism*, 25.

5 Wotschke, 220; Kot, *Socinianism*, 32; Wilbur, 355; Z, 440-41. See Williams, "Anabaptism . . . ," 245-50, for a solidly detailed interpretation of the Hutterian-Polish Brethren encounters between 1567 and 1571, from the standpoint of the Polish Brethren.

6 "A Treatise Not Against the Apostolic Community . . . ," *Transactions of the Unitarian Historical Society*, XII (1959), No. 3, 90-104; Kot, *Socinianism*, 32; Kot, "Polish Brethren," 39-41; Z, 441-42.

7 Z, 443-46.

8 Wotschke, 224; Kot, "Polish Brethren," 45-49; Kot, *Socinianism*, 35-41; Williams, *Radical Reformation*, 757-63; see also Chapter II, where the Treatise is mentioned.

9 Kot, *Socinianism*, 29-30; Z, 446-48.

10 Z, 446.

11 Z, 446-58. See Robert Friedmann, "Reason and Obedience: An Old Anabaptist Letter of Peter Walpot (1571) and Its Meaning," *MQR*, XIX (1945), 27-40, for an English translation of the original.

12 Z, 448. On the idea of "Noah," from the standpoint of Polish Brethren thought, see Williams, "Anabaptism . . . ," 232-33.

13 Z, 451-52; Friedmann, "Reason and Obedience," 32-33; Kot, *Socinianism*, 42.

14 Kot, *Socinianism*, 45; Kot, "Polish Brethren," 50-52.

15 Z, 457; Friedmann, "Reason and Obedience," 36; Kot, *Socinianism*, 44.

16 Wotschke, 298; Z, 858-59; Beck, 486-92; *ME*, IV, 1051; *ML*, IV, 647-48.

17 Kot, "Polish Brethren," 41, 44, 50.

18 *Ibid.*, 41.

## Chapter 8

1 See the extensive listings for this period in Hans Joachim Hillerbrand (ed.), *A Bibliography of Anabaptism, 1520-1630* (Elkhart, Ind., 1962).

2 See John H. Yoder (ed.), *The Legacy of Michael Sattler* (Scottdale, Pa., 1973), 27-54, esp. 47; Friedmann, *Schriften*, 24, 27, 33, 60, 69, 71, 135.

3 See Cod. 740-1-e (Amsterdam) where the scattered nature of the Swiss Brethren movement is documented, as well as the fact that members of non-Swiss origins had joined the movement. See also Zeman (1969), 254, 258, 287, and *passim* about the Swiss Brethren movement within Moravia.

4 Z, 45-49; Cod. 740-1-e, fol. 234r-234v. The original 160 page Swiss communication to the Hutterites, to which the Hutterites responded in 1567, is no longer extant.

5 Claus-Peter Clasen, *Anabaptism: A Social History, 1525-1618* (Ithaca, N.Y., 1972), 244.

6 See Robert Friedmann, "Peter Riedemann: Early Anabaptist Leader," *MQR*, XLIV (1970), 9-14. See also Chapter VII.

7 Beck, 71, 152; J. K. Zeman, "Historical Topography of Moravian Anabaptism," *MQR*, XLI (1967), 155, 159. Zeman has shown Beck to be wrong in his statement about "einige unbedeutende Reste der Schweizer Brüder" still existing in Moravia and Austria after 1565. The movement was stronger than had earlier been acknowledged.

8 Z, 193-94; 357-67; *KGB*, 45.

9 Z, 415-19; *ME*, II, 313; *ML*, I, 632.

10 Z, 548-49; 553; *KGB*, 114.

11 Beck, 396; Z, 701, 758, 765; *KGB*, 151.

12 Cod. 3844 (Wolfenbüttel), fol. 43-70.

13 Cod. 740-1-3, fol. 177r-199v; Z, 422.

14 We noted in Chapter Seven how the Polish Brethren had seen this towering strength within Hutterianism, and had hoped to gain the secret of such a group ordering process of discipline and unity.

15  Cod. 740-1-e, fol. 201r-201v.

16  *Ibid.*, fol. 201r-224r, 233v. Recent works on the Jubilee include André Trocmé, *Jesus and the Nonviolent Revolution* (Scottdale, Pa., 1973); and John H. Yoder, *The Politics of Jesus* (Grand Rapids, Mich., 1972). The list of other brotherhoods, presented here, is worthy of quotation: "Ir sollet doch bey euch selb warnemen wohin alle völckher / nur zu unsern zeiten / sy seien Spitl, Männisth, Austerlitzer, Sabather, Gabrielish, Philiper, unnd ir selber komen sein / wölliche auff dem thodten buechstaben wie ir yetzt gelegenn / nichts anders erwegen / unnd daraus dem fleisch die thier zu seiner (aber nit götlichen) freihait auffgethon haben / was sich hat mit inen zue tragen / wz sy vernumen / in vil und manigerlay zerthailet / in irrigen sinn gewachsen / unnd vast der welt in irem leben gleich worden / on dz etlich noch des kindstauffs und götzenns halben etwas ansteen." (Fol. 217r-217v.) See *ME*, and *ML*, for articles on these various groups. It should be noted that in 1665, when the Hutterites themselves were destitute, they turned with perhaps a bit more humility than was the case in the Golden Years to the Mennonites of Holland their "dearest friends and brethren in the Lord." (Z, 890).

17  *Ibid.*, fol. 224r-236r. A booklet mentioned in Article One by Melchior Rinck, entitled in the Hutterian codex (fol. 234r-234v), Zue widerlegung des vermainten Euongelisten Glaubens, schreibet in 33 Articl gestellt ... [von] Melchior Runckhen," is apparently no longer extant. Here Peter Walpot speaks for a restitution of Christian community of goods, rather than for its historical continuity.

18  *Ibid.*, fol. 236r-255r.

19  *Ibid.*, fol. 257v-258v.

20  *Ibid.*, fol. 255r-271v. See *ME*, IV, 642-43; *ML*, IV, 255-56.

21  See Chapters IX and VI.

22  Cod. 740-1-e, fol. 288v, 289r-290v.

23  *Ibid.*, fol. 272r-301v.

24  Although Hutterites in the twentieth century still maintain their own day schools, children now live with their parents as single family units.

25  Cod. 740-1-e, fol. 302.r-319v.

26  *Ibid.*, fol 319v-337v. See John H. Yoder, *Sattler*, 71-73, for Sattler's views on the Turks.

27  Cod. 740-1-e, fol. 338r-341v, given here in condensed form.

28  "Wer ainen schweitzer in od. und. d. welt verloren het / der kundt in nimer finden." *Ibid.*, fol. 347v. We have not been able to locate this song, although it is included in an "Aussbundt" dating from the 1560s or before.

29  *Ibid.*, fol. 341v-361r.

30  *Ibid.*, fol. 361r-366r.

31  Z, 423.

32  See my article in the *MQR*, XLIV (1970), 45-58, where an adaptation of this section has been published with extensive footnotes.

33  Bossert, 207, 221, 362-67, 412; Cod. Hab. 17 (Bratislava B), fol. 305r-315v; *Protocoll. Das ist / Alle handlung des gesprechs zu Franckenthal* ... (1571), 44.

34  Bossert, 364.

35  Cod. Hab. 17, fol. 310v.

36  Bossert, 207.

37  Cod. Hab. 17, 311v-319r.

38  Reproduced in *MQR*, XLIV (1970), 56-57.

39  The best volume on the historical development of Anabaptism, in the area of history of ideas, is Robert Friedmann, *Mennonite Piety through the Centuries: Its Genius and Its Literature* (Goshen, Ind., 1949).

## Chapter 9

1  For the economic and social implications of Hutterian history, see Frantisek Hrubý, "Die Wiedertäufer in Mähren," *ARG*, XXX (1933), 1-36, 170-211; XXXII (1935), 1-40; see also John A. Hostetler, *Hutterite Society* (Baltimore and London: The Johns Hopkins University Press, 1974); and John W. Bennett, *Hutterian Brethren* (Stanford, Cal., 1967).

2 See Robert Friedmann, "Peter Riedemann: Early Anabaptist leader," *MQR*, XLIV (1970), 5-44, for a keen analysis of the development in the thought of Riedemann.

3 See J. C. Wenger (ed.), *Conrad Grebel's Programmatic Letters of 1524* (Scottdale, Pa., 1970). The word "programmatic" is advisedly included in the title, for the substance of the Anabaptist faith (love, nonresistance, and discipleship) and the vehicle to carry this faith (the gathered brotherhood-church) are clearly defined at this early date in Grebel's letter.

4 Philip Weber established communal life at Auspitz in 1529. Wilhelm Reublin, one of the original Zurich Anabaptists who had also been in contact with Michael Sattler, joined the communal movement there. See *ME*, IV, 304-07.

5 This view differs from that held by scholarship heretofore. But Part One does not make sense as a document prepared for Prince Philip of Hesse. Riedemann would not have written such a charter for the Landgrave while in prison. Part One, for example, makes use of sources such as Hubmaier's works (see Friedmann, "Peter Riedemann ...," 37), which could hardly have been made available to a prisoner. Furthermore, in the "Conclusion of this Book" (p. 233), where Riedemann summarized what he wrote in his "book," he only speaks about Part Two (pp. 139 ff.) of the printed Rechenschaft, ending his Conclusion with: "Thus, we have given an account, with sufficient reason, of the truth concerning the points and articles most called in question in the land of Hesse" (p. 224); German [1938], 244-45). Part One therefore was written at the earliest in 1542 soon after Riedemann returned to Moravia.

6 Friedmann, *Glaubenszeugnisse II*, 39-42.

7 E.g., Riedemann, *Confession of Faith*, 140 (Germ., 150-51).

8 We disagree with Friedmann about the relative insignificance of Part Two (Friedmann, "Peter Riedemann ...," 32). The wealth of biblical references in itself is highly significant for biblical interpretation, in view of how the biblical citations are woven together.

9 Riedemann, *Confession of Faith*, 9-136.

10 For Friedmann's views on the significance of a strong leadership, see John W. Miller, "Robert Friedmann: In Appreciation," *MQR*, XLVIII (1974), 183.

11 See Robert Friedmann, "Second Generation Anabaptism as Illustrated by the Walpot Era of the Hutterites," *MQR*, XLIV (1970), 390-93, where there is a description of the Neumühl center (p. 392).

12 See *ME*, I, 402.

13 Published for the first time in Friedmann, *Glaubenszeugnisse II*, 59-317.

14 Cod. II-295 (Esztergom), fol. 1r.

15 *Ibid.*

16 *Ibid.*, 1v-2r. Scriptural references included in this affirmation of unity are: Eph. 4:4-6; Jer. 3:28; Mt. 7:14; Jn. 14:8; Jn. 1:4; 2 Cor. 6:7; 2 Jn. 1:9 f.; Gal. 1:8; 1 Cor. 10:6; Jn. 10:9; Mt. 7:13; 1 Pet. 2:25; Eph. 1:22; Mt. 23:10; Acts 2:41; 2 Esd. 5; Acts 4:32; Phil. 2:5; 3:15; Rom. 12:2; 15:5; 2 Cor. 13:11.

17 See Friedmann, "Eine dogmatische Hauptschrift," 99. Other versions of the first three articles, highly condensed, are ascribed to Walpot in several codices, e.g., Cod. 3844 (Wolfenbüttel).

18 "Es ist noch zu bemerken, dass das Artikelbuch neben der grossen Rechenschaft Peter Riedemanns die wichtigste dogmatische Schrift der Brüder darstellt." Friedmann, *Schriften*, 143. See *Ibid.*, 129, 143, and Friedmann, *Glaubenszeugnisse II*, 54-58, for the various extant forms of the Five Articles.

19 Cod. II-295 (Esztergom), fol. 157v-158r.

20 The same idea is expressed in the Great Chronicle, in a section written around 1585/90. See *Z*, 430-40 and Appendix (below), pp. 244-52.

21 Cod. III-150 (Esztergom), fol. 1r-237v.

22 See Friedmann, *Schriften*, 129-30, for a discussion of the problem of date and authorship. As with the Great Article Book, it is possible that Walpot wrote parts of the manuscript in 1576 or 1577, incorporating some materials from Dax's papers, and some from other sources.

23 Cod. III-150, fol. 2v.

24 *Ibid.*, fol. 145r-147r.

25  *Ibid.*, fol. 147r.

26  *Ibid.*, fol. 168r.

27  *Ibid.*, fol. 171v-173v.

28  *Ibid.*, fol. 201r-204r.

29  *Ibid.*, fol. 209v-222v.

30  *Ibid.*, fol. 222r-222v.

31  See Friedmann, *Schriften*, 170-72; *ME*, II, 454-55. The older general code of the 1550s is mentioned in Codex III, 96 (Alba Iulia), fol. 47r.

32  See "Sobotiste," *ME*, IV, 557.

33  One missing item is the hymns of Leonhard Dax; see Z, 425.

34  See *ME*, IV, 504-06.

35  *E.g.*, in 1661 the Hutterite chronicler notes that through much anxiety and tribulation "ist vns doch Gott der Allmechtig bey gestanden / vnd hat vns beschutzt." Z, 866.

36  See *ME*, I, 83-84, 517-19; IV, 557-58, 887. The Hutterites discontinued the practice of community of goods for a time in Transylvania, as well as in Russia; most of them firmly reestablished this basic tenet in the New World.

37  See *ME*, IV, 882-83.

38  See Robert Friedmann, "A Hutterite Census for 1969: Hutterite Growth in One Century, 1874-1969," *MQR*, XLIV (1970), 100-05.

39  Z, 437.

# Glossary of German Terms

Diener des Evangeliums:
> The Hutterite missioner sent to witness to seekers (individuals and groups) in other lands.

Diener der Notdurft:
> An economic leader or manager of a Hutterian Haushaben (Hutterian community).

Diener des Wortes:
> Minister or spiritual leader of a Haushaben.

Gelassenheit:
> The state of yieldedness and obedience to God, and the giving of oneself to the vision of the gathered people of God; a term which, for the Hutterites, also includes the idea of community of goods.

Gemeinde:
> The congregation of believers; a gathered, voluntaristic church; the Brotherhood.

Gemeindeordnung (Or Ordnung):
> Brotherhood code; a social-economic-political set of Brotherhood regulations.

Haushaben:
> Individual, close-knit, Hutterian communities, in some instances comprised of up to five hundred or more individuals, each community having its own social, economic, and political structure, but sharing with all other Hutterian communities a common way of life and a common faith.

Haushalter:
> General manager; "Housekeeper" of a Hutterian community; steward (Diener der Notdurft).

Nachfolge:
> Discipleship; literally, "following after" Jesus, including his way of life, his message and his commission.

Ordnung:
> The state of orderliness within life, whether for the gathered church as a whole, or for the individual within the group, effected through Brotherhood codes and regulations, built upon a common view of truth.

Rechenschaft:
> Confession of faith; a defense or account of one's faith.

Vorsteher:
> The head leader or elder of the whole Brotherhood.

# Index of
# German/Čzech (Slovakian)
# Place Names

| | |
|---|---|
| Altenmarkt | Břeclav Stará |
| Auspitz | Hustopeče |
| Austerlitz | Slavkov |
| Brünn | Brno |
| Damborschitz | Dambořice |
| Eibenschitz | Ivančice |
| Gross Meseritsch | Velké Meziříčí |
| Kromau, Märisch | Krumlov Moravský |
| Lundenburg | Břeclav |
| Neumühl | Nové Mlýny |
| Niemtschitz | Němčice |
| Nikolsburg | Mikulov |
| Oberwisternitz | Horní Věstonice |
| Olmütz | Olomouc |
| Pressburg | Bratislava |
| Rossitz | Rosice |
| Sabatisch | Sobotiste |
| Schaidowitz | Žadovice |
| Seelowitz | Židlochovice |
| Stignitz | Trstěnice |
| Teikowitz | Tavíkovice |
| Tracht | Strachotín |
| Unterwisternitz | Dolní Věstonice |
| Wastitz | Vlasatice |

(Source: Jarold Knox Zeman, "Historical Topography of Moravian Anabaptism," *MQR*, XLI [1967], 40-78, 116-60.)

# Bibliography

Ammann, Hartmann. "Die Wiedertäufer in Michelsburg im Pusterthale und deren Urgichten." *Programm des k. k. Gymnasiums zu Brixen,* Vol. XLVI (1896).

Arndt, Karl J. R. " 'Dauer im Wechsel': Grimmelshausen's ungarische Wiedertäufer and Rapp's Harmoniegesellschaft." *Traditions and Transitions: Studies in Honor of Harold Jantz.* Munich, 1972, 79-86.

*Aussbund Etliche schöne Christliche Geseng, wie die in der Gefengnus zu Passaw im Schloss von den Schweitzern, und auch von anderen rechtgläubigen Christen hin und her gedicht worden: Allen und jeden Christen, welcher Religion sie auch seyen, unparteilich und fast nützlich zu brauchen.* (1564, 1583, many editions.)

Bainton, Roland H. "The Anabaptist Contribution to History." *Studies on the Reformation.* Boston: Beacon Press, 1963.

_____. *Christian Attitudes toward War and Peace: A Historical Survey and Critical Re-evaluation.* New York: Abingdon Press, 1960.

_____. "The Left Wing of the Reformation." *Studies on the Reformation.* Boston: Beacon Press, 1963.

_____. *The Reformation of the Sixteenth Century.* Boston: Beacon Press, 1952.

_____. "The Struggle for Religious Liberty." *Studies on the Reformation.* Boston: Beacon Press, 1963.

_____. *The Travail of Religious Liberty.* Philadelphia: Westminister Press, 1951.

Baum, Ruth Elizabeth. *The Ethnohistory of Law: The Hutterite Case.* Ann Arbor, Mich.: University Microfilms, 1978.

Beck, Josef, ed. *Die Geschichts-Bücher der Wiedertäufer in Oesterreich-Ungarn,* ... *1526-1785.* Vienna, 1883 (2nd. ed. Nieuwkoop: B. de Graaf, 1967).

Bender, Harold S. "The Anabaptist Theology of Discipleship." *MQR,* XXIV (1950), 25-32.

_____. "The Anabaptist Vision." *MQR,* XVIII (1944), 67-88.

_____. *Conrad Grebel, c. 1498-1526: The Founder of the Swiss Brethren Sometimes Called Anabaptists.* Goshen, Ind.: Mennonite Historical Society, 1950.

_____. "Discipleship." *ME,* IV, 1076-77.

_____. ed., "Hutterite School Discipline of 1578 and Peter Scherer's Address of 1568 to the Schoolmasters." *MQR,* V (1931), 231-44.

————— "New Discoveries of Important Sixteenth Century Codices." *MQR*, XXX (1956), 72-77.

————— " 'Walking in the Resurrection': The Anabaptist Doctrine of Regeneration and Discipleship." *MQR*, XXXV (1961), 96-110.

Bennett, John W. *Hutterian Brethren: The Agricultural Economy and Social Organization of a Communal People.* Stanford, Calif.: Stanford University Press, 1967.

Benrath, Karl. *Geschichte der Reformation in Venedig.* Schriften des Vereins für Reformationsgeschichte, Vol. V. Halle, 1887.

————— "Wiedertäufer im Venetianischen um die Mitte des 16. Jahrhunderts." *Theologische Studien und Kritiken*, 1885, pp. 9-67.

Bergmann, Cornelius. *Die Täuferbewegung im Kanton Zürich bis 1660.* Leipzig, 1916.

Bergsten, Torsten. *Balthasar Hubmaier: Seine Stellung zu Reformation und Täufertum, 1521-1528.* Kassel: J. G. Oncken, 1961.

Blanke, Fritz. *Brüder in Christo.* Zurich: Zwingli-Verlag, 1955 (Eng. trans.: *Brothers in Christ.* Scottdale, Pa.: Herald Press, 1961).

————— "Täuferforschung: Ort und Zeit der ersten Wiedertaufe." *Theologische Zeitschrift*, VIII (1952), 74-76.

————— "Täufertum und Reformation." *Reformatio*, 1957, 212-23 (Eng. trans.: "Anabaptism and the Reformation." *The Recovery of the Anabaptist Vision.* Guy F. Hershberger, ed. Scottdale, Pa.: Herald Press, 1957).

Bossert, Gustav, ed. *Herzogtum Württemberg.* Quellen zur Geschichte der Wiedertäufer, Vol. I. Leipzig, 1930.

Braght, Tieleman Jansz van. *Het Bloedigh Tooneel der Doops-Gesinde en Weereloose Christenen* ... Dordrecht, 1660 (Eng. trans.: *The Bloody Theatre, or Martyrs Mirror of the Defenseless Christians* ... Scottdale, Pa.: Mennonite Publishing House, 1951).

Caldwell, Mark Stuart. *Ideological and Institutional Reflections of the Benedictine Ideal in Sixteenth-Century Hutterites: A Study in Ecclesiastical Ecology.* Ann Arbor, Mich.: University Microfilms, 1977.

Clasen, Claus-Peter. *Anabaptism: A Social History, 1525-1618.* Ithaca, N.Y.: Cornell University Press, 1972.

————— "The Anabaptists in Bavaria." *MQR*, XXXIX (1965), 243-61.

————— *Die Wiedertäufer im Herzogtum Württemberg und in benachbarten Herrschaften: Ausbreitung, Geisteswelt und Soziologie.* Veröffentlichungen der Kommission für Geschichtliche Landeskunde in Baden-Württemberg, Reihe B Forschungen, Vol. XXXII. Stuttgart: W. Kohlhammer, 1965.

Conkin, Paul K. *Two Paths to Utopia: The Hutterites and the Llano Colony.* Lincoln, Neb.: University of Nebraska Press, 1964.

Correll, Ernst H. *Das schweizerische Täufermennonitentum.* Tübingen, 1925.

Davis, Kenneth Roland. *Anabaptism and Asceticism.* Scottdale, Pa.: Herald Press, 1974.

Dedic, Paul. "The Social Background of the Austrian Anabaptists." *MQR*, XIII (1939), 5-20.

DeWind, Henry A. "A Sixteenth Century Description of Religious Sects in Austerlitz, Moravia." *MQR*, XXIX (1955), 44-53.

Egli, Emil, ed. *Actensammlung zur Geschichte der Züricher Reformation in den Jahren 1519-1533.* 3 vols. Zurich, 1879.

Ehrenpreis, Andreas. *Ein Sendbrief,* . . . 1652 (2nd. ed.: Scottdale, Pa.: Hutterischen Brüdern in Amerika, 1920).

Ehrenpreis, Andreas, and Felbinger, Claus. *Brotherly Community: The Highest Command of Life.* Rifton, N.Y.: Plough Publishing House, 1978.

d'Elvert, Christian. *Geschichte der Studien-, Schuel-, und Erziehungs-anstalten in Mähren und Oesterreich—Schlesien.* Brünn, 1857.

Erhard, Christoph. *Gründliche kurtz verfaste Historia Von Münsterischen Widertauffern: und wie die Hutterischen Brüder so auch billich Widertauffer genent werden, im Löblichen Marggraffthumb Märhern, deren uber die sibentzehen tausent sein sollen, gedachten Münsterischen in vilen ähnlich, gleichformig und mit zustimmet sein.* Munich, 1589.

Fast, Heinold. *Der linke Flügel der Reformation: Glaubenszeugnisse der Täufer, Spiritualisten, Schwärmer und Antitrinitarier.* Klassiker des Protestantismus, Vol. IV, Sammlung Dieterich, Vol. 269. Bremen: C. Schünemann, 1962.

Fischer, Christoph Andreas. *Antwort auff die Widerlegung so Clausz Breütel* . . . *hat gethan auff das Buch, Von der Widertauffer verfluchten Vrsprung.* . . . Closter Bruck a. d. Teya, 1604.

————. *Der Hutterischen Widertauffer Taubenkobel, in welchem all ihr Wüst, Mist, Kott vnnd Vnflat* . . . *zu finden verfasset, Auch dess grossen Taubers, dess Jacob Hutters Leben* . . . *angehenckrischen Widertauffer* . . . Ingolstadt, 1607.

————. *Vier vnd funfftizig Erhebliche Vrsachen Warumb die Widertauffer nicht sein im Land zu leyden.* Ingolstadt, 1607.

————. *Von der Wiedertauffer verfluchten Vrsprung, Gottlosen Lehre, vnd derselben gründtliche widerlegung. Nach welcher gefragt wirdt,*

*Ob die Wiedertauffer im Land zu leyden sind oder nicht?* Bruck a. d. Teya, 1603.

Fischer, Hans. *Jakob Huter: Leben, Froemmigkeit, Briefe.* Newton, Kan.: Mennonite Publication Office, 1956.

Franck, Sebastian. *Chronica, Zeytbuch und geschychtbibel von anbegyn bisz inn disz gegenwertig M. D. xxxj jar.* . . . Strassburg, 1531.

Franz, Günther, ed. *Thomas Müntzer, Schriften und Briefe.* Gütersloh: Gerd Mohn, 1968.

————, ed. *Wiedertäuferakten 1527-1626.* Urkundliche Quellen zur hessischen Reformationsgeschichte, Vol. IV. Marburg: N. G. El-wert'sche Verlagsbuchhandlung, 1951.

Friedmann, Robert. "Die Briefe der österreichischen Täufer (Ein Bericht)." *ARG,* XXVI (1929), 30-80, 161-87.

————. "Claus Felbinger's Confession of 1560." *MQR,* XXIV (1955), 141-61; addendum in XXX (1956), 78.

————. "The Doctrine of Original Sin as Held by the Anabaptists of the Sixteenth Century." *MQR,* XXXIII (1959), 206-14.

————. "Eine dogmatische Hauptschrift der hutterischen Täufergemeinschaften in Mähren." *ARG,* XXVIII (1931), 80-111, 207-40, (Ergänzung der Bibliographie) 240-41; XXIX (1932), 1-17.

————. *Glaubenszeugnisse oberdeutscher Taufgesinnter.* Vol. II. Quellen zur Geschichte der Täufer, Vol. XII. Gütersloh: Gerd Mohn, 1967.

————. "Die Habaner in der Slowakei." (Offprint from) *Wiener Zeitschrift für Volkskunde,* XXXII (1927).

————. "Hutterite Physicians and Barber-Surgeons (Additional Notes)." *MQR,* XXVII (1953), 128-36.

————. *Hutterite Studies: Essays by Robert Friedmann, Collected and Published in Honor of His Seventieth Anniversary.* (Harold S. Bender, ed.) Goshen, Ind.: Mennonite Historical Society, 1961.

————. tr. and ed. "Hutterites Revisit European Homesteads: From the Diary of David Hofer." *MQR,* XXXIII (1959), 305-22, 346.

————. "Jacob Hutter's Epistle Concerning the Schism in Moravia in 1533." *MQR,* XXXVIII (1964), 329-43.

————. *Mennonite Piety through the Centuries: Its Genius and Its Literature.* Goshen, Ind.: Mennonite Historical Society, 1949.

————, ed. "A Newly Discovered Source on the Transmigration of the Hutterites to Transylvania, 1621-1623." *MQR,* XXXV (1961), 309-14.

————, "A Notable Hutterite Document Concerning True Surrender and Christian Community of Goods." With an Introduction by Robert

Friedmann; translated by Kathleen Hasenberg. *MQR*, XXXI (1957), 22-62.

_____. "Old Evangelical Brotherhoods: Theory and Fact." MQR, XXXVI (1962), 349-54.

_____. "The Oldest Church Discipline of the Anabaptists." *MQR*. XXIX (1955), 162-66; addendum in XXXII (1958), 236-37.

_____. "The Oldest Known Hutterite Codex of 1566: A Chapter in Anabaptist Intellectual History." *MQR*, XXXIII (1959), 96-107.

_____. "Peter Riedemann: Early Anabaptist Leader." *MQR*, XLIV (1970), 5-44.

_____. "The Philippite Brethren: A Chapter in Anabaptist History." *MQR*, XXXII (1958), 250-97.

_____. "The Re-establishment of Communal Life Among the Hutterites in Russia (1858)." *MQR*, XVI (1942), 82-98.

_____. *Die Schriften der huterischen Täufergemeinschaften: Gesamtkatalog ihrer Manuskriptbücher, ihrer Schreiber und ihrer Literatur, 1529-1667.* Vienna: Hermann Böhlaus Nachf., 1965.

_____. *The Theology of Anabaptism.* Scottdale, Pa.: Herald Press, 1973.

Fries, Lorenz. *Die Geschichte des Bauernkrieges in Ostfranken.* Edited by August Schäffler and Theodor Henner. 2 vols. Würzburg, 1876-83.

Grolig, M. "Die deutschen Handschriften der Studienbibliothek in Olmütz." *Zeitschrift des deutschen Vereins für die Geschichte Mährens und Schlesiens*, XXXI (1929), 85-113.

Gross, Leonard. "Dialogue Between a Hutterite and a Swiss Brother." *MQR*, XLIV (1970), 45-58.

_____. "Jakob Huter: Ein christlicher Kommunist." *Radikale Reformatoren*. Hans-Jürgen Goertz, ed. Munich: Verlag C. H. Beck, 1978, 137-45.

_____. "Leonhard Dax's Encounter with Calvinism, 1567/68." *MQR*, XLIX (1975), 284-334.

_____. "Newly Discovered Codices of the Hutterites." *MQR*, XLII (1968), 149-55.

_____. "Nikolaus Geyersbühler, Hutterite Missioner to Tirol." *MQR*, XLIII (1969), 283-92.

Gross, Paul, ed. *The Defence against the Prozess at Worms on the Rhine in the Year 1557.* n.p., n.d. (4th. ed.: Pincher Creek, Alta., 1955).

_____. *The Hutterite Way: The Inside Story of the Life, Customs, Religion, and Traditions of the Hutterites.* Saskatoon, Canada: Freeman Pub. Co., 1965.

Harada, Mary Ault. *Family Values and Child Care During the Reformation Era: A Comparative Study of Hutterites and Some Other German Protestants.* Ann Arbor, Mich.: University Microfilms, 1977.

Harnack, Adolf von. *Lehrbuch der Dogmengeschichte*, Vols. III and IV. 4th ed. Tübingen, 1910.

Hassinger, Erich. *Religiöse Toleranz im 16. Jahrhundert.* Vorträge der Aeneas-Silvius-Stiftung an der Universität Basel, Vol. VI. Basel and Stuttgart: Helbing and Lichtenhahn, 1966.

Hege, Christian. *Die Täufer in der Kurpfalz: Ein Beitrag zur badischpfälzischen Reformationsgeschichte.* Frankfurt am Main, 1908.

Heimann, Franz. "The Hutterite Doctrines of Church and Common Life: A Study of Peter Riedemann's Confession of Faith of 1540," *MQR,* XXVI (1952), 22-47, 142-60.

Hershberger, Guy F., ed. *The Recovery of the Anabaptist Vision: A Sixtieth Anniversary Tribute to Harold S. Bender. Scottdale, Pa.: Herald Press, 1957.*

Hillerbrand, Hans Joachim. "Anabaptism and the Reformation." *Church History,* XXIX (1960), 404-24.

_____. *Bibliographie des Täufertums, 1520-1630.* Quellen zur Geschichte der Täufer, Vol. XII. Gütersloh: Gerd Mohn, 1962. (Parallel Eng. ed.: *A Bibliography of Anabaptism, 1520-1630.* Elkhart, Ind.: Institute of Mennonite Studies, 1962.)

_____. "The Origin of Sixteenth-Century Anabaptism: Another Look." *ARG,* LIII (1962), 152-80.

_____. *The Reformation: A Narrative History Related by Contemporary Observers and Participants.* New York: Harper and Row, 1964.

_____. "Ein täuferisches Missionszeugnis aus dem 16. Jahrhundert." *Zeitschrift für Kirchengeschichte,* LXXI (1960), 324-27. (Eng.: "A Sixteenth Century Anabaptist Evangelistic Testimony," *MQR.* XXXV [1961], 314-17.)

Hochhuth, Karl Wilhelm Herman. "Landgraf Philip und die Wiedertäufer." *Zeitschrift für die historische Theologie,* XXVIII (1858), 538-644; XXIX (1859), 167-209.

Horsch, John. *The Hutterian Brethren, 1528-1931: A Story of Martyrdom and Loyalty.* Goshen, Ind.: Mennonite Historical Society, 1931.

Hostetler, John A. *Hutterite Society.* Baltimore: Johns Hopkins University Press, 1974.

Hostetler, John A., Gross, Leonard and Bender, Elizabeth. *Selected Hutterian Documents in Translation, 1542-1654.* Philadelphia, Pa.: Communal Studies Center (222 Gladfelter Hall, Temple University,

Philadelphia, Pa. 19122), 1975.

Hrubý, František. "Die Widertäufer in Mähren." *ARG*, XXX (1933), 1-36, 170-211; XXXI (1934), 61-102; XXXII (1935), 1-40. (Also as offprint.)

Jäkel, Joseph. *Zur Geschichte der Wiedertäufer in Oberösterreich und speciell in Freistadt mit einer Einleitung über Entstehung und Wesen des Täuferthums überhaupt.* In: Bericht über d. Museum Francisco-Carolinum Linz XLVII (1889), 1-82.

Jedelshauser, Hans. *Zwelff wichtige vnd starke Vrsachen Hansen Jedelshausers. . . .* Ingolstat, 1587.

Jenny, Beatrice. "Das Schleitheimer Täuferbekenntnis 1527." *Schaffhauser Beiträge zur vaterländischen Geschichte*, XXVIII (1951).

Klaassen, Walter. *Anabaptism: Neither Catholic nor Protestant.* Waterloo, Ont.: Conrad Press, 1973.

Klusch, Horst. "Die Habaner in Siebenbürgen." *Forschungen zur Volks- und Landeskunde*, XI (1968), 21-40.

Köhler, Walther. *Reformation und Ketzerprozess.* Tübingen, 1901.

_____. "Die Zürcher Täufer." *Gedenkschrift zum 400 jährigen Jubiläum der Mennoniten.* Ludwigshafen, 1925.

Kot, Stanislaw. "Polish Brethren and the Problem of Communism in the Sixteenth Century." *Transactions of the Unitarian Historical Society*, XI (1956), 38-54.

_____ *Socinianism in Poland: The Social and Political Ideas of the Polish Antitrinitarians in the Sixteenth and Seventeenth Centuries.* Boston: Starr King Press, 1957.

_____, ed. "A Treatise not against that Apostolic Community, formerly in Jerusalem and described and commended by the New Testament, which should exist among the true followers of Christ, but against such as has been recommended by one of the numerous sects which multiplied from the teaching of Jesus after His Ascension, known as the 'Communists' in Moravia. *Extra quam*—they say—*non est salus.*" *Transactions of the Unitarian Historical Society*, XI (1957), 90-104.

Krajewski, Ekkehard. *Leben und Sterben des Zürcher Taüferführers Felix Mantz. . . .* Kassel: J. G. Oncken, 1957.

Kraus, František. *Nové Príspevky k dejinám Habánov na Slovensku.* Bratislava, 1937.

Krebs, Manfred, ed. *Baden und Pfalz.* Quellen zur Geschichte der Täufer, Vol. IV. Gütersloh: C. Bertelsmann, 1951.

Krisztinkovich, Bela. "Unbekannte Messerschmied-Kunstwerke der Ungarischen Habanen." n.d. (Copy in the Mennonite Historical Library, Goshen, Ind.)

Krisztinkovich, Maria H. "Anabaptist Book Confiscations in Hungary During the Eighteenth Century." *MQR*, XXXIX (1965), 125-46.

_____. "Some Further Notes on the Hutterites in Transylvania." *MQR*, XXXVII (1963), 203-13.

Kühn, Johannes. *Toleranz und Offenbarung: Eine Untersuchung der Motive und Motivformen der Toleranz im offenbarungsgläubigen Protestantismus. Zugleich ein Versuch zur neuerer Religion- und Geistesgeschichte.* Leipzig, 1923.

Lecler, Joseph. *Histoire de la Tolérance au siècle de la Réforme.* Paris: Editions Montaigne (F. Aubier), 1955. (Eng.: *Toleration and the Reformation.* New York: Association Press, 1960.)

*Die Lieder der Hutterischen Brüder.* . . . Scottdale, Pa., 1914.

Liliencron, Rochus v. "Zur Liederdichtung der Wiedertäufer. . . ."*Abhandlungen der K. Bayer. Akad. d. Wissenschaften,* Cl. III, Vol. XIII, Div. I. Munich, 1875.

Littell, Franklin H. *The Anabaptist View of the Church.* . . . 2nd. ed. Boston: Starr King Press, 1958. (Republished as *The Origins of Sectarian Protestantism.* . . . N.Y.: Macmillan, 1964.)

_____. *Landgraf Philipp und die Toleranz.* . . . Bad Nauheim: Christian-Verlag, 1957.

Loserth, Johann. *Der Anabaptismus in Tirol.* Vienna, 1892.

_____. "Der Communismus der mährischen Wiedertäufer im 16. und 17. Jahrhundert: Beiträge zu ihrer Geschichte, Lehre und Verfassung." *Archiv für österreichische Geschichte,* LXXXI (1894), 137-322.

_____. "The Decline and Revival of the Hutterites." *MQR*, IV (1930), 93-112.

_____. *Doctor Balthasar Hubmaier und die Anfänge der Wiedertäufer in Mähren.* Brünn, 1893.

_____. *Georg Blaurock und die Anfänge des Anabaptismus in Graubündten und Tirol.* Berlin, 1899.

_____. "Die Stadt Waldshut und die vorderösterreichische Regierung in den Jahren 1523-1526." *Archiv für österreichische Geschichte,* LXXVII (1891).

_____. "Zur Geschichte der Wiedertäufer in Mähren." *Zeitschrift für Allgemeine Geschichte, Kultur-, Litteratur- und Kunstgeschichte,* I (1884), 438-57.

Lubieniesus, Stanislas. *Historia Reformationis Polonicae.* Freistad, 1685.

Mais, Adolf. "Gefängnis und Tod der in Wien hingerichteten Wiedertäufer in ihren Briefen und Liedern." *Jahrbuch des Vereins für Geschichte der Stadt Wien,* Vol. XIX/XX (1963/64), 87-182.

─────, ed. "Das Hausbuch von Neumühl 1558-1610, das älteste Grundbuch der huterischen Brüder." *Jahrbuch der Gesellschaft für die Geschichte des Protestantismus in Oesterreich,* LXXX (1964), 66-88. (Eng.: "The Hausbuch of Neumühl 1558-1610, the Oldest Land Register of the Hutterian Brethren." *MQR,* XLVIII [1974], 215-36.)

Mecenseffy, Grete. *Geschichte des Protestantismus in Oesterreich.* Graz: Hermann Böhlaus Nachfolger, 1956.

─────. "Die Herkunft des oberösterreichischen Täufertums." *ARG,* XLVII, (1956), 252-59.

─────. *Österreich, I. Teil.* Quellen zur Geschichte der Täufer, Vol. XI. Gütersloh: Gerd Mohn, 1964.

─────. *Österreich, II. Teil.* Quellen zur Geschichte der Täufer, Vol. XIII. Gütersloh: Gerd Mohn, 1972.

Meihuizen, H.W. "Who Were the 'False Brethren' Mentioned in the Schleitheim Articles?" *MQR,* XLI (1967), 200-222.

*The Mennonite Encyclopedia.* 4 vols. Scottdale, Pa.: Mennonite Publishing House, 1955-59.

*Mennonitisches Lexikon.* 4 vols. Frankfurt/M. and Karlsruhe, 1913-67.

Meyer, Christian. "Zur Geschichte der Wiedertäufer in Oberschwaben. I: Die Anfänge des Wiedertäufertums in Augsburg." *Zeitschrift des historischen Vereins für Schwaben und Neuburg,* I (1874), 207-53.

Müller, Lydia, ed. *Glaubenszeugnisse oberdeutscher Taufgesinnter.* Vol. I. Quellen zur Geschichte der Wiedertäufer, Vol. III. Leipzig, 1938.

─────. *Der Kommunismus der mährischen Wiedertäufer.* Schriften des Vereins für Reformationsgeschichte, Vol. XLV. No. 1. Leipzig, 1927.

Muralt, Leonhard von, and Schmid, Walter, eds. *Quellen zur Geschichte der Täufer in der Schweiz.* Vol. I. Zürich; S. Hirzel Verlag, 1952.

Neumann, Gerhard. "Nach und von Mähren. Aus der Täufergeschichte des 16. and 17. Jahrhunderts." *ARG,* XLVIII (1957), 75-90.

─────. "'Rechtfertigung' und 'Person Christi' als dogmatische Glaubensfragen bei den Täufern der Reformationszeit." *Zeitschrift für Kirchengeschichte,* LXX (1959), 62-74.

Neuser, Wilhelm. *Hans Hut, Leben und Wirken bis zum Nikolsburger Religionsgespräch.* Berlin, 1913.

Ott, Johannes Heinrich. *Annales Anabaptistici, hoc est, Historia universalis de Anabaptistarum. . . .* Basel, 1672.

Oyer, John S. *Lutheran Reformers against Anabaptists: Luther, Melanchthon and Menius and the Anabaptists of Central Germany.* The Hague: Martinus Nijhoff, 1964.

Padover, Saul K. *The Revolutionary Emperor: Joseph II of Austria.* Hamden, Conn.: Shoe String Press, 1967.

Paulus, Nikolaus. *Protestantismus und Toleranz im 16. Jahrhundert.* Freiburg im Breisgau, 1911.

Peters, Karl Andreas. *Factors of Social Change and Social Dynamics in the Communal Settlements of Hutterites, 1527-1967.* Ms. n.d. (Copy in the Mennonite Historical Library, Goshen, Ind.)

Peters, Victor. *All Things Common: The Hutterian Way of Life.* Minneapolis: University of Minnesota Press, 1965.

*Protocoll. Das ist, alle handlung des gesprechs zu Franckenthal inn der Churfürstlichen Pfalz, mit denen so man Widertäuffer nennet....* Heidelberg, 1571.

*Prozess, wie es soll gehalten werden mit den Wiedertäuffern. Durch etliche gelerten—so zu Wormbs versammlet gewesen, gestellet.* Worms, n.d.

Purcell, John F. "The Moravian Hutterites, 1529-1622: Their Theology and Way of Life." 1976. (Copy in the Mennonite Historical Library, Goshen, Ind.)

Reddaway, W.F., et al., eds. *The Cambridge History of Poland,* Vol. I. Cambridge: The University Press, 1950.

Redekop, Calvin W. *The Free Church and Seductive Culture.* Scottdale, Pa.: Herald Press, 1970.

Rhode, Gotthold. *Geschichte Polens.* Darmstadt, 1966.

Riedemann, Peter. *Rechenschaft unserer Religion, Lehr und Glaubens, von den Brüdern, so man die Hutterischen nennt, ausgangen durch Peter Rideman.* Ashton Keynes, Wilts, England, 1938. (Eng. *Account of Our Religion, Doctrine and Faith, Given by Peter Rideman of the Brothers Whom Men Call Hutterians.* Suffolk, England, 1950; Rifton, N.Y.: Plough Publishing House, 1974.

Ritschl, Albrecht. *Geschichte des Pietismus in der reformierten Kirche.* Bonn, 1880.

Runzo, Jean Ellen Goodban. *Communal Discipline in the Early Anabaptist Communities of Switzerland, South and Central Germany, Austria, and Moravia, 1525-1550.* Ann Arbor, Mich.: University Microfilms, 1978.

Saliger, W. "Peter Scherers (Schörers) Rede, welche er mit anderen Aeltesten den Schulmeistern zu Niemtschitz in Mähren am 15. November 1568 gehalten hat, und die Schulordnung vom Jahre 1578." *Mitteilungen der Gesellschaft für deutsche Erziehungs- und Schulgeschichte,* XI (1901), 112-27.

Scharnschlager, Leupold. "A Church Order for Members of Christ's Body,

Arranged in Seven Articles." *MQR*, XXXVIII (1964), 354-56, 386.

Schäufele, Wolfgang. *Das missionarische Bewusstsein und Wirken der Täufer: Dargestellt nach oberdeutschen Quellen.* Neukirchen: Neukirchener Verlag des Erziehungsvereins, 1966.

Schraepler, Horst W. *Die rechtliche Behandlung der Täufer in der deutschen Schweiz, Südwestdeutschland und Hessen, 1525-1618.* Schriften zur Kirchen- und Rechtsgeschichte, Vol. IV. Tübingen, 1957.

Schwabe, Ludwig. "Ueber Hans Denk." *Zeitschrift für Kirchengeschichte*, XII (1891), 452-93.

Seebass, Gottfried. *Müntzers Erbe: Werk, Leben und Theologie des Hans Hut.* Quellen und Forschungen zur Reformationsgeschichte. Vol. XLIV. Gütersloh: Gerd Mohn, 1974.

Sommers, John L. "Hutterite Medicine and Physicians in Moravia in the Sixteenth Century and After." *MQR*, XXVII (1953), 111-27.

Stayer, James M. *Anabaptists and the Sword.* Lawrence, Kan.: Coronado Press, 1972.

Troeltsch, Ernst. *Die Soziallehren der christlichen Kirchen und Gruppen.* Tübingen, 1912. (Eng.: *Social Teachings of the Christian Churches.* London, 1931.)

Wagner, Ernst. *Historisch-Statistisches Ortsnamenbuch: Mit einer Einführung in die historische Statistik des Landes.* Cologne-Vienna: Böhlau Verlag, 1977.

Waltner, Gary James. *The Educational System of the Hutterian Anabaptists and their Schulordnungen of the 16th and 17th Centuries.* [Vermillion, S.D.], 1975. (Master's Thesis, University of South Dakota. Copy in the Mennonite Historical Library, Goshen, Ind.)

Wappler, Paul. *Die Stellung Kursachsens und des Landgrafen Philipp von Hessen zur Täuferbewegung.* Münster, 1910.

_____. Die Täuferbewegung in Thüringen von 1526-1584. Jena, 1913.

Wenger, John C. ed. *Conrad Grebel's Programmatic Letters of 1524. . . .* Scottdale, Pa.: Herald Press, 1970.

_____, ed. "Schleitheim Confession of Faith." *MQR*, XIX (1945), 243-53.

Wengierski, Adalb (Wojciech), ed. *Chronik der Evangelischen Gemeinde zu Krakau von ihren Anfängen bis 1657.* Breslau, 1880.

Westin, Gunnar and Bersten, Torsten, eds. *Balthasar Hubmaier Schriften.* Quellen zur Geschichte der Täufer, Vol. IX. Gütersloh: Gerd Mohn, 1962.

Widmoser, Eduard. "Das Täufertum im Tiroler Unterland." Dissertation, Leopold Franzens Universität, Innsbruck, 1948.

_____ "Die Wiedertäufer in Tirol." Part One: *Tiroler Heimat*, XV (1951), 45-89; "Das Tiroler Täufertum." Part Two: *Tiroler Heimat*, XVI (1952), 103-28.

Wilbur, Earl Morse. *A Bibliography of the Pioneers of the Socinian-Unitarian Movement in Modern Christianity, in Italy, Switzerland, Germany, Holland.* Rome, 1950.

_____ *A History of Unitarianism, Socinianism and Its Antecedents.* Cambridge, Mass.: Harvard University Press, 1945.

Williams, George Huntston. "Anabaptism and Spiritualism in the Kingdom of Poland and the Grand Duchy of Lithuania: An Obscure Phase of the Pre-History of Socinianism," Ludwika Chmaja, ed., *Studia Nad Arianizmen* (Warsaw, 1959), 215-62.

_____ *The Radical Reformation.* Philadelphia: Westminster Press, 1962.

_____ and Mergel, Angel M., eds. *Spiritual and Anabaptist Writers.* The Library of Christian Classics, Vol. 25. Philadelphia: Westminster Press, 1957.

_____ "Studies in the Radical Reformation (1517-1618): A Bibliographical Survey of the Research since 1939." *Church History*, XXVII (1958), 46-69, 124-60.

Wiswedel, Wilhelm. "Die alten Täufergemeinden und ihr missionarisches Wirken." *ARG*, XL (1943), 183-200; XLI (1948), 115-32.

_____ *Bilder und Führergestalten aus dem Täufertum: Ein Beitrag zur Reformationsgeschichte des 16. Jahrhunderts.* 3 vols. Kassel: J. G. Oncken, 1928-52.

_____ "Das Schulwesen der huterischen Brüder in Mähren." *ARG*, XXXVIII (1940), 38-60.

Wolkan, Rudolf, ed. *Geschicht-Buch der Hutterischen Brüder.* Macleod, Alta.: Standoff-Colony, 1923.

_____ *Die Hutterer: Oesterreichische Wiedertäufer und Kommunisten in Amerika.* Vienna, 1918.

_____ *Die Lieder der Wiedertäufer: Ein Beitrag zur deutschen und niederländischen Litteratur- und Kirchengeschichte.* Berlin, 1903.

Wotschke, Theodor. *Geschichte der Reformation in Polen.* Leipzig, 1911.

Yoder, John Howard, ed. *The Legacy of Michael Sattler.* Scottdale, Pa.: Herald Press, 1973.

_____ "The Prophetic Dissent of the Anabaptists." *The Recovery of the Anabaptist Vision.* Guy F. Hershberger, ed. Scottdale, Pa.: Herald Press, 1957.

_____ *Täufertum und Reformation im Gespräch.* Zurich: EVZ Verlag, 1968.

_____ *Täufertum und Reformation in der Schweiz, I: Die Gespräche zwischen Täufern und Reformatoren, 1523-1538.* Karlsruhe: Mennonitischer Geschichtsverein, 1962.

_____ "The Turning Point in the Zwinglian Reformation." *MQR,* XXXII (1958), 128-40.

_____ "Zwingli." *ME,* IV, 1052-54.

Zath, Peter von. "Studien zur Entstehung der sozialen Ideen des Täufertums in den ersten Jahren der Reformation." Unpublished Ph.D. dissertation, Freiburg University, 1942.

Zeman, Jarold Knox. *The Anabaptists and the Czech Brethren in Moravia, 1526-1628: A Study of Origins and Contacts.* The Hague: Mouton, 1969.

_____ "Historical Topography of Moravian Anabaptism." *MQR,* XL (1966), 266-78; XLI (1967), 40-78, 116-60.

Zieglschmid, A. J. F., ed. *Die älteste Chronik der Hutterischen Brüder.* . . . Philadelphia: The Carl Schurz Memorial Foundation, 1943.

_____, ed. *Das Klein-Geschichtsbuch der Hutterischen Brüder.* Philadelphia: The Carl Schurz Memorial Foundation, 1947.

# Description of
# the Brotherhood[1]

During these years God gave his people quiet times. For after the Lord had purified his church in various ways, allowing it to experience all kinds of tribulation, misery, and poverty for many years (as can be found above in this book), God then took it upon himself (which we cannot help but describe separately, in honor and remembrance of him) also to grant his people quiet times and rich blessings, as he did to the devout Job after his temptation. This he did to see how they would act in the same, and also so that his work and establishment would be publicly carried out and become known to all people, resounding afar. This God did. And he gave his people good quiet times, contrary to the intentions of the whole world, so that there was no general tribulation or persecution for twenty years and more (except what happened from time to time) as will be seen below.

However, in these times many charges and resolutions were pronounced by emperor and king at the Imperial Diets, and also in the provincial diets, the latter consisting of various social classes and faiths. Although they were otherwise quite disunited, in this they all agreed: that this people is to be exterminated and not tolerated anywhere. But the Lord prevented this in many a way and at many times (Acts 4[:5-22]; Is. 8[:5-15], 19[:1-24]; Ps. 33[:8-22]). Once he gave them something else to worry about; another time he took away their courage to carry out their plans. For the Lord can make the flag fly according to his wind.

Many appeared who resolved not to lay their heads on a pillow until they had expelled and exterminated [God's people]—even receiving power

1 This interpretive historical account of the Hutterian Brotherhood was incorporated into the Great Chronicle (Z, 430-40) as a description of the life and times of the movement during the late 1560s. It is a vivid picture of Hutterianism, interpreted from the vantage point of the 1580s or early 90s. The past tense is used throughout this portrayal, as if the Golden Years had already passed their prime, and in some ways had already come to an end. Tribulation (1592 ff.) may have already set in, and the smell of change was in the air. The account is written with a gilded pen, where the olden times were well nigh hallowed as an epoch approaching perfection. The unfolding story of the Walpot Era as portrayed throughout this volume provides criteria by which to judge this rose-tinted, somewhat nostalgic portrait.

(but not from God) for this purpose. But the Lord destroyed them before they could begin. Many intended to inflict suffering [on God's people], but only brought harm to themselves (Jer. 2[:14-37]).

There was a great deal of discussion. One counseled that they should all be hanged; another wanted to burn them; a third called for the apprehending of the elders, thereby destroying them at the roots. A fourth wished he had power over them; he would know how, by this means or that, to deal properly with them so that they would be removed from the earth. But such people often lived only for a short time after that, and death prevented their adding many more years to their lives; this we have experienced and could tell about with names.

The tribe of priests continuously incited the powers that be wherever they could, as is still the case. But the Lord our God stood in the way, the Archangel Michael, who stands before the children of his people; otherwise his people would long since have been swallowed up and devoured like bread. But as a hen gathers her young under her feathers and wings, protecting them, snapping and pecking at all that want to attack her own— indeed, as an eagle hovers over his young—this and much more God did for the sake of his people to the point that even the unbelievers often had to recognize and acknowledge that God did not desire this people to be annihilated or driven out (Dan. 12[:1-3]; Ps. 124; 2 Esd. 1[:28-32]; Mt. 23[:37-39]; Deut. 32[:1-43]).

They dwelt in the land which God had provided especially for them. They were given the wings of a great eagle (Rev. 12[:14]) and flew to the place which God prepared for them, and were established and sustained there as long as it pleased God. Thus they gathered in peace and unity, taught and preached the gospel and the Word of God publicly; twice a week, sometimes more often, they held meetings to proclaim the Word of God (Heb. 10[:25]; 2 Tim. 2[:1-2]). In these meetings the communal, united prayer was offered to God, asking him for all the needs of the Brotherhood and giving joyful thanks for all the good things they enjoyed. Likewise, intercession was made for emperor, king, princes, and worldly powers, that God might make them consider the office entrusted to them and conduct it properly for the protection of the devout and for peaceful government [1 Tim. 2:1-2].

Furthermore, the Christian ban was used against the wicked when they were discovered in the Brotherhood. The Brotherhood banned, separated, and punished the wicked, each according to his transgressions; when they showed true repentance, they were reaccepted into the Church (Mt. 18[:15-18]; 1 Cor. 5[:9-13]).

In accordance with the Lord's command and the practice of the apostles, Christian baptism was given to people who were grown up, who could hear the Word of God and could understand, accept, and believe it, infant baptism being totally false and opposed to [the apostles' teaching] (Mt. 28[:16-20]; Mk. 16 [:16]; Acts 2[:38-41]; 8[:36-39]; 10[:44-48]; 16[:33-34]; 19[:1-7]).

The people assembled and celebrated the Lord's Supper to remember and continually refresh the holy memory of the suffering and death of Jesus Christ, who through his death redeemed us, who were otherwise lost, and brought us back, making us of one mind to be members of his body. It was a celebration of thanksgiving for his love and unspeakable kindness for what he has done for our sakes; this we in turn should do for his sake, in thanksgiving. Such a celebration of the Lord's Supper stands opposed to the idolatrous sacrament of the priests (Mt. 26[:17-29]; Lk. 22[:7-19]; Acts 2[:42, 46]; 20[:7]; 1 Cor. 10[:14-22]; 11[:17-34]).

Christian community of goods was practiced as Christ taught it and lived it with his disciples, and as the first apostolic church practiced it. No one was permitted to be above the others. Those who earlier had been poor or rich now shared one purse, one house, and one table; yet the healthy [were cared for] as healthy, the sick as sick, and the children as children (Mt. 19[:16-22]; Lk. 14[:7-14]; Jn. 13[:1-20]; Acts 2[:43-47]; 4[:32-37]; 5[:1-11]).

Swords and spears were forged into pruning knives, saws, and other useful tools and were so used. There was no musket, saber, halberd, or any weapon made for defense. Rather, each was completely a brother to the other, a thoroughly peaceful people who never helped—much less took part actively—in any war or in bloodshed, or in the payment of war taxes. They did not resort to revenge; instead, patience was their weapon in all strife (Mt. 23[:29-36]; Mt. 5[:21-26, 43-48]; Rom. 12[:14-19]).

They were subject to the authorities and obedient to them in all good works, in all things that were not against God, their faith, or their conscience. They paid their taxes, annual dues, interest, tithes, customs, and supplied labor and services. They honored the government because of its divinely ordained office, as necessary in this wicked world as daily bread (Rom. 13[:1-7]; 1 Pet. 2[:13-17]).

In conclusion, all Twelve Articles of the Christian apostolic faith were confessed and observed, and everything that is founded upon Holy Scripture.

They carried out Christian mission according to the command of the Lord: "As my Father has sent me, so I send you," and also: "I have chosen and established you that you go out and bear fruit." Therefore each year servants of the gospel and their helpers were sent out into the lands where there was a call. They visited those who desired to live better lives, and who sought and inquired after the truth. These they led out of their land by day and by night according to their desire, heedless of constable and hangman, so that many gave their lives for this cause. Thus they gathered God's people in a manner befitting good shepherds (Mt. 10[:1-23]; 28[:16-20]; Mk. 16[:14-17]; Jn. 15[:18-27]; 20[:19-23]).

They separated themselves from the world and its evil, unjust life; they especially also shunned the false prophets and false brethren (2 Cor. 6[:1-10]; Rev. 18[:4-8]; 2 Cor. 5[:1-10]; 2 Jn. 1[:10-11]).

No cursing or blasphemous swearing was heard, without which the world cannot speak. No oaths or vows were made. There was no dancing, gambling, carousing. They did not make fancy, fashionable, and immodest clothes; such things were done away with. They did not sing shameful, immoral songs of which the world is full, but instead sang Christian and spiritual songs, and songs of Bible stories (Mt. 5[:33-37]; Jas. 5[:7-12]; Eph. 5[:1-20]; Col. 3[:1-17]).

The places of responsibility were held by elders, men who led the people with the Word of God by reading, teaching, and exhorting them through Scripture. They practiced admonition and reconciliation, putting right any mistakes and wrongdoings (Tit. 1[:5-9]; Acts 6[:1-7]; 1 Tim. 4[:6-16]).

Men were carefully chosen to be in charge of the management of temporal affairs; they made and received payments, provided for food and supplies, and did the buying and selling. Others were in charge of arranging the work and sending each one to the job he knew and could do well, in the field or wherever necessary. These were the field managers ("Weinzierl"). Others were in charge of the table service. The meals began with prayer and thanksgiving to God, and thanks were given at the end before returning to work. Thanksgiving and prayer was offered at bedtime and again in the morning upon arising before going out, each one to his job. Others were responsible for the school. Together with the sisters appointed for the care and instruction of young children, they were in charge of the education and discipline of the children.

There was no usury or taking of interest, no buying and selling for gain. There was only honest work to earn a living with the daily toil of those working as stonemasons and farmers, in the vineyards, fields, meadows, and gardens (Eph. 4[:17-32]; 2 Thess. 3[:6-13]). Many carpenters and builders went out, not only within Moravia, but even into Austria, Hungary, and Bohemia to build many substantial mills, breweries, and other buildings at just wages for the lords, nobles, citizens, and other people. For this purpose a brother was specially assigned, an experienced builder who organized the carpenters, accepted work, bargained, and made arrangements with people on behalf of the Brotherhood.

Many were millers; and many mills in the land, owned by the lords and others, upon their request were leased to the brethren. These looked after the grinding, for which a just agreement was reached, a third or a fourth, according to the custom of the land. Therefore, a brother was appointed to take on such mills on behalf of the Brotherhood with the advice of the elders, to bargain and make agreements with the mill owners, to assign the millers, and in general to see to it that the mills were staffed and functioning well.

For a long time the lords and noblemen (especially those on whose land we dwelt) employed our people to run their farms and dairies, some for a third, some for wages, whatever was acceptable to both parties. A brother was responsible for taking on such dairy farms in response to the landlords' requests, which could not always be met immediately. This brother saw to it that enough people were available to staff the dairy farms.

In short, no one was idle; each did what was required and what he was able to do, whether he had been poor or rich, noble or commoner, before. Even the priests who joined the Brotherhood learned to labor and work.

Then there were all sorts of honorable, useful trades: mason, scythe-smith, blacksmith, coppersmith, locksmith, clockmaker, cutter, plumber, tanner, furrier, cobbler, saddler, harness maker, bag maker, wagon maker, cooper, joiner, turner, hatter, clothmaker, tailor, blanket maker, weaver, rope maker, sieve maker, glazier, potter, beer brewer, barber-surgeon, physician. In each work department one brother was in charge of the shop, received orders and planned the work, then sold the products at their fair value and handed the proceeds over to the Brotherhood.

Everyone, wherever he was, worked for the common good, to supply the needs of all, and to give help and support wherever it was needed. It was indeed a perfect body whose living members served and helped one another.

Just as in the ingenious works of a clock, where one piece helps another to make it go so that it serves its purpose; or as in a colony of bees, those useful little animals who work together in their common hive, some making wax, some the honey, some fetching water, or working in other ways, until their precious work of making sweet honey is done, not only for their own needs but that people may also be supplied—so it was among them. There has to be an ordered life in all areas of existence, for the matters of life can be properly maintained and furthered only where orderliness reigns—even more so in the House of God who is himself the Master Builder and Establisher. When there is no order, there is disorder and collapse, and there God does not dwell.

Furthermore, the Brotherhood became widely known on the one hand through those who again and again were imprisoned for the sake of their witness to Jesus Christ and his truth, both servants of the Word and other brothers who in many different ways were painstakingly asked about the basis of their faith. This happened throughout the German lands, since the brothers were imprisoned in many places and often for long periods of time; in word and deed, in life and by death, they witnessed that their faith was the truth. On the other hand, emperors, kings, princes, lords, and those at their courts, especially in the German lands, became acquainted with the Brotherhood's religion, practice, teaching, faith, and life; they often came to see for themselves, and in this and other ways learned of the Brotherhood's harmlessness, finding that the evil reports about the brothers were untrue. Many were convinced and praised them as a devout people that must have been established by God. It would otherwise have been impossible for so many to live together in unity, whereas among others, where only two, three, or four live together they are daily in each other's hair and quarrel until they run from one another.

Some would have liked nothing better than to employ them for their services and work. Here they were appreciated more than other people; so there were too few of them in the land, since—because of their faithfulness—everyone wanted them for his own benefit. But because of their religion there were always too many of them in the land.

And so it was a remarkable affair. Some lords were angry and ill-disposed to them because of their faith and did not want them to be tolerated in the land; others were angry when they were not given more people to work for them, although for many years they kept asking. In short, some wanted to have them accepted, others wanted to have them expelled; some said the best about them, others the worst.

The whole world was unwilling to tolerate them, yet it had to. God divided the sea—the raging nations of this world—so that people could be gathered from all lands and dwell together in great numbers, acting without fear. This was the work of the Lord, opposed to the devil and the world. Indeed, it is an amazing work of God, whoever thinks about it. Some people thought [the Hutterian way of life] was good and right for those who could do it, others wished they too could live like that; still others, the great majority, in their blindness saw it as error and seduction, or as a human undertaking (Is. 11[:10-16]; 49[:8-13]).

Yet all the world hated and envied them so that they might have said with David, "We have more enemies than hairs on our head" (Ps. 69[:4]). As soon as they stepped outside the door they were slandered and abused, called "Anabaptists, two-time baptizers, new baptizers, schismatics, agitators," and all kinds of insulting names. Everywhere people disparaged them, despised and mocked them with gruesome lies and accusations, such as that they ate children and other horrible things, which would have grieved us deeply had we even dreamed of them, much less done them. Many slanderous accusations of things that are not human, let alone Christian, were brought against the Brotherhood to lay them open to suspicion and hatred (Mt. 5[:11-12]; Lk. 6[:22-23]; 2 Cor. 6[:4-5]; 1 Pet. 4[:12-19]).

The world hated and persecuted us solely for the sake of Christ's name and of his truth because we followed him, and for no other reason. And this was a true sign: if a person traveled about with only a staff in his hand as a sign that he did not want to do harm to anyone, or if he prayed when he was about to eat, he was called an Anabaptist, a heretic, this and that—so coarse is the devil! But as soon as one deserted the Church and walked according to the ways of the heathen, a sword at his side and musket on his shoulder, from that moment on he was welcome to the world and "a good Christian" in their eyes.

One who went about without a ruffle round his neck or other signs of vanity on his clothes, saying that gambling, pride, haughtiness, gluttony, drunkeness, and carousing are sin, evil, and against God, and conducting himself in a quiet way with patience and other qualities befitting a disciple of Christ—such a one was reckoned by the world to be a heretic, a sectarian, a deceiver, a fool, etc. He was hated and despised by people who had never even seen him before and knew of no wrongdoing of which to accuse him, since he had wronged no one nor had any wish to do so. To such a pass have things come in the world!

But one who forsook [the Brotherhood], joined the world once more, and stepped into the inn saying, "Boys, I will treat you to a drink," singing immoral songs, drinking wildly in their company, sticking a silly plume in his hat as a fool's sign; if he then indulged in gambling and dancing, wearing a huge ruff around his neck, baggy trousers, and clothes with ornamental slits, making a show of their many and much-honored sacraments, spreading syphilis and other dreadful curses, and swearing and blaspheming God—from that moment on, such a person was loved and befriended by the world and recognized as one of them; they were satisfied with him and praised him, saying, "Well done! You were right to leave the brethren, to be converted and become a good Christian. Now you have the true faith, do not let yourself be led astray from the Christian Church. You did well to leave the brethren and separate yourself from this sect," as they say. Wherever he goes he will find good friends. People like him and accept him even if they have never seen or known him before. They can see all his wicked deeds and vices and still he is liked by the world because he has forsaken the truth of God.

From all this it is clear that they hate and persecute us simply because we are devoted to God uniquely for the sake of God's truth—the cause of their hatred occasioned by envy which stems from the serpent of old. Although no one wants to admit it, there is no denying it.

Then there was no little hate coming from the people who lived round about us in envy, as Esau envied Jacob, on account of the blessings God allowed to flow to us besides what we earned with the toil of our hand. We had what we needed in house and home and—thank God—food, while they for the most part had to make do with very little because they spent it all on drink; they wasted their time and often spent money before it was earned, and loved a life of leisure and laziness.

Finally, we should relate how the false brethren and congregations themselves seemed to take greater interest in complaining about the taking to task the Brotherhood of God than they did anyone else. They specifically and grievously maligned the Brotherhood, and viewed it as highly offensive. Rude and overt expressions of hate and resentment have been the consequence of our reproving them for their mistakes and deviations into which they had fallen. The verse in the gospel is still appropriately true where Christ speaks about his own, that "you will be hated by all for my name's sake." (Mt. 10[:22]; 24[:9]). Because the Lord's Word truly applies to us, all of this simply reassures and strengthens us all the more.

The Lord also strengthens and gives us, his Church, a great witness through those who fall away from truth and again return to the world. Many of them—however long they live outside—are given no quiet and peace in their hearts month after month, whether they advance in society or regress. No matter what they set themselves to do, their conscience constantly smites them, and they constantly have a pounding in their hearts for falling away. Many return deeply convicted, and with weeping and tears, repent and confess their sins, and seek peace with God and his Church rather than to lose their lives through forsaking or compromising the truth.

Indeed the many experiences we have had in this regard grant us a deep sense of security, our having heard and seen for ourselves the despair of the backsliders and their great dread and heartfelt sorrow, individuals who had once confessed and accepted such truth of God, but then deviated from it—that when God seized them in sickness, and when death hovered over them (at which time all things are revealed to man) how they then lamented so deplorably with fruitless, belated regrets that they, as apostates, had turned from the truth of God, and now had to die in their apostasy.

Some saw their reward and punishment before their very own eyes, and carried on frightfully, crying out damnation upon themselves as being among those who could no longer be helped. Others related how they themselves with their own feet had now pushed the door of heaven shut in front of them. Still others admitted that if they would still have been brethren, and would have repented, then they would gladly die and part from this life. Many prayed and pleaded anxiously that God would permit them one more single chance to regain their health. They would repent and return to what they had forsaken. Many who recovered did indeed return without a moment's hesitation. Many, however, were never able to reach or experience such reconciliation, but rather, as already stated, died with heavy conscience and in the state of deep dread, passing on with those who had mocked God one too many times. For when God called to them, they were not interested. Now when they pleaded, it was the Lord's turn not to show interest (Jer. 7; Prov. 2[:1-15]; Ps. 81[:6-16]).

With this we want to bring the section to a close, and return again to the relating of other things.

# Index of
# Biblical References

# Index

# The Author

Since 1970, Leonard Gross has served as executive secretary of the Historical Committee of the Mennonite Church and director of its archives and historical research program located on the campus of Goshen College, Goshen, Indiana. From 1968 to 1970 he taught history at Western Michigan University, Kalamazoo, Michigan.

He studied as a Fulbright Scholar at the University of Basel and completed his doctoral examinations there in 1968 in the areas of church history, general history, and New Testament.

From 1959 to 1964 he taught history and sociology at Bethany Christian High School, Goshen, Indiana. From 1955 to 1957 he was engaged in youth work in North Germany on assignment with Mennonite Central Committee.

Gross has published articles and essays in various North American and European journals and books. His latest essay is: "Jakob Huter. Ein christlicher Kommunist," *Radikale Reformatoren: 21 biographische Skizzen von Thomas Müntzer bis Paracelsus*, ed., Hans-Jürgen Goertz (Munich, 1978, Verlag C. H. Beck).

He holds a BA degree from Goshen College and a BD degree from Goshen Biblical Seminary. In addition to studies leading to his PhD degree from Basel, he has done graduate work at the University of Chicago and the University of Hamburg.